~ 2 ~

"WAS" SATAN UNLEASHED IN THE C.I.A.

*

"WAS" SATAN UNLEASHED IN THE C.I.A.

*

(BASED ON A TRUE STORY)

SOME NAMES HAVE BEEN CHANGED FOR THE PROTECTION OF THE INNOCENT

BY

MARCEL L. GARCIA JR.

~ 5 ~

WAS SATAN UNLEASHED IN THE C.I.A.

Published By

The Wu Dao Muay Thai Academy, LLC

Copyright © 2010 by Marcel L. Garcia Jr. / Second Edition in 2013

Book Cover Designed By; Marcel L. Garcia Jr. (Author)

Graphic Design Support By; Mr. Benjamin Young

All rights reserved. No part of this book may be reproduced or transmitted in any form or by any means, electronic or mechanical, including photocopying, recording or by any information storage and retrieval system, without written permission from the author, except for the inclusion of brief quotations in a review.

UPC 682097

~ 6 ~

To my beloved and devoted

CHILDREN

My Daughter; Jacqueline C Garcia Rivera

My Son; Marcel L Garcia III

My Granddaughter; Serenity J. Rivera

faithful companions of our Lord Yahshua,

this book is affectionately dedicated.

FOREWORD

*

This is the real life experience of a secret hero.
Based on a true story of
Ernest Garcia
A former O.S.S./C.I.A. Covert Actions Operator
(Since the early 1940's)

Rarely has one man's "true life story" centered on such a controversial topic, with the potential to resonate on such a grand "global scale." Former O.S.S./C.I.A. covert actions operator "Ernest Garcia is the first man" to petition the American Congress and win the right to tell his classified story. Mr. Garcia now stands poised to release startling information regarding the unspeakable horrors and injustices committed and covered-up by the U.S. intelligence community. "Documented evidence never before seen or even imagined by the International community."

Plus

"Vital Information That May Harrow In the Most Terrifying Events Yet To Come, and DECEIVED in Jesus name."

INTRODUCTION

The documentary of Mr. Ernest Garcia reveals documented "historical evidence" that is educational along with his own personal perspectives and experiences for the faculty of seeing all the relevant data in a meaningful relationship, while serving as a O.S.S./C.I.A. covert actions operator. Mr. Ernest Garcia contributed the freedom of information, by contractual agreement between Ernest Garcia and his cousin Marcel L. Garcia Jr.

The twentieth century has been an unprecedented period of change. At no time in history have more changes occurred in science and in a single year than formerly occurred in a century.

The events of the twentieth century have done much to change human life. Two world wars have torn our world. The advent of atomic weapons and missile warfare has shrunk its size and put it in jeopardy of another world war, which is imminent.

Events of the twentieth century have alerted many to the tremendous potential for fulfilled prophecy. Just the introduction of the concept of a world government, made real by the United Nations, also paints a scenario that is in harmony with prophecy concerning a future world government.

~ 10 ~

Recent events in Europe have highlighted rapid political change and introduced the possibility of democracy becoming a major factor in the political scene. Though this is not a special subject of prophecy, it is entirely possible that people will discover that democracy does not have the answer to our world's problems and may succumb to dictatorship, this is exactly as the Bible predicts for the end of the age. "But the prophecy of God's word will prevail."

~ 11 ~

Reports From

103d Congress, 2d Session-Committee Prints. Prt. 10397
A Staff Report Prepared For The Committee On Veterans' Affairs, United States Senate, Washington, DC, December 8, 1994.

United States General Accounting Office, Washington, DC 20548, National Security and International Affairs Divisions B251258, February 18, 1993, 556465 Released.

The Ethics of Clandestine Scientific Research – A Rejoinder to the Advisory Committee on Human Radiation Experiments, Jean Maria Arrigo, Center for Organizational and Behavioral Sciences, Claremont Graduate School, Claremont, CA 91711.

Mr. Ernest Garcia approved and contributed all of his information given for the benefit of education, and the "support" from all of the above, plus the information obtained from the interviews and the knowledge obtained from the author's personnel research (Marcel Garcia Jr.), and the "support" of The Freedom of Information Act. The expanded versions will be identified; along with all the statements made as to where the information was established and confirmed, referrals will also be implemented, along with in-depth scene-by-scene script.

Table of Contents

FOREWORD 8

INTRODUCTION 9

REPORTS FROM 11

LIMIT OF LIABILITY/DISCLAIMER OF WARRANTY 17

GAS CHAMBER EXPERIMENTS...20

    THE POTENTIAL INCENTIVE 20
    WHERE IT ALL BEGINS..20
    IN THE ORIENTATION ROOM IN ABERDEEN MARYLAND 22
    MAN BREAK TEST 26
    IN THE GAS CHAMBER 27

RADIATION EXPOSURE AND THE EBOLA VIRUS 30

    RADIATION EXPOSURE...30
    EBOLA VIRUS..33

DEADLY VIRUSES RELEASED IN AMERICAN CITIES 37

    A DRAMATIC SCENE PORTRAYED BY MR. GARCIA 38
    DEADLY VIRUSES RELEASED IN MINNEAPOLIS, SAN FRANCISCO, AND NEW YORK 42

SATAN'S HIDDEN TREASURE 49

EROSION / EXISTENCE 57

    ANOTHER SCIENTIST IS DEPRIVED OF EXISTENCE 58

THE CAPTURE OF THE "ANGEL OF DEATH" 62

    ILLEGAL DRUG DEALS IN THE GOVERNMENT......................................89
    A GREATER HOLOCAUST IS IMMINENT...93

REGRESSIVE SCIENCE 95

Snow Witnessed Physicists Fall From Grace in World War II 95
The Final Report of the Advisory Committee on Human Radiation Experiments 97
Scientist as Tools of Intelligence Agencies 101
Pieces Missing from the Final Report. 105
Discordant Views of Explanation by Regressive Science 107
Theory Evaluation of Regressive Science 109
A Methodological Note on the Policy Science Approach 112

INTELLIGENCE AS A NECESSARY EVIL 115

The Protection Industry 115
Delivery by Intelligence as a Protection Agency 117
The Theory of Coercion 120
Reputation and Advertising 123
Advertising for the Protection Industry 125
Evaluation of the Explanation of Intelligence as a Necessary Evil 127
Methodological Note on Theory and Analogy 129

U.S. ARMY AND CIA INTERROGATION MANUALS 130

Army Manuals 130
CIA Manuals 132
The 1983 Manual and Battalion 316 135

PROJECT MKULTRA 139

Title and Origins 140
Aims and Goals 143
   Budget *144*
   Experiments *145*
Drugs 145
   LSD *145*
   Other drugs *146*
Hypnosis 147
   Canadian experiments *147*
Revelation 149
Deaths 154
Legal Issues Involved Informed Consent 155

EXTENT OF PARTICIPATION 158
NOTABLE SUBJECTS 158
CONSPIRACY THEORIES 159

MIND CONTROL **161**

THEORETICAL MODELS AND METHODS 162
   Robert Lifton 's Thought Reform Model *162*
   William Sargent's Theories on Mind Control *164*
   Margaret Singer's Conditions for Mind Control *165*
   Steven Hassan's BITE model *172*
MIND CONTROL AND THE BATTERED PERSON SYNDROME 177
   Social Psychology Tactics *177*
   Social Psychological Conditioning by Stahelski *179*
   Subliminal Advertising *179*
CULTS AND MIND CONTROL CONTROVERSIES 180
   Scholarly points of view *180*
   Mind Control, Exit Counseling, and Deprogramming *184*
   Mind Control and Recruitment Rates *185*
   Mind Control and Faith *186*
   Counter-cult Movement and Mind Control *187*
LEGAL ISSUES 188

BRAINWASHING **192**

TERMINOLOGY 192
POLITICAL 195
   Korean War (19501953) *195*
   Criticism of claims *202*
CULTS 203
PROTO-BRAINWASHING 206
   The APA, DIMPAC, and Theories of Brainwashing *207*
   Other views *211*
NEW RELIGIOUS MOVEMENTS 212
TRUTH DRUG 215
   Substances *216*
APPLICATIONS 216
   Russian secret services *216*
   CIA *217*
   CBI *217*

Reliability	218
HUMAN SUBJECT RESEARCH	**219**
Research subject	219
History	220
Ancient History	221
Middle Ages	*221*
Early Modern Times	*221*
Early 20th Century	*222*
Second Sino-Japanese War and World War II	*223*
After World War II	*225*
In the United States	*226*
Human vivisection	228
Ongoing Issues	*229*
Questionable Psychological Experiments	229
Human Radiation Experiments	230
Experiments performed in the United States	*230*
Fallout Research	*232*
Strontium	234
PROJECT SUNSHINE	**237**
The Advisory Committee on Human Radiation Experiments	238
Human Rights Issues Remain for the Radiation Victims	242
The Story According to Military and Political Intelligence	244
Project Sunshine	247
TORTURE – SEC/RET	**296**
Restrictions	296
The Theory of Coercion	296
Arrest	*298*
Detention	*299*
Deprivation of Sensory Stimuli	*299*
Threats and Fear	*301*
Debility	*302*
Pain	*302*
Heightened Suggestibility and Hypnosis	*303*
Narcosis	*305*
The Detection of Malingering	*306*

Conclusion 308
TERRIFYING EVENTS YET TO COME 329
   WEAPONS OF MASS DESTRUCTION 329
      Early Uses of the Term 330
      Evolution of its use 332
      Definitions of the term 334
   WMD USE, POSSESSION AND ACCESS 336
      Nuclear weapons 336
      Nuclear Terrorism 338
      Radiological Weapons 339
      Radiological Assassinations 339
      Allegations of Preparations to Nuclear Sabotage 340
      Allegations of Privately Owned Nuclear Weapons 341
      Planned and Attempted Attacks 342
   THE "COVENANT WITH DEATH" AND THE "AGREEMENT WITH HELL" 362
   REVIVED ROMAN EMPIRE 365
Deceived in Jesus name.. 476

"*Israel seems to have sold Jerusalem to the Vatican!!!*" **494**

~ 17 ~
LIMIT OF LIABILITY/DISCLAIMER OF WARRANTY

THE PUBLISHER AND THE AUTHOR MAKE NO REPRESENTATIONS OR WARRANTIES WITH RESPECT TO THE ACCURACY OR COMPLETENESS OF THE CONTENTS OF THIS WORK AND SPECIFICALLY DISCLAIM ALL WARRANTIES, INCLUDING WITHOUT LIMITATION WARRANTIES OF FITNESS FOR A PARTICULAR PURPOSE. NO WARRANTY MAY BE CREATED OR EXTENDED BY SALES OR PROMOTIONAL MATERIALS. THE ADVICE AND STRATEGIES CONTAINED HEREIN MAY NOT BE SUITABLE FOR EVERY SITUATION. THIS WORK IS SOLD WITH THE UNDERSTANDING THAT THE PUBLISHER IS NOT ENGAGED IN RENDERING LEGAL, ACCOUNTING, OR OTHER PROFESSIONAL SERVICES. IF PROFESSIONAL ASSISTANCE IS REQUIRED, THE SERVICES OF A COMPETENT PROFESSIONAL PERSON SHOULD BE SOUGHT. NEITHER THE PUBLISHER NOR THE AUTHOR SHALL BE LIABLE FOR DAMAGES ARISING HEREFROM. THE FACT THAT AN ORGANIZATION, WEBSITE, OTHER AUTHORS, OTHER PUBLISHERS, ARTICLES OR UNITS OF GOVERNMENT IS REFERRED TO IN THIS WORK AS A CITATION AND/OR POTENTIAL SOURCE OF FURTHER INFORMATION DOES NOT MEAN THAT THE AUTHOR OR THE PUBLISHER ENDORSE THE INFORMATION THE ORGANIZATION, WEBSITE, OTHER AUTHORS, OTHER PUBLISHERS, ARTICLES OR UNITS OF GOVERNMENT MAY PROVIDE OR RECOMMENDATION IT MAY MAKE. FURTHER, READERS SHOULD BE AWARE THAT REFERRALS MAY HAVE CHANGED OR DISAPPEARED BETWEEN

~ 18 ~

WHEN THIS WORK WAS WRITTEN AND WHEN IT IS READ.

"WAS" SATAN UNLEASHED IN THE C.I.A.

1

GAS CHAMBER EXPERIMENTS

The Potential Incentive

Mr. Ernest Garcia was born in 1928 in a poor farm community near Los Alamos New Mexico, a talented boy who picked up several languages from his Indian and immigrant neighbors. His mother died in his childhood, and his severely abusive father demanded extreme obedience. Mr. Garcia tells of Mr. Albert Einstein and Mr. Robert Oppenheimer giving him pennies when they occasionally came to Jemez Springs for meals.

Where It All Begins

Mr. Ernest Garcia lied about his age to get into the service; he was just 16 years old when he started the service. When I interviewed Mr. Garcia, I asked him if he ever felt the conviction of the Holy Spirit while involved in some of the most horrifying missions in the history of the United States. He said, oh God yes, it was horrible; you could sense the presence of the demonic spirits working through the government. When I worked on mind control, I could see through the other person's eyes and I could recognize that the seed of the devil was just planted within that person. It was not until I got out of the service when I became a Christian and brought two of my friends to Christ. Ernest and I prayed before my interview with him, but he just couldn't hold back the tears.

I remember when it all started; I was sitting on the back seat of an Army military vehicle while an officer was driving down a busy street in Fort Blitz Texas around 1946. I saw a preacher standing at the corner of the street staring at me and saying; from the gospel of Luke, Jesus said, "Satan has asked for you, that he may sift you as wheat." But I have prayed for you. This preacher kept staring at me even as we passed by him and continued to say. That your faith should not fail; and when you return to me "strengthen your brethren." Then we got to the train station and the officer told me; Mr. Garcia, you'll be going to Virginia now – good luck.

When I got to Virginia and while I was walking out of the train, I was greeted with a salute from Sergeant Barkley, he introduced himself and said; an officer declared you here, and you're going to do covert operations. There are four of you that are going to Maryland, in a place called Aberdeen, and then they will separate you for special services.

In The Orientation Room in Aberdeen Maryland

Ernest Garcia's Personal Statement

As Ernest Garcia entered the orientation room he was greeted by a commanding officer, the commanding officer told Garcia to have a seat. The commanding officer then walks to the front of the orientation room and faces the officers that are sitting down at their desk.

Commanding Officer: Welcome to Aberdeen Proving Grounds, gentlemen you have been specifically chosen to work in this project. You are to be introduced to the new weapons of the future.

While the commanding officer crossed his arms and placed his right hand on his chin, he walked across the room to his left side and then he pointed to the German defector who was standing at the corner of the room.

Commanding Officer: At this time, I want to introduce you to this German defector into our country. This gentleman is a scientist that developed a lot of the process that we will be working with here today.

Garcia has a shocking expression of fear and curiosity. The German defector then went around the room and shook hands with the American officers. Meanwhile the commanding officer is shuffling papers at the podium in the front of the room.

Commanding Officer: Gentlemen, it is time to tell you what you will be doing here. Many of you have heard – but may
not know what we are about to tell you today.

The commanding officer pauses while he walks around to the front of the podium, and then points his right index finger at the officers. The officers are starring at the commanding officer as he starts to raise his voice.

Commanding Officer: From this point on we are going to impose the highest form of confidentiality and the Top Q Clearance! Nothing seen, talked or discussed with anybody, including members with this meeting, and at any time in duty or off duty! Except! With the person you are assigned with, under the penalty of the strictest Federal Law!

Then one of the trainee's with fear on his face speaks out of order.

Trainee: I do not understand what I am doing here, would you explain?

The commanding officer then gets angry, with a stern look on his face, with tension rising in his body.

Commanding Officer: Gentlemen, I will tell you in due time and "do not" ask any questions at this time!

The commanding officer then pauses and starts to walk around the front of the room, again crossing his arms and placing his hand on his chin. Then he stops and brings his arms down and faces the officers, then takes a deep breath.

Commanding Officer: We are here to introduce you to chemical warfare. You have specifically been selected and assigned to handle these chemicals and to use them where they are needed, "i.e. the Battlefield."

U.S. Senate
Committee on Veterans' Affairs

During the last 50 years, hundreds of thousands of military personnel have been involved in human experimentation and other intentional exposures conducted by the Department of Defense (DOD), often without a service member's knowledge or consent. Thousands of World War II veterans who originally volunteered to "test summer clothing" in exchange for extra leave time, found themselves in gas chambers testing the effects of mustard gas and lewisite. Several

Persian Gulf War veterans interviewed by Committee staff reported that they were ordered to take experimental vaccines during Operation Desert Shield or "face prison."

United States
General Accounting Office

We identified three military research projects that were conducted secretly by the services between 1942 and 1975 that exposed service members to hazardous substances. The three projects are as follows: (1) In the World War II era, the U.S. Navy conducted test of clothing and equipment, exposing sailors to mustard and lewisite agents; (2) in the same era the U.S. Army tested clothing, equipment, and weapons that exposed soldiers to mustard agent; and (3) in the Cold War era, the U.S. army's experiments exposed soldiers and some U.S. Air Force personnel to incapacitating agents, such as nerve agents, nerve agent antidotes, and psychochemical, including lysergic acid diethylamide (LSD).

U.S. Senate
General Accounting Office

In addition, the Army developed and tested offensive chemical weapons and evaluated the effectiveness and persistency of mustard agents in different environments. Test documents located at the Army's Chemical Research, Development and Engineering Center document that gas chamber tests and skin tests were conducted at 11 locations – Bushnell Field, Florida; Fort Pierce, Florida; Dry Tortugas, Florida; San Jose Island, Panama; Camp Sibert, Alabama; Dugway Proving Grounds, Utah; Camp Polk, Louisiana; Gulfport, Mississippi El Centro, California; San Carlos, California; and, Fort Richardson, Alaska.

Man Break Test

Mr. Garcia stated that he went through this horrible experience of going through the chamber of hell, so called the "gas chamber" I went through it 6 times. Even after living through it, I felt tortured through life because of just this one experience. This was just the physical contribution given to me by the government, this does not compare to the mental suffering that was contributed through the inhuman missions that I was ordered to do, that I carried on my shoulders through life. Along with this came an attachment of a threat if I did not obey, that even carried on to my family years later.

U.S Senate
Committee on Veterans' Affairs

The Department of Defense (DOD) conducted numerous "man break" tests, exposing soldiers to chemical weapons
in order to determine the exposure level "that would cause a casualty," i.e. "break a man."(Note

3) Similarly, hundreds of soldiers were subjected to hallucinogens in experimental programs conducted by the DOD in participation with, or sponsored by, the CIA. Most Americans would agree that the use of soldiers as unwitting guinea pigs in experiments that were designed to harm them, at least temporarily, is not ethical.

Although military personnel are the logical choice as human subjects for such research, it is questionable whether the military hierarchy allows for individuals in subordinate positions of power to refuse participating in military experiments. Moreover, the evidence suggests that they have not been adequately monitored for adverse health effects after the experimental protocols end.

In The Gas Chamber

Mr. Garcia gives an example of just one experience that he witnessed. An officer was misrepresented to believe that he was brought over to test Navy summer clothing, in exchange for a 3day pass. The look on this officer's face when they were putting on the gas mask and clothing was of dismay and of pure surprise and fear, especially when they locked him in the gas chamber alone and started releasing the mustard gas and lewisite. He was seen pacing faster and faster around the gas chamber, with extreme nervousness and fear, while his hands are stretched out before him, not knowing where to go or what to do. Then within moments later the officer starts to become violently ill, and he called for the corpsman through the intercom, to release him from the chamber. The officer was seen pressing the intercom button with intensity, crying out "let me out of here," "I'm getting sick." The corpsman in control of the releasing of the officer in the gas chamber responded by saying "No!" The officer then walked away from the intercom button, grasping his chest and coughing. He immediately turns back to press the intercom button. The officer has the right hand on the intercom button and he is pounding with his left fist on the glass of the exit door. The officer requested, "I request to be released from here immediately." The corpsman responded by saying, "No, your request is denied." The officer then turns around and suddenly takes a hold of his throat and his stomach and then falls to the floor, while his body starts to shake, then passes out.

The corpsman then said, "Alright, get this officer out of here, and give him his three day pass, and let's get the next one in. Now rise up the exposure level, and let's see if we can break this one, "Alright, who's next?"

Meanwhile two officers are together in a military vehicle, pulling aside a private road. Both officers go to the back of the vehicle and pull out this officer, while he is still passed out, and then they tossed him on the side of the snowy road. Fortunately this officer lived to tell his side of the story and Mr. Garcia has this testimony on video.

U.S. Senate
Committee on Veterans' Affairs

Additionally, some of these human subjects were threatened with imprisonment at Fort Leavenworth if they discussed these experiments with anyone, including their wives, parents, and family doctors. (Note 15) For decades, the Pentagon denied that the research had taken place, resulting in decades of suffering for many veterans who become ill after the secret testing.

2

RADIATION EXPOSURE AND THE EBOLA VIRUS

Radiation Exposure
U.S. Senate
Committee on Veterans' Affairs

From 1945 to 1962, the United States conducted numerous detonation tests: Crossroads (Bikini); Sandstone, Greenhouse and Ivy (Eniwetok Atoll); Castle (Bikini Atoll); Pacific Ocean 400 miles southwest of San Diego; Redwing and Hardtack I (Eniwetok and Bikini Atolls); Argus (South Atlantic); and Dominic (Christmas Island, Johnston Island, 400 miles west of San Diego). (Note 28) The main goal was to determine damage caused by the bombs;
however, as a result, thousands of military personnel and civilians were exposed to radioactive fallout. Similar tests were conducted within the continental United States, including sites in New Mexico and Nevada. Some "atomic veterans" believe they were used as guinea pigs to

determine the effects of radiation from various distances.

Dugway Proving Ground is a military testing facility located approximately 80 miles from Salt Lake City. For several decades, Dugway has been the site of testing for various chemical and biological agents. From 1951 through 1969, hundreds, perhaps thousands of open-air tests using bacteria and viruses that cause disease in humans, animals, and plants were conducted at Dugway.

In 1968, approximately 6,400 sheep died following the intentional release of a deadly nerve gas from a plane. According to a veterinarian who evaluated the sick and dying sheep, there was little doubt that the sheep had been poisoned with nerve gas. (Note 24) The sheep and other animals in the area had depressed cholinesterase levels, suggesting organophosphate nerve poisoning. Initially, the Department of Defense denied any responsibility for the accident, stating that the sheep died from organophosphate pesticides sprayed on a nearby alfalfa field. However, the nerve agent VX was identified when the poisoned sheep were autopsied, which made it clear that the deaths were not caused by pesticides.

It is unknown how many people in the surrounding vicinity were also exposed to potentially harmful agents used in open-air tests at Dugway. In 1969, concerns were expressed at a congressional hearing about the possible public health implications of the VEE virus testing at Dugway. (Note 26)

U.S. Senate
Committee on Veterans' Affairs

When the Department of Defense began preparations for Desert Shield and Desert Storm in 1990, officials were extremely concerned that Iraq would use chemical and biological weapons against the United States. Despite years of study and billions of dollars, the DOD lacked drugs and vaccines that were proven safe and effective to safeguard against anticipated chemical nerve agents and biological toxins. Therefore, DOD officials wanted to use a medication (pyridostigmine bromide) and vaccine (botulinum toxoid) that they believed might protect against chemical nerve agents and botulism. Because the safety and effectiveness of pyridostigmine bromide and botulinum toxoid had not been proven for their intended use, these products were considered investigational drugs.

Pyridostigmine bromide is a chemical which enhances the effectiveness of two drugs, atropine and 2PAM, which are proven effective for the treatment of nerve agent poisoning. (Note 44) Pyridostigmine is also a nerve agent itself. Nerve agents exert their biological effects by binding to, and inhibiting, the enzyme acetyl cholinesterase (AChE) which normally shuts off the neurotransmitter, acetylcholine (Ach). When levels of Ach increase, stimulation are excessive, "death can result."

The bromide that is included in pyridostigmine bromide pills is known to sometimes cause problems referred to as "bromide intoxication" when used for the treatment of myasthenia gravis. (Note 53) Bromide intoxication may cause confusion, irritability, tremor, memory loss, psychotic behavior, ataxia, stupor, and coma.

U.S. Senate
Committee on Veterans' Affairs

Mr. Garcia stated: Most of the training that we got was how to handle work around scientist, how to work with scientific instructions, scientific chemicals. I was mustered into Panama. They had one of the most sophisticated laboratories, because all these chemicals have a different behavioral pattern that is consistent with heat and barometric pressure in the tropics.

Ebola Virus
Mr. Garcia Stated

Marcel: Mr. Garcia, after your experiments in Aberdeen Proving Ground, you were assigned to a scientist, who developed the Ebola Virus, whose name was Dr. Frank Olsen.

Mr. Garcia: Oh yes, Frank Olsen was himself an extremely knowledgeable person, very kind, and very willing to open to a lot of things. We had our opinions that we kept secluded that we thought the conditions were dangerous. When Frank Olsen developed the Ebola Virus, he really became concerned then. But he developed other things that I cannot remember the exact numbers. But once he found out the effects of these viruses he destroyed them by fire. The people that stole that story they couldn't of known that, no way in the world, except when I was saying it to the Congress, they tried to portray it like that. But I don't know if you have seen the movie "Outbreak" they mention Albuquerque, New Mexico that is a form of trying to portray the activities being connected to us or something else. It was all distorted, it was pretty bad.

Marcel: Yes, Warner Brothers produced that film; I forgot the actors' name.

Mr. Garcia: One of the actors was Dustin Hoffman. You know the writer that put that program together; I later found out that he was from Arizona. You see how dangerous it is to supply a lot of the story, because they will just steal it from you just like that.

Marcel: And like you said it was all distorted just made out of assumption. Now what really took place was you, a scientist, and four American military guardsmen departed from a military airport and flew into the jungles of Africa. There the guardsmen unloaded a dead dog that was sealed in a bag. All of you pursued to carry the animal into a cave in one of the high mountains there. And then the guardsman removed the animal from the bag that was contaminated with a rare killer virus (Ebola Virus). Then you tracked some of the animals that ate upon this dead dog, one of them happen to be a large bat the size of a cat.

Mr. Garcia: That is right the bats there are huge. The animals there that got contaminated, had inherited a very aggressive manner. We watched a large bat come down aggressively and attack this native while he was working in his field. Then we were informed that this person had gotten a scratch on his ear from the attack of this bat. This native within hours had received a very serious and deadly illness. With just his presence and through his breath it was air born. The virus started to spread within his home. By morning, the native and his whole family were dead in their home. That included his wife and three children.

Marcel: Mr. Garcia you had mentioned to me previously that the scientist Dr. Frank Olsen had disappeared while he had gone fishing by a lake near his home. And that search teams had gone into the lake to look for him for days, but were unable to find him.

Mr. Garcia: That is right, and months later the family requested another search in the same location, and then all of a sudden the search team found his body. After tests were taken on Dr. Olsen, the results showed that they found seawater in his system, but yet his body was in a freshwater lake. What does that tell you?

Marcel: Well what it tells me is exactly what you told me before that Dr. Olsen did not want to release the information on how he developed the Ebola Virus to the government, because the government wanted to use it as a chemical weapon. So they may of done away with Dr. Olsen?

Mr. Garcia: That is exactly right, can you imagine this chemical being used as a weapon, or getting into the wrong hands. People would be dying in a matter of hours, not days, hours.

Marcel: As inhumane that this world has gotten, the evil of it, would have loved it, they would have lusted and drooled over the idea of obtaining it. The darkness of this world will not prevail. What is my concern is; what "spirit" will every living human being choose to feed, the good or the bad? This will determine the person's destination.

3

DEADLY VIRUSES RELEASED IN AMERICAN CITIES

U.S. Senate
Committee on Veterans' Affairs

Page 36 – For example, the military has released chemicals and biological agents through outdoor "open air" test for over four decades. Some of these supposedly safe chemicals and biological agents, referred to as simulants, were also released over populated areas and cities. (Note 158) Although scientific evidence suggested that the tests may have caused illnesses to exposed citizens, the Army repeatedly claimed that these bacteria and chemicals were harmless until adverse health effects convinced them to change the simulants used. The "death" of Edward J. Nevin "was" associated with the release of one simulant, "Serratia marcescens," over San Francisco in 1950. (Note 159) A subsequent court trial revealed that on September 26 and 27, 1950, the Army sprayed "Serratia marcescens" from a boat off the coast of San Francisco. (Note 160) On September 29, patients at the Stanford University Hospital in San Francisco began appearing with "Serratia marcescens" infections. Although the judge denied the validity of the plaintiffs' claim that the exposures were related to the death of Mr. Nevin, the trial raised frightening questions about the selection of simulants. Serratia marcescens is no longer used by the military as a simulant.

A Dramatic Scene Portrayed By Mr. Garcia

The citizens in the city of San Francisco are seen coughing and holding their forehead, some were vomiting while walking down the busy sidewalks downtown, while the overhead spraying was going on.

(Names have been changed)

James a 60 yr. old man and his wife Elisabeth a 53 year old woman, are seen walking down this busy San Francisco sidewalk. James stops walking and leans over, while holding on to the corner of a building and starts to cough, while he inhaled, the coughing got more intense. James's wife follows him with one arm on his back and the other arm on his shoulder.

Elisabeth: James are you all right? Honey, are you ok?

Elisabeth starts to cough lightly while she is still leaning on James.

Elisabeth: Oh my God James there must be something in the air.

James starts to vomit, and then he slowly starts to bend his knees, as he comes closer to the ground, while he still is holding on to the corner of the building.

James: Elisabeth, honey, I don't know what's going on call an ambulance!

James's voice starts to fade, as his eyes start to close.

James: Call an ambulance, please honey call an ambulance quick!

As Elisabeth is looking over her left her left shoulder with tears starting to come out of her eyes and with fear in her voice, she screams for help.

Elisabeth: Somebody help! Somebody call an ambulance! Help me please!

~ 40 ~

A group of people that were walking on the sidewalk close by came to help. Even the groups of people coming to help were coughing, yet some of the people had handkerchiefs over their mouths. Just then James collapsed to the ground and passed out. Elisabeth then falls to her knees on the ground and places her hands on his shoulder and cries out.

Elisabeth: James, wake up honey! Wake, up!

Inside the Stanford University Hospital in San Francisco just moments later, nurses and doctors are scrambling around patients in the hallways at the Stanford University Hospital.

Doctor Reyes, says to Doctor Patricia Jones.

Doctor Reyes: Doctor Jones, these numerous patients are all coming in with the same symptoms!

Doctor Jones: That's right! What do you think it is?

Doctor Reyes: I believe a chemical must have been released out there. Call the authorities right away!

Doctor Jones: Yes sir, I'll get to that right now.

Then suddenly, down the same hallway a nurse is seen pulling a gurney and she is yelling out.

Nurse: Everyone, clear the way! Doctor, doctor! This gentleman needs your help immediately!

This drew the attention of both the doctors, as they both looked at the nurse coming down the hallway. The nurse approaches the doctors.

Doctor Reyes: Nurse, what is the problem with this gentleman?

While the nurse has one hand on the gurney, she points to the patient on the gurney with her other hand. It is James, the gentleman whom passed out on the sidewalk, with his wife Elisabeth holding on to the gurney at the opposite end.

Nurse: Doctor, this gentleman is unconscious, and his heart rate is dropping dramatically.

Doctor Reyes: Nurse, take him to the emergency room immediately!

Four days later a funeral is taking place, a casket is being carried out of the entrance of a church and Elisabeth is seen crying while she follows the casket.

Deadly Viruses Released In Minneapolis, San Francisco, and New York

Marcel: Documents indicate that you Mr. Garcia directly participated in extremely top-secret operations involving the deployment of deadly viruses in large cities, such as Minneapolis, San Francisco and New York. Mr. Garcia you have access to actual sample film footage of how lethal bacteria was released into the subway systems, and sewers, endangering the American populace.

Mr. Garcia: Yes, this was an extremely top-secret operation involving the deployment of a deadly virus in those cities. Well, we had all the clearance in the world, but let me tell you how we did this. This is now no more dangerous now days then to learn how to build a bomb from the Internet.

While inside a science lab, Mr. Garcia and a scientist are mixing chemicals, dressed in chemical protection outfits. The scientist had a very strong German accent. The scientist hands over two 8oz. clear glass containers, with deadly chemicals inside them.

Scientist: Mr. Garcia, mix these two chemicals very slowly and make sure none of it spills over.

Mr. Garcia: Yes doctor, I will be very, very careful.

Mr. Garcia gets two glass containers with one being a clear liquid and the other being a yellowish color substance. Then he pours them into a larger clear container, about quart size, and then Mr. Garcia starts to mix them very slowly with a clear gas stirring stick. Meanwhile the scientist is seen walking to the side of this large table that they are working on, and reaches to grab a tray of secured vials and a box of syringes.

Scientist: Now, if you would Mr. Garcia pour this deadly chemical into these vials and keep them secured, plus take a few of these syringes with you. Once you inject the chemical into these light bulbs tape them so there would not be any leakage. The moment you disperse this virus in the subways and sewers, get the hell out, you understand?

Mr. Garcia: Oh, I understand very clearly doctor, I definitely understand, and I will get the others to follow with extreme caution.

The scientist then turns away and waves from over his shoulder as he intends to walk out of the lab.

Scientist: Now, you be careful Mr. Garcia, and I will see you soon.

Mr. Garcia: I will be doctor, thank you.

Mr. Garcia and three other CIA agents are inside a hotel room in San Francisco – Morning – 5:00am. – Winter.
Mr. Garcia is advising the other agents what to do while giving them the chemically filled light bulbs. He hands them the light bulbs very

carefully. The agents are wearing long trench coats.

Mr. Garcia: Gentlemen, each one of you will take four of these chemically filled light bulbs, place one in a separate pocket in your coat. Please handle these with extreme caution.

The agents start to place the light bulbs in their coats with extreme caution.

Mr. Garcia: One of you will be driving the van while the rest of us will be dropped off in three different locations at the substations. While on the way to these substations we will throw a bulb in numerous sewers. You will throw and burst these light bulbs at every 20ft. on the subway tracks. Then get the hell out, and then you will be picked up, and then we will be on our way on a plane to Minneapolis. Let's get going guys and do a good job.

The agents are each seen in their own location throwing the light bulbs on the clear subway tracks. A light yellowish green chemical color is seen coming out of the explosion of the light bulbs. And when the subway train came in, it only dispersed the chemicals even more. The van is seen picking up the agents, as Mr. Garcia climbs in he says.

Mr. Garcia: Mission accomplished lets head for Minneapolis

~ 45 ~

Mr. Garcia and his team are seen exiting the van at the subway station in Minneapolis – Morning – 5:00am – winter.

Mr. Garcia: Minneapolis, here is your wake up call.

The agents hit Minneapolis with a series of chemicals on the subways and sewer systems, all done in a matter of a few hours. As Mr. Garcia is walking into the passenger side of the van, he says.

Mr. Garcia: All right Big Apple, it's your turn, New York City here we come!

An agent is exiting the side of the van outside of the subway station in New York City – Morning – 5:00am – winter

As agent Smith is walking out of the van, Mr. Garcia is looking out of the passenger window and telling him.

Mr. Garcia: Agent Smith, you're doing a great job for your country, this mission is almost over, see you soon.

Agent Smith: Yes Sir, thank you sir.

Agent Smith then salutes agent Garcia, and then walks towards the entrance of the New York subway station. Moments later agents Smith is seen taking out a light bulb from his trench coat, then leans back to throw it, he then comments.

Agent Smith: Here, is a Big Apple! Just made special for New York City!

Agent Smith then is seen throwing the light bulb at the subway tracks. Then he is seen running down the side of the walkway throwing the light bulbs every 20ft., the chemicals fill the air inside the subway station. Meanwhile the other agents are hitting other areas of the subway station, while the driver is hitting the sewer systems with more chemicals.

Moments later all of the agents are in the van, Mr. Garcia turns around while seating on the passenger seat and looks at the other three agents in the back of the van and says.

Mr. Garcia: Gentlemen, your mission has been successfully accomplished, and a mission well done. Let's head back to headquarters for our next assignment.

While we return back to the interview with Marcel in Mr. Garcia's office, Marcel then says;

Marcel: Well, that was quite an endeavor; thank God all of this is history.

Mr. Garcia: It was so strange, once I got to headquarters, I heard of a rather unusual circumstance, which occurred in Utah, at the Dugway Proving Ground. Here I'll read it from the document.

U.S. Senate
Committee on Veterans' Affairs

Dugway Proving Ground has been a site for "open air" testing of chemical and biological agents for decades. The purpose of the tests is to determine how the agent spread and survive, and their effect on people and the environment.

Earl Davenport is a veteran who participated in tests at Dugway Proving Ground in Utah, first as a military employee and later as a civilian employee. He became ill in 1984 after being exposed to a chemical simulant called DMMP (dim ethyl methyl phosphate). He had been spraying the chemical into the path of a laser beam when a sudden change in wind blew the chemical all over his face and hair before he was able to put on a protective mask. Although he was "wheezing and coughing" the next day, and his symptoms lasted for weeks, the Dugway Army Hospital merely gave him cough medicine and antibiotics. The Dugway Safety Office assured him that the chemical was safe. However, by 1988, officials at Dugway had reevaluated the simulant's danger, and were becoming concerned that DMMP could cause cancer and kidney damage.

THE FEDERAL GOVERNMENT HAS FAILED TO SUPPORT SCIENTIFIC STUDIES THAT PROVIDE INFORMATION ABOUT THE REPRODUCTIVE PROBLEMS EXPERIENCED BY VETERANS WHO WERE INTENTIONALLY EXPOSED TO POTENTIALLY DANGEROUS SUBSTANCES.

Mr. Garcia had eight children, six of whom were born dead and deformed. The government confiscated and "disposed" of the fetuses.

Mr. Steve Miller, an Army nurse who also testified at a Committee hearing on August 5, 1994, said he had no problems with burning semen, but his son was born with extensive birth defects, including having only one eye and one ear. Mr. Miller believes that his son's birth defects could be related to his use of investigational drugs or vaccines, perhaps in combination with pesticide exposures.

4

SATAN'S HIDDEN TREASURE

Mr. Garcia Reveals
Satan's Hidden Treasure

Mr. Garcia: Marcel let me tell you about this assignment that I went on, which was pretty much an adventure than an assignment. It took place in the Philippines, a place I call the Satan's Treasure.

There is a boat by the shore in the Philippines – Day
Mr. Garcia is getting suited up with a scuba outfit. Along with him are his guide and two other CIA agents. The guide was the only one suited up to go with Mr. Garcia; the other two agents had to remain on the boat. Mr. Garcia's guide was named Robert, who was from the Philippines.

Mr. Garcia: So Robert, what was it that you called me here for that is so top secret?

Robert: I will only reveal that secret to you only, and that will be when we get to our destination. But for now, I can say that it will be a very extraordinary surprise. But you must promise me that you will keep secret the information that you will be given, and the things that you will see to yourself, and no one else must know of this, do you understand?

Mr. Garcia: Yes Robert, of course I do, you know that you can trust me; I have always been there for you.

Robert: Mr. Garcia, I think you're the only person that I can really trust, and it is true, you have always been there for me.

Mr. Garcia: Ok Robert, where do we go from here?

Robert: We are going to go 80ft. straight down, and stay close by me and just follow me.

Mr. Garcia and Robert are seen diving straight into the water, while under the deep water Robert directs Mr. Garcia with hand gestures. Now, that they are getting close to 80ft. below the water.

Robert: (Makes a hand gesture to Mr. Garcia, that they are getting close)

Mr. Garcia: (Makes a hand gesture back to Robert, with a thumb up signal).

After about 5 minutes have passed by, Robert and Mr. Garcia now come to a large steel gate made of metal bars and steel frame that is approximately 7ft. tall and 6ft. wide, which cover the entrance to a cave. Robert now signals with a hand gesture to Mr. Garcia that they made it to a certain point.

Robert: (Puts both thumbs up and then points to the gate).

Mr. Garcia: (Puts both thumbs up and nods his head of approval).

Robert now reaches to his pouch attached to his belt and pulls out a ring with two keys; he then places the keys into two different keyholes and turns them simultaneously, the gate now unlocks.

Robert: (Signals to Mr. Garcia to come and help him pull the gate open).

They continue to swim into the water filled cave, about 100ft. straight ahead, and then they reached a wall.

Robert: (Signals to Mr. Garcia with his hand to swim upward).

Mr. Garcia: (Signals back to Robert with both thumbs up).

Just before they get to the surface of the water, there was a ladder anchored by cement into the wall of dirt, the ladder was just wide enough for one person to climb up on.

Robert: (Signals to Mr. Garcia to start climbing the ladder).

They start to climb the ladder and about 7ft. up they reached the surface of the water, they now raised their goggles to their forehead and remove their mouthpiece from the oxygen tanks, But they yet need to go up 10 more ft. to reach the cave that leads into the hidden treasure. Robert then says.

Robert: We made it to this point Mr. Garcia; we just need to climb up 10 more ft. and then grab the handrail and then we will be at the entrance of the hidden treasure.

Mr. Garcia: Well you definitely have my attention let's keep going.

They reached to the top of the ladder and then grabbed the handrail and pulled themselves to the surface of the cave. The entrance to the hidden treasure was just 30ft. away straight ahead. The door covering the entrance was made of solid steel.

Robert: Mr. Garcia, just 30 more ft. to go and we will be at the entrance of the hidden treasure. But I must tell you, don't touch anything unless I give it to you. You must not leave your fingerprints on inappropriate material, or set off any alarms.

Mr. Garcia: I understand Robert, and I'll follow your instructions as you request.

~ 53 ~

Robert reaches back into his pouch to get the keys, while he is unlocking the door with both keys he comments to Mr. Garcia, as he now places the keys back in his pouch.

Robert: Prepare yourself for an unusual experience.

Mr. Garcia: Possibly, a rather unusual experience Robert?

Robert: Yes, an experience that I have never before felt, or the sense of evil that I had never experienced, until I came here.

Due to the weight of this door, Robert had to push the door with both hands. As they both walk in Mr. Garcia is amassed at the amount of treasure chests that are piled up on one another, and the room was so huge.
Just as Mr. Garcia walked into the room, he starts to feel a very strong and a deep dark presence of evil in the room. Then he places both of his hands on each side of his head.

Robert: Mr. Garcia, are you ok?

Mr. Garcia: My God, I got so dizzy; I can feel a very strong and powerful presence of Satan in this room, it feels so evil in here, this is horrible, I even have an upset stomach from the powerful presence in this room, the pressure is intense.

~ 54 ~

As Robert points to one of the treasure chest on the floor, he says.

Robert: When I show you what is inside of this, then you will be confirmed of the presence that you are now experiencing, as Satan's hidden treasure.

Robert then reached back into his pouch and pulled out a skeleton key and waved it back and forth for Mr. Garcia to recognize.

Robert reached down with the skeleton key and unlocked the treasure chest and then lifted the lid all the way open. Mr. Garcia's eyes opened up with amassment while his jaws dropped.

Mr. Garcia: Oh my God! Look at all that gold!

Robert reaches down to get a bar of gold to show Mr. Garcia the inscription on the gold.

Robert: Mr. Garcia, look at the inscription on this bar of gold, and then tell me if this does not coincide with the presence of what you felt just a while ago.

Mr. Garcia: Oh, this definitely coincides with what I felt all right.

Robert: Well tell me, what do you see?

Mr. Garcia: What I see is the mark of the Beast! The mark is 666 engraved right on center of all of these bars of gold.

Mr. Garcia then takes a deep breath and then says.

Mr. Garcia: Robert who does this gold belongs to?

Robert: Mr. Garcia, all of this gold and treasure belongs to the United Nations.

Mr. Garcia: I believe it, you know I was present when the United Nations first announced that they were going to build a One World Government and control the world. The mark just coincides with whom all of this was inspired by.

Robert: That surely is going to be amazing, now I can see who inspired them, Satan himself inspired them.

Mr. Garcia: That surely is going to be Hell on earth, and it is not too far away. Let's lock this place up and get the hell out of Satan's treasure.

Mr. Garcia: Marcel, after President Bush became president in the year 2000, a navy ship was seen in that location. I do not know what may have occurred to the treasure after that.

5

EROSION / EXISTENCE

Marcel: Mr. Garcia, you told me before about the current chemical and nuclear containers have been wearing out from the inside out.

Mr. Garcia: Oh yes, as a matter of fact there is a place in Missouri, where they have an ammunition dump there and they have tons of mustard gas and lewisite and all that kind of stuff. And they are so dangerous, and right now they are starting to leak and they don't know what the hell to do with them. So they are talking about the possibility of exploding a nuclear device and burning them in there. That is what the proposal was and there was a lot of controversy about that, but of course this was not made public. They had asked us to try to help neutralize that problem.

Marcel: Mr. Garcia how about the nuclear bombs, what risk do they impose?

Mr. Garcia: Some of the nuclear bombs that we have here something needs to be done with them. They are not dangerous for a bomb to explode that takes a special trigger to do that. If they start to release the radiation from inside, it could be very dangerous.

Marcel: Because they've been sitting there so long?

Mr. Garcia: Yea, because they're getting pretty old. I don't care how much they are maintained, eventually they are going to deteriorate from the inside out, they may look in good shape from the outside, but they are rotting their way through. And they knew about it before they started to use plastic containers for chemicals.

Marcel: That is amazing and nothing more than pure ignorance.

Mr. Garcia: Anyhow, when we were in Panama we were there at this time to test ballistics that had a nuclear load on them. They wanted us to test them just to see if they would work. We placed them in an island close by there.

Marcel: What is the name of that island?

Mr. Garcia: It was San Jose Island, in which it was totally inhabitable. Many different kinds of weapons are there and eventually they will explode, and no one can go in there.

Because the poisons that we threw and released in there was incredible. It would cost billions of dollars to try to clean that up.

~ 58 ~

Another Scientist is Deprived of Existence

Marcel: Mr. Garcia, you had indicated that there was nine out of ten scientists deprived of existence, and yet you being the only one from the CIA left as a witness to tell the truth, no wonder the government still threatens your life and your family's life at the age of 80 yrs. old.

Mr. Garcia: This is what they do when they have gotten what they need from you. Well, let me tell you about this other scientist and what happened to him and his unfortunate friend.

(Names Have Been Changed)

   While inside the home of Dr. Warrensburg –
Night –
The phone is ringing in the kitchen and the scientist answers the phone (with a German accent).

Dr. Warrensburg: Hello, this is Dr. Warrensburg.

   The call was coming from Commander McClellan.

Commander McClellan: Dr. Warrensburg, this is Commander McClellan.

Dr. Warrensburg: Yes sir, what can I do for you sir.

~ 59 ~

Commander McClellan: I would like to have you come to the lab building, you left some important documents on your table. I need you to come and pick them up immediately.

Dr. Warrensburg: Yes sir, I will be right there.

Dr. Warrensburg hung up the phone and walked to the living room, with a look of dismay on his face wondering what documents he was talking about. While Dr. Warrensburg walked into the living room he informed his company and his wife that he had to leave for just a few minutes, he then looks at his wife Kelly and says;

Dr. Warrensburg: Honey, I need to leave for just a few minutes, a commander just called indicating that I need to pick up some documents from the lab, and I'll be right back.

Kelly: Ok, but be back soon.

Dr. Warrensburg's guests are Carlos and his wife Marie.

Dr. Warrensburg: Carlos would you like to go with me; this should only take a minute?

Carlos: Sure, why not, Marie I'll be right back.

Marie: All right, but be careful Carlos, I love you.

Carlos: I love you to babes.

In front of the lab building – Night –

In the lighted parking lot, in front of the lab building, Dr. Warrensburg and Carlos are seen walking out of Dr. Warrensburg's car.

Dr. Warrensburg: This will not take long; we'll just get the documents and leave.

Carlos: No problem.

Dr. Warrensburg is seen unlocking the door. The moment he opened the door, the smoke filled room of a deadly chemical comes pouring out of the building through the door.

Mr. Garcia: The inhalation from the sudden surprise caused an inhaling horror of sudden death, from an extremely deadly chemical. Within seconds Dr. Warrensburg and Carlos are seen collapsing to their death.

6

THE CAPTURE OF THE "ANGEL OF DEATH"

Next to the Rio Negro River
In The Amazon Jungles of South America

A military team of 20, U.S. Army soldiers are being led by Officer Ernest Garcia, are united together to prepare to meet their objective.

We went after the Nazis there as they tried to regroup themselves there in the jungles. We were on the edge of the Rio Negro River, getting ready to get on our small boats.

Mr. Garcia: Officers we are here to infiltrate this territoryand subdue the Nazis that have regrouped here and there are some extraordinary criminals that need to be neutralized. We will break up in groups of four and take these five small boats down the Rio Negro River. Everyone stay close together and just follow me.

The soldiers are seen getting into the boats and starting their way down the Rio Negro River. While going down the river Mr. Garcia's sitting on the front of the boat, and the other boats are in a V shape behind him. Mr. Garcia is looking deeply into the jungle, while the boats are moving slowly down the river. Then all of a sudden Mr. Garcia saw something on the edge of the river.

Mr. Garcia: Randy take a look at this, it looks like a rusty metal object.

Randy: Well, it's rusty all right.

Charles: Maybe it's a boat of some sort.

James: Let me try to get us a little closer.

James takes the boat closer towards that object. Mr. Garcia comments.

Mr. Garcia: Take a look at that, it's a submarine. It looks like it got hung up in the sand. They sure did travel a long ways to try to hide out. Come on let's pull over to the side over here and get off. James wave to the other officers and tell them to follow us.

James is waves at the other officers on the other boats, to follow him off the river. James: Come on guys, let's pull over!

The officers are now seen walking together into the jungle Mr. Garcia is reminding them of a little history, and what to expect.

Mr. Garcia: Now officers if you recall at the time of the Holocaust when one of the big honchos there in Germany was Adolf Eichmann.

That caught Randy's attention; he now starts to look at Mr. Garcia and responds by saying.

Randy: How could anyone forget that bastard?

Mr. Garcia: Well he was the one that ordered to have the Jewish people almost starved to death, and then placed them in cages like rabbits, and it was cold, and they were just skin and bones, but they were still alive. Then they got them out of there, when they saw that they weren't going to make it. Then they put them in a basket, and then they were thrown on a conveyor system where they would be conveyed all the way into those furnaces, while they were still alive, and that was the end of that.

Charles: Then the Nazis were sent to the Nuremberg Trials and convicted of war crimes and were sentenced to death.

Mr. Garcia agrees and then continues to his story.

Mr. Garcia: Yes, that is right and these ones escaped because they were on the list and needed to get the hell out. And these guys are notorious criminals.

As James comments he raises his arms up with a fist on both hands.

James: And these Nazis might be here, and we are going to neutralize them, in other words we are going to kill them!

As Mr. Garcia responds, he then points to go forward.

Mr. Garcia: You got that right James, now let's go get them!

They travel deep into the jungle, after a few hours Mr. Garcia noticed a small village in the valley of these mountains, it is now 6:00pm and the sun is about to set.

Mr. Garcia: All right guys hold it; there is a small village just up ahead.

Mr. Garcia, pulled out his binoculars and is focusing in on this small village, he then declares that.

Mr. Garcia: There is a couple of Nazis walking out of a building.

Mr. Garcia is putting the binoculars down to his side while he looks at Randy and then tells him.

Mr. Garcia: Randy, I want you to get your sniper rifle ready and climb up on that tree, and you will take out those men that are on the outside. But wait for my signal or for me to commence firing first. There are five buildings there, in which could house about ten men each. I want four other sniper men equally spaced across the brush ahead of those buildings. Then there will be three men per building, and all of you will throw your grenades inside those buildings. Be sure and confirm that they are housed with soldiers. Wait for my signal that will indicate that we are all ready. Then we will fire at the same time so that no one will escape.

Mr. Garcia taps Randy on the shoulder and points to the tree that he was indicating previously.

Mr. Garcia: But if you see Eichmann, do not kill him, I want him alive, and that goes for all of you. So look into the building first before you throw your grenades, is that understood?
Randy: Yes sir!

The rest of the officers commented the same as they nod their heads yes, and salute to Mr. Garcia, and he salutes back to the officers.

Mr. Garcia taps Randy on his back this time and tells him.

Mr. Garcia: Now, go Randy, and show them your skills and just wait for my signal and make every shot count.

Randy takes off running towards the tree, keeping his head low.

Mr. Garcia: Charles and James come with me, the rest of you know your jobs, now let's kick some butt, for what they did to the Jews, and their judgment day has now come.

The teams of soldiers were strengthened by his words, inspiration and vigor rose within them with intensity, and all the soldiers said; Yes!

The soldiers hide on the side of their assigned buildings – sun starts to set – moments later.
The officer's use hand signals to communicate to one another. There are three soldiers per team and ready to meet their objective.

Team A) Mr. Garcia signals to team B to look in the window for Adolf Eichmann, so Garcia points with two fingers at his eyes, and then he points to the window just above him.

Team B) Received Garcia's signal, and raises one thumb up to confirm that he received it, then he signaled to the second person behind him to go to the back of the building and pass the message to the others.

Team C) was hiding underneath an old horse trailer, while receiving the signal from team B. One soldier raised one thumb up to confirm, then he tapped the soldier next to him, to follow the instructions. He crawls out from underneath and is seen looking in the window, then moving forward to the front of the building in order to get a visual of the other officers across the opposite side. He now signals to the other soldiers.

Team D) is hiding between a small barn and a pile of hay, they receive the signal and signaled back with one thumb up.

Team E) was hiding at the back of the house between the house and the odd house. They received the signal and confirmed with one thumb up. Then this soldier moved across the side of the building to get a visual on Mr. Garcia. He saw Garcia and signaled to him with two thumbs up, signifying that everyone is ready to go. Garcia confirms back with two thumbs up.

There are three Nazis seen standing under a tree smoking cigarettes and talking away, not knowing their damnation is very near.

Mr. Garcia now signals to James next to him, to prepare to throw his grenade through the window. Then right after that Garcia taps Charles on the shoulder to come with him to the front door of the building, immediately Charles responds to Garcia's order.

There are four Nazis seen inside the building playing cards around the coffee table in the living room. All of the Nazis suddenly turned their heads towards the thrusting sound of the front door being burst open by Garcia and Charles right by his side.

Mr. Garcia: Here's your straight flush Nazis!

Garcia and Charles are seen throwing their grenades at the Nazis. The Nazis responded by standing straight up from their chairs. But unfortunately another grenade comes flying in through the window right in the middle of them. The Nazis are seen at a glance looking around with a look of surprise and fear on their face, and unfortunately for the Nazis that is all they had remaining was a glance.

Garcia is seen jumping out of the front door while Charles is descending through the air right after him.

Then all at the same time intense explosions go off while all of the buildings are being demolished, with the Nazis.

Then all of a sudden a series of shots go off:

- A) The two Nazis walking across the field, one gets shot in the head that takes a part of his head off and then causes him to take a sudden step to the side, then goes to the ground.
- B) The other Nazis next to him got hit with a storm of bullets causing him to shiver

where he stands for a second and then he drops to the ground.
C) The three Nazis by the tree looked up suddenly with a surprise look on their faces, but it was too late.
D) The one in the far right of them got hit on the forehead, then three times in the body and then dropped.
E) The one in the middle got hit in his left eye and twice in the body and then he collapsed to the ground.
F) The one in the far left still had the cigarette in his mouth, he got hit in the throat and smoke came out and a series of shots were stormed through his body.

With the sun setting behind the hills brings a glow of yellow/reddish color, which highlights a background for a spectacular scene from the explosions of the buildings.

The soldiers are back together and gathered around Mr. Garcia a few 100ft. from the explosion; the smoke is still seen on the background, while the sun starts to set.

Mr. Garcia: I must commend you guys, you did a wonderful job back there, and not one man is missing, that was beautiful team work and perfect timing. The snipers came in with precision shooting and we all came out victorious.

The Soldiers: Yea, we kicked some butt, yea!

James: Now, that is called getting down!

Mr. Garcia: Now, that was funny James, but there is still a problem.

Randy: What is the problem sir?

Mr. Garcia: Adolf Eichmann was not there. I still need to capture this notorious criminal known as the "Angel of Death."

Randy: The "Angel of Death" wow!

Mr. Garcia: Well of course, look how many Jews Eichmann and Hitler the Satanist himself had killed.

James: I guess if a person kills for Satan, he deserves a disgusting title as that.

Mr. Garcia: Well let's move forward, we will find a place to camp while I pursue to conquer my objective.

They walk deeper into the jungle – dark – one hour later.

The full moon is lighting the jungle in the early of the night. The team of soldiers notices a small village of natives close by with a small campfire between the center of the huts and the small adobe houses. With James and Randy on each side of Garcia, and the other soldiers behind them, Garcia recognizes the small village and proclaims to the officers what is ahead of them.

Mr. Garcia: There is a small village ahead of us that looks to have just a few natives living there.

Mr. Garcia turns his head and looks at Randy and says.

Mr. Garcia: Randy, go take a closer look around that village to see if there are any Nazis there and report right back.

Randy: Yes sir, I'll be right back with my report sir.

Randy is seen spying around the village – moments later.
Randy then comes back to give Mr. Garcia the report and tells him.
Randy: Mr. Garcia, the village is clear from Nazis. There are only a few natives there.

Mr. Garcia: Ok, thank you Randy now let's move forward.

As the soldiers are seen walking in the village with Randy on Garcia's left side and James and the other soldiers behind him.
The messenger is seen once again, this time he is sitting on the ground leaning his back against the tree. Then the messenger raises his head and looks directly at Mr. Garcia's eyes, while the light

from the campfire reflects and gleams from the messenger's eyes and then he says.

Messenger: Vengeance is mine, says the Lord.

Mr. Garcia has an expression of curiosity on his face; while the messenger's words pierced his heart.

While they continue walking passed the messenger, Mr. Garcia then turns his eyes downward towards the ground while placing his right hand on his chest, remembering that he had seen this person before.
James while he is walking and looking at Mr. Garcia, he is pointing back to the messenger with his right hand, he then says to Mr. Garcia.

James: Now what kind of message was that? What the hell did he mean by that?
Mr. Garcia then places his hand down from his chest, while he continues to walk, he then raises his head up and is now looking forward and then proclaims.

Mr. Garcia: It's not what he meant, but where the message came from that matter.

James is seen throwing both arms up in the air, not understanding what Garcia meant.

James: Well whatever, you got me on that one.

After walking about a half a mile, Mr. Garcia points to the flat ground off to the side of them and directs the soldiers.

Mr. Garcia: All right soldiers, I want you to set up camp right here while Randy, James, Charles and I are going to the other side of that mountain that is about a mile away and see what is over the other side, and I'll keep you informed.

The Soldiers: Yes sir, Mr. Garcia sir (salute).

After a mile of traveling, Mr. Garcia and his three officers are now crossing over the mountain that they were trying to get to. They now find themselves close to a camp, and suddenly hear some banging noise of some kind of metal coming from inside a single building nearby. Garcia starts to speak with a very low voice to his officers.

Mr. Garcia: What the hell is that noise, coming from inside that building? It sounds like someone banging metal together.

The group of officers is now gathered together to discuss this matter.

Charles: That is exactly what it sounds like, someone pounding metal together.

Mr. Garcia: Let's walk forward a little more.

~ 74 ~

Mr. Garcia slowly starts to walk forward while the others follow. They ended up walking to a chain link fence mixed with bob wire that was about seven ft. high.

Randy: Check this out guys, but look about 10ft. beyond the fence. That looks like a large ditch of water all the way around this camp also.

Charles: From what I can see those gates are very securely locked from the inside and the gate becomes the bridge that is held up by a rope and it must be released from the other side of the ditch in order to cross over that ditch.

Mr. Garcia: I do not see anyone around the outside of this
building, and I'll bet you there are probably Nazis inside that building.

Randy: I wouldn't doubt that at all Mr. Garcia, but we need to get one of us over to the other side of this fence and unlock the gate. Who is going to go in there first?

Mr. Garcia: Well guys, I guess we better turn ourselves into superheroes.

They all reached into their fatigue clothes and took out a small vile and drank it.

James: Now come on guys, who is going to be the one to fly over this fence?

They paused for a moment with a smile on their faces while looking at each other wondering who is going to the other side.

Charles: The shorter guy here is Garcia. How about it Mr. Garcia?

Mr. Garcia: Well, we came here to do a job, so let's get this done.

The two bigger soldiers are Charles and Randy; they are the ones that will throw Mr. Garcia over the fence.

Charles: Alright Randy let's do this together and show Mr. Garcia what flying is really like.

Randy: Let's do it my man, let's do it.

Randy and Charles squatted down low and took a hold of each other's hands and are now ready for Mr. Garcia.

Charles: Alright Mr. Garcia we are ready, you know what to do sir.

Mr. Garcia starts to place his feet on Charles's and Randy's hands and then Garcia squats down a little to help him with his jump.

Mr. Garcia: I'm ready guys, let's go.

~ 76 ~

Charles and Randy threw Mr. Garcia clearly over the top of the fence and to the other side. It was unfortunate though that Garcia landed on his head.

Charles, Randy and James: Start to laugh.

Right after Mr. Garcia landed on his head he got extremely serious, because all of a sudden he heard some dog barking close by.

Mr. Garcia: Oh, shit!

Mr. Garcia is seen running to the gate; Garcia starts to cut the rope that is attached to the gate. Just when he finished cutting the rope, the gate collapsed to the ground. Then suddenly a dog started biting into Garcia's right hand and obtained a good grip on Garcia. The dog was large enough to drag Mr. Garcia on the ground from his right hand and tearing deeply into the skin with its firm grip.

Mr. Garcia: Damn it! Where and the hell is my knife?

Mr. Garcia is desperately moving his left hand around his body looking for his knife. Garcia found his knife on his right hip; he pulls out the knife with a firm grip on the handle and then leans over to his right side while being pulled by the dog. Garcia bent his right elbow in to bring the dog closer to him and then sliced the dog's throat by reaching from Garcia's right side to the left side. Blood was all over Garcia's wrist from the dog bite, and all across his right side from the blood of the dog's neck. Garcia is seen getting up from the ground.

There was very little light from an oil lamp hanging on the pole by the entrance of the building and inside the building an oil lamp was also lit up.

Charles, Randy and James are now crossing over the collapsed gate and entering into the camp. Randy is looking at Garcia and notices all the blood on him and asked him.

Randy: Damn Mr. Garcia, are you all right?

Mr. Garcia: Yea, I think so, everything happened so fast.

James: Mr. Garcia, your certainly soaked in blood.

Mr. Garcia is seen looking at himself, wondering if all that blood came from the dogfight or was he also shot.

Mr. Garcia: I am certainly soaked in blood, I wonder if maybe I got shot also.

The soldiers start looking around to see if the enemy is anywhere around them.

Charles: Put your hand inside your shirt and see if you're shot.

Mr. Garcia is putting his left hand inside his shirt and trying to see if he got shot.

Mr. Garcia: No, I do not feel any bullet holes; all of that blood must have come from that dogfight.

Randy takes out a small first aid kit.

Randy: Here Mr. Garcia, let me wrap that wrist for you.

While Randy is wrapping Mr. Garcia's wrist, the banging noise inside the building continues, no wonder they did not hear the struggling outside.

Mr. Garcia: Well obviously whoever is inside that building was not distracted by the noise out here? They are still clanging on that metal.

Just when Randy was completing the wrapping on Mr. Garcia's wrist and placing the tape over the wrap, Mr. Garcia was enthusiastic about pursuing his objective.

Mr. Garcia: All right Randy, are you finished?

Randy: Yes sir, you're ready to go.

Mr. Garcia is now standing before the ditch, and while he is looking at the ditch he then places an order.

Mr. Garcia: Ok guys, let's cross over the ditch and take cover right along the side of the ditch.

The soldiers are seen obeying Mr. Garcia's command.

The soldiers are now taking cover along the other side of the ditch. Mr. Garcia is with them, except one of his feet is digging into the water. Mr. Garcia suddenly jumps up away from the ditch.

Mr. Garcia: What the hell was that! Something in this water was biting on my boot, ether a piranha or a gator; I don't know what the hell it was.

James: Mr. Garcia, you sure are prime bait for the animals tonight.

While Mr. Garcia is pointing at the building he says.

Mr. Garcia: Whoever is in there sure knows how to set up a trap. Come here guys gather around here.

The soldiers are seen gathering around Mr. Garcia.

Mr. Garcia: There might be some resistance when we go inside this building.

James is seen pulling out a hand grenade.

James: Let me just throw this baby in there and take out who ever are in there.

Mr. Garcia: Don't even think about it that would be the last resort. What we are going to do is stand by each side of the door and talk out loud in Spanish and English. This will get them to come out, and then we will see if we have any resistance.
Now guys let's get to that door and have your guns drawn out but be patient to see who is inside.
　The soldiers are talking out loud at the same time in both Spanish and English with their guns drawn out while standing on each side of the door. The door begins to open and sure enough it was "Adolf Eichmann" himself the "Angel of Death" stands boldly at the door. There was another Nazi soldier standing right behind him. Adolf Eichmann had a surprise look on his face, and then changed the look on his face with a look of arrogance. While Adolf Eichmann is starring at Mr. Garcia, Mr. Garcia then steps in front of his soldiers and stares right back at Adolf. Mr. Garcia then pushes Adolf back with his left arm, while he is holding a gun to his head on his right hand.

Mr. Garcia: All right you cocky son of a bitch! You're under arrest! The notorious "Angel of Death" is now busted.

Charles: You're the man Garcia, you caught Adolf Eichmann, and this is now history in the making.

The other soldiers had their guns drawn out and were aiming at the Nazis. Then suddenly a "clashing of noise" came from behind them as if there was someone crossing over the gate. As the soldiers turned behind them to look where the noise was coming from, a sudden force of three Israeli soldiers were pushing the American soldiers from behind and made their way into the building with large machine guns aiming at the heads of the Americans.

Israeli Soldier: Put your guns down!

Mr. Garcia: Ok, ok, all right guys lower your guns.

The American soldiers are seen putting their guns down.

After the American soldiers had put their guns down they started moving out of the way of the Israeli soldiers as they walked up to Adolf Eichmann.

Israeli Soldier: Hay we know whom this is!

The Israeli soldier at that time is pointing his right index finger straight at Eichmann's face.

Israeli Soldier: And we want him! He is going with us!

The Israeli soldier then uses the same hand and points his thumb at himself.
While Mr. Garcia raises his palm up to stop the Israeli soldier he said.

Mr. Garcia: Well wait a minute here! Who and the hell are you? Quepasa?

The Israeli soldier moved his palm upward signifying that he did not understand what Mr. Garcia just said. The Israeli soldier strongly points his thumb back to himself again to get his point across and says.

Israeli Soldier: We want him! And we are going to take him! And we are willing to kill!

The Israeli soldiers then raised their machine guns a little higher at the American soldiers as preparing to shoot them.
Mr. Garcia is seen raising his right palm at himself and his left palm up in the air and moves his head side to side (as a meaning of no).

Mr. Garcia: You know, I got so many brothers and sisters back in the states and I would like to live long enough to go back and see them.

Mr. Garcia then stepped to the side and pointed to Adolf Eichmann.

Mr. Garcia: Let the bastard go; let them have him the hell with it.

The Israeli soldiers then take down the two Nazis and start to restrain them.

Just outside the Nazi building – dark – moments later.

All three of the Israeli soldiers had horses and Adolf Eichmann is seen lying on the ground tied up to a rope and about to be dragged by the soldiers' horse. They started to move down a trail, which took them down this mountain. The third Israeli soldier rode his horse at the back end of the other two soldiers while the Nazis were being dragged.

Back inside the Nazi camp building – moments later.
Mr. Garcia is seen setting a plan with his troops, he turns around and looks at his officers and says.

Mr. Garcia: Two of us will follow these guys to see where they are going and the other two stay here. Now do not handle any of the contents underneath that tarp there. We will check that out when we get back. Randy you come with me.

Randy: Yes sir lets go.

Mr. Garcia and Randy are hiding behind some brush at the base of the mountain watching the Israeli soldiers untying the Nazis from the horses while standing next to their private plane. Then by surprise the local armed law enforcement surrounds them and takes over.

Randy: Now take a look at that, the local law enforcement just surrounded the Israelis and the Nazis and just took over.

Mr. Garcia: Well look at what these Israelis did, they made themselves so conspicuous by dragging those Nazis down this mountain for everyone to see now that was foolish.

Randy: What do you think will happen next?
Mr. Garcia: I think it will be a political game for quite a while but I believe that the Israelis will get the upper hand and end up with the Nazis.

Randy: Your probably right sir.

Mr. Garcia: Well let's head back.

Mr. Garcia and Randy are now entering into the Nazi building – one hour later.

Mr. Garcia: All right guys let's take that tarp off and see what is underneath that baby.

Mr. Garcia points at the tarp and walks over to it, the rest of the soldiers follow and help pull the tarp off. Right after they pulled the tarp off, they all end up with a look of amazement in their eyes.

Mr. Garcia: Wow, look at all of this gold!

Charles: My God, this is quite a treasure.

Mr. Garcia: Wait a minute, what is inside these individually wrapped packages?

Mr. Garcia starts to walk over to the wrapped packages leaning on the side of the blocks of gold, the packages were about 4ft. x 4ft. x 2in. thick in size.

Mr. Garcia: James hand me your knife so I can cut this canvas wrapping, my knife is full of blood still from that dam dog attack.

James is taking his knife out of his sheathe on the side of his belt.

James: I will be more than happy to oblige sir.

Mr. Garcia takes the knife from James and smiles.

Mr. Garcia: I'll bet you are.

While Garcia is cutting the canvas wrapping Randy was standing on the backside of this package.

Mr. Garcia: Randy would you help me pull the backside of this wrapping off?

Randy: Sure Mr. Garcia.

There was another look of amazement on the soldiers eyes as the wrapping slowly starts to come down.

Charles: Oh my God, look at this beautiful famous painting.

Randy is seen looking at the back area where the blocks of gold are, he then says.

Randy: Yea, and that's not all, there are more of those packages back here behind this gold.

While James is standing there he is shaking his head back and forth and then says.

James: My mama is going to be proud of me when I take some of this back home. I can see my mama crying right now.

Mr. Garcia: Yea, I can see your mama crying as I tell you guys sorry, but all of this has to be reported, none of it goes to mama.

Charles, James and Randy all suddenly get a bummed out look on their faces and they all made negative statements.

As we return back to the interview with Marcel in Mr. Garcia's office.

Marcel: Now some of that gold you showed me a while ago, did that come from there or from the Philippines?

Mr. Garcia: (Laughs) no all that gold was taken by the government. It would have been nice though, there was about twenty two tons of gold there. They had the German symbol on the bars of gold called the swastika.

Marcel: So Mr. Garcia what happened to Adolf Eichmann?
Mr. Garcia: The reports show that the Israelis took Adolf Eichmann to Israel and hung him there.

Marcel: I believe that you're capturing of Adolf Eichmann should be recorded and documented in the history books as you being the one who captured and arrested Adolf Eichmann.

Mr. Garcia: Yea, that would be nice but it's unfortunate that the officers of the CIA do not get that kind of recognition.

Marcel: Now shortly after that mission you were sent to Panama.

Mr. Garcia: Yes they were having a big shindig, it must have been Christmas or New Years, and they had an Officer's Club out there.

Illegal Drug Deals In The Government

New Year's party in Panama – night – in the late 1940's. The Officers Club was full of officers and women celebrating New Year's night.

Mr. Garcia: Although we did not have the privilege to expose ourselves very much there, we did not want anyone to know who and the heck we were or what we were doing there. Then this Commander came up to me and gave an order that I had to do, he said.
Commander: Officer Garcia, you're going for a little ride
with this pilot here, you guys have a little mission to do.

Mr. Garcia: Where to?

Commander: Well I don't know really, but you'll go with the pilot and you'll know when you get there. You are required to deliver this box to where you are going and then you will be picking up another one and bring that one back.

In the same area of the Officers Club, at the airstrip – moments later.

~ 89 ~

The Commander, the pilot and Garcia are standing next to a fighter plane and a government car parked right behind them in which they came in.

Mr. Garcia: My God, this is a fighter plane, how am I supposed to carry that box in the plane?

Commander: Oh, you'll make room for it somehow.

Mr. Garcia: We made room for it all right, let me tell you this pilot was ether drunk or on drugs, but this pilot was stupid. This pilot was doing all kinds of tricks in the air and flying upside down close to the ocean water, he was crazy. When we landed we landed in Mobile, Alabama.
   The airport in Mobile Alabama and the fighter plane is being refueled.

Mr. Garcia: While the pilot was refueling the plane, I met up with the connection. The connection involved four men, one walking ahead of the other three while they were approaching me one of them said.

Group Leader: Are you from Panama?

Mr. Garcia: Yea, I'm from Panama, who are you?

Group Leader: We are your connection over here, and we need that box that's wrapped and we have another one that you're going to take back.

Mr. Garcia: Ok.

Back at the airstrip in Panama, a couple of hours later. Mr. Garcia is seen walking away from the fighter plane caring the other package.

Mr. Garcia: Sure enough when we landed back into Panama there comes all those assholes.

The Commander and several other Officers are seen coming to greet Mr. Garcia as they meet up with Garcia. Garcia makes the first comment.

Mr. Garcia: I don't believe this shit! I risk my ass to take all that stuff over there, this is bullshit, here is your dam box I do not want anything to do with this.

Commander: Ok Garcia, just give me the box.

The Commander is seen opening the box; the box is full of cash.

The scene changes back to the interview with Marcel in Mr. Garcia's office. Mr. Garcia continues to say what he felt about that experience and what became of it.

Mr. Garcia: There was no accountability what so ever, if you had a high rank you could almost do anything you wanted to and if you talk its bad news.

Marcel: So what was it that you delivered to Alabama, cocaine?

Mr. Garcia: Well we found out later on that it was cocaine and that is the truth. We tried to tell the government about it and in return we got threatened if we exposed stuff like that. Later there were some statements made by some of those pilots that were involved in this all the time, they exposed it and it was on the records.

Marcel: And that was all she wrote.

Mr. Garcia: Well you see the government places these things on the record just to cover their ass, you see.

Marcel: Yes, but what I also do see on these documents is that you were a candidate for the Nobel Peace Prize, for what you had done for the veterans across this nation you should have received it.

Mr. Garcia: Now that would have been nice unfortunately they gave it to a person that was involved with "Project Sunshine."

Marcel: It is amazing how some people value immoral attributes over integrity. That just comes to tell you how sick this world has gotten. But I must say that justice will prevail.

A Greater Holocaust Is Imminent

Marcel: The president of Iran (Mahmoud Ahmadinejad) seems to be calling for another Holocaust, he proclaims that he had been chosen by Allah to become Iran's leader and hasten the coming of the Islamic messiah known as the Twelfth Imam or the Mahdi by launching a final holy war against Christians and Jews. He publicly promised to annihilate the United Sates and wipe Israel "off the map." He proclaimed in the year of 2006 that the end of the world was just two or three years away, it is now 2009. Western intelligence agencies and experts predict that Iran could have operational nuclear weapons within that same time period.
    With a nuclear Iran they can threaten the west in ways that are unimaginable; they can take over the Persian Gulf and control most of the oil. Iran would subordinate Iraq in two seconds.
    What Hitler did in a time period of six years, the president of Iran could do in just six minutes and that is to annihilate six million Jews and leave only a remnant to survive.
    Hitler embarked on a world conflict and sought to achieve nuclear weapons, where as the leading radical Islamic regime Iran is seeking to first acquire nuclear weapons and then embark on the world conflict. Which "needs" to be understood and if it is understood why isn't it acted upon. We need to wake up; otherwise it will be too late.

"This is bigger Nazism"

~ 93 ~

"This is unbelievably dangerous"

Garcia, Ernest, (Since July 18, 2008). An OSS/CIA covert actions operator. Oral history interview conducted by Marcel L. Garcia Jr.

7

REGRESSIVE SCIENCE

The Ethics of Clandestine Scientific Research –
A Rejoinder to the Advisory Committee on Human
Radiation Experiments
Center for Organizational and Behavioral Science

The 1960 address of British physicist and author C.P. Snow to the American Association for the Advancement of Science (AAAS) expresses confidence in the progressive ethics of science.

English author and physicist, PH.D. Cambridge 1930. A concern which he expresses in his essay "The Two Cultures and the Scientific Revolution"…..Snow was knighted in 1957 for his services during the Second World War.

Snow Witnessed Physicists Fall From
Grace in World War II

Most scientist thought then that Nazism was as near absolute evil as a human society can manage. That being so, Nazism had to be fought, and since the Nazis might make fission bombs – which we thought possible until 1944, well, then we had to make them, too. But the trouble is, when you get onto any kind of moral escalator, you never know whether you're ever going to be able to get off.

Snow held scientists, not military personnel, to the task of getting off the escalator. For obedience is the "foundation of morality" in the military, but "Scientists have to question and if necessary to rebel."

Snow spoke more confidently of science ethics than advocates would venture now, after revelations of postwar radiation, psychochemical, and behavioral experiments on unwitting human subjects. But other researchers have kept alive his vision. In 1997, AIDS researcher Charles F. Farthing convinced that "a vaccine is the only realistic means of combating the worldwide AIDS epidemic," announced his decision to undergo test vaccination himself. Farthing's example drew others: "I have been joined by about 300 physicians, AIDS researchers, AIDS activists, and other public-spirited citizens confounding some critics who have said we would never be able to recruit human subjects for such a study."

Farthing, Charles F. (1997, October 27). Putting my body on the line: A physician explains why he and hundreds of colleagues will test an AIDS vaccine on themselves. "The Washington Post National Weekly Edition." P. 21.

With explanation by *Regressive Science*, abuses of subjects in clandestine research are products of a less enlightened era, or the fact that scientist sometimes lose their moral bearings when caught up in national defense projects. The National Academy of Science, in its 1991 ethical assessment of chemical warfare experiments on American soldiers in World War II, first tried to understand the historical context: "It was a war and the experiments were conducted before the Nuremberg Code of 1947 established formal principles to govern the proper treatment of human subjects." President Clinton's January 1994 Advisory Committee on Human Radiation Experiments conducted oral histories of eminent physicians from the 1940s and 1950s to determine ethical standards then. Committee members fiercely debated whether it was even fair to make retrospective moral judgments on government sponsored radiation experiments because standards they believe ethical standards have risen. In this view, the solution to the moral problems of clandestine research is to develop stronger institutional norms for ethical practice in the scientific community. This spirit of a high moral calling for scientists and the wherewithal to carry it off animated the 1994 Advisory Committee on Human Radiation Experiments.

The Final Report of the Advisory Committee on Human Radiation Experiments

In March 1945, J. Robert Oppenheimer, director of the Manhattan Project, authorized a tracer study of plutonium on terminal patients, who were expected to die before the plutonium harmed them.

The urgent military purpose for injecting these patients with plutonium was to determine the rate of bodily excretion so as to gauge the plutonium risk to bomb production workers. However, this urgency did motivate Manhattan Project scientists to test themselves, as the AIDS epidemic motivated Farthing and his colleagues. The secret experiment on unwitting subjects achieved notoriety in 1993, when the Albuquerque Tribune portrayed the afflictions to some victims who had unexpectedly survived for decades. Under the leadership of Department of Energy Secretary Hazel O'Leary and goaded by public uproar President Clinton appointed an Advisory Committee to "tell the full story to the American public" about government sponsored "human" radiation experiments.

The fourteen Committee members were mainly biomedical scientists and supporting academics in ethics, history of science, law, and so on. As a context for ethical review, the Committee embedded the radiation experiments in the history of radiation medicine from the discovery of X-rays in 1885, to the use of radioisotopes as tracers in 1913, and so on. The Committee reviewed 4,000 radiation studies from the period 1944 to 1974, taking as its cutoff date the year of the Department of Health, Welfare, and Education

Regulations on "Human Subjects Research." The Committee's Final Report in October 1995 condemned many studies as unethical and recommended compensation and apologies to some victims. "No researchers though were accused of scientific misconduct."

The monumental empirical investigation by the Advisory Committee left two major legacies of data and public policy.

First, thousands of declassified documents were deposited in the National Archive, on the Internet, and in supplemental volumes to the Final Report. Second, the Clinton Administration responded to the Committee's recommendations with policies for "openness in government," "protecting future human subjects," and "righting past wrongs," in a bulletin called "Building Public_Trust." For progress in science ethics, the Committee's triumph was the Human Research Subject Protection Act of 1997. Federal funding studies now require informed consent of all human subjects, and consent cannot be waived, as in the past, for national security interests. Violation is a *criminal* offense. But the National Association of Radiation Survivors would say that the Nuremberg Code already made that point. The problem remains at the level of monitoring and enforcement.

Pechura, C.M., & Rall, D.P. (Eds.) (1993). Veterans at risk: The health effects of mustard gas and lewisite. Washington, DC: National Academy P. vii.

Committee member Ruth Macklin described this debate during a question period. Mastroianni, A. & Kahn, Jeffrey (Cochairs), (1996, November). Post War government sponsored radiation research. Symposium conduction at the meeting of the American Association of Bioethics, San Francisco, CA. (Official conference recordings from HMR Duplications, 4252 Coolidge Ave., Oakland, CA 94602).

Final Report.

U.S. Government Human Radiation Interagency Working Group. (1997, March). Building public trust: Actions to respond to the report of the Advisory Committee on Human Radiation Experiments. (DOE/EH0542: Stock No. 061000008802.) Washington, D.C.: U.S. Government Printing Office.

Scientist as Tools of Intelligence Agencies

In explanation by *Regressive Science*, scientists are the protagonists in abuses of clandestine research: scientists therefore are the potential saviors, Ernest Garcia, a former OSSCIA covert actions operator, challenged the notion of the autonomy of scientists, in his oral history interview. Garcia was variously involved with scientists in the late 1940s and early 1950s as manipulator, project field assistant, and involuntary experimental subject.

Mr. Garcia: What the operators do is they tease scientists on their projects sufficient to get them interested to where they can't remove themselves out of it.
This is my personal observation. And once they become involved to that extent, it becomes their baby and they don't want to let go of it. With that in mind, I think that they become submissive to whatever is necessary. They allow themselves to be manipulated.

Garcia also disagreed with the assumptions that science ethics are progressive and that scientists, as Snow said, are "just perceptibly more morally admirable....."

Garcia, Ernest, (1995, October 21 & 22). An OSSCIA covert actions operator. Oral history interview conducted by Jean Maria Arrigo, Albuquerque, NM. –See Appendix for a copy of Garcia's release from secrecy by Secretary of Defense William Perry in 199_.

Garcia does not distinguish between the OSS (Office of Strategic Services) and its successor, the CIA (Central Intelligence Agency) in conduct of operations.

Arrigo: The scientific community and the public have the idea that in order to control scientist's experimentation on people, that they could institute some kind of codes of ethics. And I wonder if you can estimate whether there are any kinds of codes or safeguards or guidelines which would serve in secret research?

Mr. Garcia: I can truthfully tell you this, from my personal experience that's been involved in both ends of the area (as covert operator and victim). It's very interesting that you would bring that up. But I have made it a point to study the obedience of a commitment by other professionals. And I have not found anybody that is less sensitive to its commitment than the scientific community. They are willing to prostitute themselves, to totally disregard their oaths in the name of secrecy or the name of the betterment of humanity, when in fact it is a sham—it is not true at all.

Garcia said that he was at Nuremberg briefly during the war crimes trials to round up Nazis to bring back to the United States. He reported his later, nearly fatal experience in mustard gas and psychochemical experiments at Edgewood Arsenal. At the time of the oral interview, he showed me a documentary film called "Bad Trip to Edgewood" with apparently original film footage of Edgewood Arsenal experiments on soldiers. Some of the original film footage of Edgewood Arsenal experiments on soldiers. Some of the original researchers and subjects were interviewed in the documentary. The apparent indifference of the researchers to the visible distress of the subjects produced a chilling effect.

Hunt, L. (1991). Secret agenda: The United States government, Nazi scientists, and Project Paperclip, 1945 1990. New York: St. Martin's. Hunt is an investigative journalist.

Arrigo: What kind of evidence brings you to this opinion?

Mr. Garcia: Well, hell, you know, the commitment made in Nuremberg, for example, was said there, and the ones that stood up and made this flamboyant commitment was the "American" community, saying that never again shall we ever see this kind of encroachment and manifestation or ugliness in mankind again. "At the same time they were plea bargaining with some of the Nazis to come to the United States and *finish their experiments on American citizens*" (at Edgewood Arsenal). That is deplorable. If that isn't an example there, I would like to find a better one.

And then that makes me very angry. They might be very talented, or they might be...And I will say this from my own personal experience, personally, I don't mind telling you, they're "pathological liars, deceivers."

In explanation by *Regressive Science*, the relationship between scientists and their subjects is believed to be the crucial link in abuses of clandestine scientific experiments, so a rule of informed consent by voluntary subjects should help to prevent abuses. Garcia and other interviewees from military and political intelligence gave a different account: scientists are tools of policy an Oppenheimer can be made, and an Oppenheimer can be unmade. In this account, scientists in clandestine research are either collaborators or tools of intelligence, but in no case are they autonomous moral agents in charge of their own projects. Because of scientists' curiosity and their fixed methods of inquiry, scientists are predictable and, therefore, manipulate able. And because of the compartmentalization of information in classified research and the routine deceptions, scientists themselves often don't know the significance or consequences of their own work, even if they should wish to inform their subject. In this account, the crucial link is between science and intelligence, not between scientist and subject. A rule of informed consent of subjects cannot resolve the moral problems in clandestine scientific research. War and appeals to the "national interest" have exigencies that override the delicacies of scientific ethics, and scientists themselves respond to these exigencies.

Pieces Missing from the Final Report.

As chair of the Contaminated Veterans of America, Garcia testified before the Advisory Committee in 1995, but he said that the Committee refused to hear his testimony about serious crimes by scientific researchers. Robert Staplton, who also testified to the Committee and sociologist Lincoln F. Grahlfs, President of the National Association of Radiation Survivors, agreed that the Committee enforced narrow constraints on topics of testimony.

The Committee itself castigated the CIA for blocking investigation, although President Clinton had ordered all federal agencies to comply with the Committee's requests for classified information. As its final recommendation for remedies for abuses in clandestine experiments, the Committee recommended that "most if not all" of the "records of the CIA bearing on programs of *secret human research*, such as MKULTRA and the related CIA human behavior projects from the late 1940s through the early 1970s" be released to the public. In an interview with The_Chronicle of Higher Education, the Committee's Executive Director, Dan Guttman, appeared to accept the response of the CIA: "It wasn't a question of if they were hiding anything, but if they could find anything,"

Garcia commented on the article:

And so here is the CIA saying to the President's Committee, "Well, we weren't very much involved with the human radiation experiment." And they're right by saying that if they was to be asked for some records that they're not going to *find* any (laughing hard), because if there is any, they're going to destroy them. The CIA was very careful on implicating themselves. They went to great lengths of using different people, not always the same people. What has been done has maybe been done in the names of other organizations and agencies, and so on, and not under their own name in any case.

Just remember one thing. "The CIA has the ability to *penetrate anything.*" It is conceivably possible that an Advisory Committee member was even a person who was selected from the ranks of the CIA.

From Garcia's perspective, no competent intelligence agency would have revealed compromising information to a public committee.

Advisory Committee on Human Radiation Experiments. (1995, October). Pp. 838839.

Wheeler, David L. (1995, October 13). Radiation probe taps records spanning 30 years. The Chronicle of Higher Education. A11 &19.P.A11.

At the executive level, if the Committee had been intended as a full investigation instead of political damage control, then sympathetic military historians, intelligence personnel, and other experts who knew the system would have been recruited to assist the science ethics committee.

Discordant views of explanation by Regressive Science

How can the position of C.P. Snow and the President's Advisory Committee be reconciled with the testimonies of covert actions operator Ernest Garcia and counterintelligence agent Ray Tegtmeyer (of Section _). A background passage from Garcia's oral history gives a sense for how his outlook might differ from theirs.

I was born in 1928 in an era of time when it was during the Depression and the opening of the Southwest, in the little valley of Jemez Springs, 18 miles from Los Alamos. We were raised under extraordinary primitive environment in today's standards – hardship, poverty, and isolation. The area was extremely diversified because of the lumber business that came there. We spoke Spanish and English, Indian, Italian; I could speak a little French, German, too. I was extremely mathematical and mechanical. My mother died when I was seven, of some kind of disease that nobody knew what it was. And I'm going to be frank here because this is times that are gone – there were a lot of unnecessary kinds of punishments and abuses.

~ 107 ~

As a child, Garcia had witnessed the construction of Manhattan Project facilities at Los Alamos, after survey of Jemez Springs as a possible site, and the glamour of secret operations with famous people.

The people that worked at Los Alamos maintained a very secluded environment. Dr. Einstein and Dr. Oppenheimer used to come to Jemez Springs on weekends for a meal. And we would always wait for them because Dr. Oppenheimer – he was a kind of frail, skinny guy – would reach into his pocket – I remember his hands trembling – and he would pick these three pennies and give them to us.
    At the end of the war I lied about my age to get into the service. I was in about a thousand of us army recruits selected to fit the CIA criteria (of obedience, stamina, intelligence and language facility). The training period was very, very aggressive. We would be in very difficult situations, terrains, or in other countries, but never, never telling us where we were going.
    Most of the training that we got was how to handle work around scientists, I was mustered into Panama. They had one of the most sophisticated laboratories, because all these chemicals have a different behavioral pattern that is consistent with heat and barometric pressure in the tropics.
    Most of the time we was working under the influence of some sort of a mind-altering drug – some of those covert operations were pretty

horrible – that we became extremely strong and fearless, over and above the capacity of humanity. And they changed us around, never kept too many of us too long at a time working together. So if one of us died, we would just go on.

The epistemology of intelligence developed in Part II provides a theoretical foundation for understanding the divergence of Garcia and Tegtmeyer's testimony from Snow and Faden's explanation of abuses in "clandestine scientific research as *Regressive Science*. Garcia could not have performed in Faden's role as chair of the Advisory Committee.

But neither could she have performed in his as "covert actions operator" – a point that is often lost in evaluating the testimony of participants. By the Epistemological Explanation, in the larger picture of national security their roles depend on each other in ways that must be invisible to be effective, for one defends individual Constitutional liberties and the other defends territory.

Theory Evaluation of Regressive Science

By Thagard's criteria of theory evaluation, *Regressive Science* fares well with respect to simplicity and analogy. The main premises are few: the practice of science tends to edify the scientific community over time, and scientists are morally autonomous in clandestine research. The basic analogy is strong: ethics progress like knowledge progresses in science. The question is how to make ethics keep pace with scientific knowledge – whence Snow's call to action in his AAAS address. "The Moral Un-Neutrality of Science." The analogy of progress prompted the Advisory Committee's Oral History Project in postwar medical ethics and led to the Human Research Subject Protections Act of 1997. The 1997 Act not only regulates on behalf of subjects, which may or may not be efficacious, but it redefines membership in the scientific community to entail progressive ethics by making violation of the Act a crime.

With respect to Thagard's criterion of consilience, *Regressive Science* is able to explain altruistic conduct in research where exploitation of subjects might seem inevitable, as AIDS vaccine trials. Ad Hoc Cynicism, in contrast, must posit hidden, self-serving motives to explain the altruistic self-trials by AIDS research Farthing and his colleagues, but such convolutions defeat its simplicity of explanation.

The analogy of progressive ethics to progressive science does structure and unify the cases explained by *Regressive Science*. But many significant cases remain unexplained, besides the unauthenticated cases of my oral history interviewees. These would include "major abuses" in clandestine scientific research, without clear justification in defense strategy, conducted by eminent scientists. An example is the CIA funded, "psychic driving" project of biological psychiatrist Ewen Cameron. Cameron was elected to the presidencies of the World, American, and Canadian Psychiatric Association, and he was one of the psychiatrists invited to Nuremberg to examine a Nazi defendant. Scholars at Snow's level had a better opinion of Cameron in the 1950s than did one of my oral history interviewees, who underwent thirteen electro and insulin shocks in Cameron's Montreal psychiatric institute.

In the United States, ethical review of government sponsored clandestine research usually occurs, if at all, decades after "alleged abuses," as in the Committee's own restriction of its ambit to 1944-1974 radiation studies. On the assumption that there are no current abuses, past abuses can be interpreted as evidence of *Regressive Science*. The Committee did conduct a survey and interview study of almost 1,900 outpatients in waiting rooms of 20 hospitals and found no significant evidence of current abuses of subjects in biomedical research.

Weinstein, Harvey M. (1990), Psychiatry and the CIA: Victims of mind control. Washington, DC: American Psychiatric Press. P. 92.

Rich, Harvey, (1996). A Zionist patient in Ewen Cameron's psychiatric institute. Harvey is a Canadian political sociologist.

However, the Committee's own studies of past abuses had shown that victims were unwitting, institutionalized, or bound by military secrecy, not witting victims who would be available in hospital waiting rooms.

In sum, explanation by *Regressive Science* is strong on simplicity and analogy but lacks consilience; it cannot account for numerous and far reaching violations of the Nuremberg Code by eminent scientists. The explanation itself guides inquiry away from contemporary abuses of clandestine scientific research that might rebut it – or interfere with current clandestine research for national security operations.

A Methodological Note on the Policy Science Approach

The Advisory Committee on Human Radiation Experiments proceeded according to a schema of enlightened policy science; (a) identification and study of a social problem; (b) design of policy, with a causal theory (progressive ethics) to achieve the desired state of affairs; (c) implementation of the policy; and (d) monitoring and evaluation. Problem study involved painstaking, multi-method, scientific empiricism – massive document analysis, oral histories of physicians, testimonies from victims and their advocates, ethics oral histories of biomedical researchers, interviews, and surveys – with tremendous political, financial, and personnel support. This investigation culminated in (a') public archival of thousands of declassified documents. (b') policy recommendations by the Committee, and (c') implementations announced by the Clinton Administration in March 1997. The oral histories of Garcia and Tegtmeyer suggest great difficulties in (d') monitoring and evaluation of policies in clandestine research.

From another perspective, the Advisory Committee functioned as an amateur intelligence agency confronting established "professionals." This could account for the criticism of the Committee's study by the Task Force on Radiation and Human Rights: "Advisory Committee Recommendations Unacceptable:" "Clinton Admin. Continues the Radiation Whitewash." Thirty or so groups of radiation survivors and their advocates comprise the Task Force.

The epistemology of intelligence in Part II reveals the obstacles to a policy science approach to abuses in clandestine scientific research. Sociologist John Lofland has described the difficulties in studying upwards on the power scale, instead of downwards – in the "underling and leisure settings of American society," occupied by mental patients and motor cyclists. People of substance "have the power not to be bothered," or, in the case of military and political intelligence, to "deceive or intimidate" inquires. The empirical method hits its limit when the topic of inquiry is contemporary clandestine scientific research. Intelligence agencies are prepared to withstand investigation by the Adversary;

investigation by a science ethics committee is not a serious challenge.

"The Administration has adopted most of ACHRE's (Advisory Committee on Human Radiation Experiments') recommendations and has acted through the government to implement them." – U.S. Government Human Radiation Interagency Working Group. (1997, March). Building public trust.

Advisory committee recommendations unacceptable. (1995, Fall). National Association of Radiation Survivors Newsletter, pp.1&3.

Clinton Admin. Continues the radiation whitewash. (1997, Spring). National Association of Radiation Survivors Newsletter, pp. 1&3.

8

INTELLIGENCE AS A NECESSARY EVIL

The Protection Industry
A Rational for Protection Industries

The *Protection Industry* explanation postulates that clandestine scientific research, including its atrocities, is an inevitable product of natural market forces in transactions among governments. "Here, intelligence personnel, not scientists, are the autonomous moral agents."

Economist Diego Gambetta's model of the "Sicilian mafia" as a *Protection Industry* inspires the interpretation of Intelligence as a *Protection Industry*. In Gambetta's account, Sicilian businesses cannot depend on civic law and judicial process for timely and effective enforcement of agreements. The "mafia" though, by means of its networks of oversight, influence, and coercion, "can offer dependability of transactions." In the Sicilian business community, "guarantee of contracts is simply a commodity with a price, for which everyone is charged (extorted) a bit, as for police, courts, and other public services." In this rational scheme, "mafia violence is not an end in itself – a manifestation of aggression – but an instrument of enforcement, as is the legitimized violence of the state." Unfortunately, the mafia exacerbates the problem it purports to solve, for those who do not pay for protection are likely to experience setbacks. Like a public utility company, the *Protection Industry* flourishes both by providing protection and by increasing the need for it.

For intelligence as *Protection Industry*, the structural analogy maps businesses to governments, the mafia to intelligence, and so on:

Businesses to Nations
Civil Law to International Law
Contracts to Treaties, Trade Agreements, etc.
Mafia to Intelligence
Guarantee of Contracts to Monitoring of Treaties, etc.
Exacerbation of Distrust to Exacerbation of Political Conflicts

For both the mafia and intelligence, a sophisticated information network is essential to the *Protection Industry*, but the real product, in Gambetta's analysis, is the *guarantee* on the information, not the information itself. Covert operations then constitute the essential backup for "clandestine collection" and analysis of information.

Gambetta acknowledged the moral challenge of his model of the *Protection Industry* as a rational economic phenomenon. The "implications have never been explored in full, perhaps owing to the difficulty of reconciling the facts that the mafia can supply a real service while being at the same time an evil that must be opposed." By analogy, the *Protection Industry* of intelligence is a political response to distrust and unreliability in transactions among governments, and the "only solution to the moral problems" of "clandestine scientific research" is a fair and efficient "world order" that obviates the need for extralegal guarantees.

Delivery by Intelligence as a Protection Agency

The "covert actions operator Ernest Garcia" gave an example of the OSS delivering as a "protection agency" just after the World War ll in Argentina.

Gambetta, Diego. (1993). The Sicilian mafia: The business of private protection. Cambridge, MA: Harvard University Press.

Gambetta, Diego. P.18

Harvard University Press. Pp. 23.

The OSS, he said, "kidnapped" and interrogated Nazis to discover the whereabouts of Allied prisoners of war whom the Soviets took the Nazis but failed to repatriate. In the *Protection Industry* model, the unenforceability of the Geneva Convention on return of prisoners of war virtually demanded an intelligence agency such as the OSS to track prisoners of war.

As the son of a German immigrant mother and a New Mexican father of Spanish origin, Garcia said he was an ideal candidate for the operation:

Mr. Garcia: Blue eyes, light complexion that is highly prevalent in Argentina. I could mingle with the Nazis very, very easily and quickly adapted to their style. I went out and someone pointed out the person and "I made sure that I delivered them." This was terrible. Many times I also participated in the actual tortures (Distressed).

Arrigo: It's important for people who are discussing these things academically and politically to understand the mechanisms. So let's put the morals aside here and just understand the mechanisms. What was the purpose of torturing them?

Mr. Garcia: For example, there was a lot of the Allied prisoners of war that weren't accounted for in Germany and that later turned out to have been taken to the Baltic, or were taken to the Russian country and later were found there tortured dead. "These people were being used for experimental forced labor," for many things "that were against the United Nations treaty." Unfortunately at that time the Kremlin was very arrogant and they couldn't get to the prisoners.

Arrigo: And so the idea was you would get information from these Nazis in Argentina that would enable you to locate the prisoners of war?

Mr. Garcia: We would get the basic information, at least enough for us to follow up.
Another thing is we would force them to tell us who ultimately had access to some of the weapons the Nazis were working on and some of the scientific information and papers that were removed from the laboratories in Germany. There were a lot of scientists and a lot of scholars. These people knew a lot of things.

Two CIA interrogation manuals used at the U.S. Army School of the Americas provided extensive scientific background for "coercive questioning." The 1963 manual presented a theory of coercion.

New evidence provides the final link in a chain the Soviet Union began building in 1945: the kidnapping of American POWs after conflicts in which the Soviet Union or its satellites were involved. When the Soviets pushed through Eastern Europe to meet American forces at the Elbe River in 1945, it "liberated" more than 20,000 Americans in Germany POW camps. They never came home. After the war, Soviet agents kidnapped American servicemen off the streets of Europe, packing them off to the phosphorous (sic) and coal mines in the gulag.... And now, we learn from eyewitnesses, the communist regime in Hanoi shipped

captive American fighting men to the Soviet Union as well.
– Charm School, The. (1991, September 5). Washington Times, P. G2.

Garcia, Ernest. (1995, October 21 & 22). An OSSCIA covert actions operator. Oral history interview conducted by Jean Maria Arrigo, Albuquerque, NM.

The Theory of Coercion

Coercive procedures are designed not only to exploit the resistant source's internal conflicts and induce him to wrestle with himself but also to bring a superior outside force to bear upon the subject's resistance....
"All coercive techniques are designed to induce regression." As Hinkle notes in "The Physiological State of the Interrogation Subject as it Affects Brain Function," the result of external pressures of sufficient intensity is the loss of those defenses most recently acquired by civilized man: "...Relatively small degrees of homeostatic derangement, fatigue, pain, sleep loss, or anxiety may impair these functions." As a result, "most people who are exposed to coercive procedures will talk."

Central Intelligence Agency (July, 1963). KUBARK Counterintelligence Interrogation. Fort Benning, GA: United States Army School of the Americas. (Released in 1997 under the Freedom of Information Act. Obtained through Psychologists for Social Responsibility, 2607 Connecticut Ave. NW, Washington, DC 20008.) P. 83.

The reference is to: Hinkle, Lawrence, E. (1961). The physiological state of the interrogation subject as it affects brain function. In A.D. Biderman & H. Zimmer (Eds.). The manipulation of human behavior (pp. 1949). New York: Wiley.Hinkle was a psychiatrist at Cornell Medical School. He was one of the chief investigators of brainwashing for the U.S. government and a formative contributor to the CIA's behavioral modification *Project MKULTRA*.Marks, J. (1979). The search for the "Manchurian Candidate" – The CIA and mind control. New York: Times Books. Pp.127127&149.

Six of the 42 citations in KUBARK Counterintelligence Interrogation were blanked out before public release.

This theory was operationalized in the 1983 manual (printed in upper case):

AS I SAID AT THE BEGINNING OF OUR DISCUSSION OF COERCIVE TECHNIQUES. THE PURPOSE OF ALL COERCIVE TECHNIQUES IS TO INDUCE REGRESSION... THE EFFECTIVENESS OF THESE TECHNIQUES DEPEND UPON THE "QUESTIONER'S CONTROL OF THE ENVIRONMENT. FOR EXAMPLE:... B: RETARDING AND ADVANCING CLOCKS:...D. DISRUPING SLEEP SCHEDULES....F: UNPATTERNED "QUESTIONING" SESSIONS:...I: REWARDING NONCOOPERATION. IN GENERAL, THWARTING ANY ATTEMPT BY THE SUBJECT TO RELATE TO HIS NEW ENVIRONMENT WILL REINFORCE THE EFFECTS OF REGRESSION AND DRIVE HIM DEEPER AND DEEPER INTO HIMSELF.

UNTIL HE NO LONGER IS ABLE TO CONTROL HIS RESPONSES IN AN ADULT FASHION.

The earlier manual described techniques Garcia had reported.

Detention makes a number of tricks possible. One of these, planting an informant as the source's cellmate, is so well-known, especially in communist countries, that its usefulness is impaired if not destroyed.
But Garcia had his own ruse:

I had tremendous control of the mind. I could get some very valuable information without having to impose any pain or injury on them.

There were times when I would actually sleep inside of the cell where they were being held and sit with them, and I could pump more information than anybody could pump under force or pain. A man can't sit right there in the cell and stare on you. I totally ignore the guy and I would act extremely angry, and it would take me whatever time it would take, even up to three days, have absolutely nothing to do with him. Eventually human nature will bend. He will try to get something from you. And that opens an extraordinary door for you.

Some of the older scientists would have methods that could be extremely assisting to pumping this information.

In Garcia's example, the *Protection Industry* draws attention to the causal links between research in coercive interrogation and the failure of the international agreement on repatriation of prisoners of war. The moral solution then would not be the solution of *Regressive Science*, ethical advance for scientists, which might leave the prisoners stranded. The solution would be, say, good monitoring systems with enforcement for repatriation of prisoners of war.

Reputation and Advertising

In the *Protection Industry*, according to Gambetta, reputation and advertising are vital. For centuries, the allegiance of the mafia to the Catholic Church, as in sponsoring festivals for saints, upheld its reputation. A parallel for intelligence would be the affiliation with science. "The front funding agency for the CIA's behavioral modification Project MKULTRA also deliberately funded conspicuously non-militarist scientists such as the humanist Carl Rogers."

My three oral history interviewees who worked at nuclear test sites were all impressed by the participation of civilian scientists. Kenneth Kendall, a mechanic for the scientists' motor pool at the "Nevada Test Site" in 1953, occasionally drove tour buses of visiting dignitaries:

~ 123 ~

The day before the bomb was to go off we had all these VIPs – admirals, generals, senators, and congressmen, and all kinds of scientists – and we'd load up a whole bunch of these buses and drive them out to the site where the bomb was going off. We took them to the exact site where they could touch the base of the tower for the bomb. And then a thousand yards away there was an underground bunker with all kinds of instruments and everything....It was a jaunt, a happy jaunt. They were going to see something that nobody else would ever get to see.

Each test had one or two or three primary major things, but each test also had a myriad of other tests. That's why we had so many scientists and doctors and VIPs. Various universities were big in this....

We knew, we believed like other guys, the low GIs, that there was something that was going to be very historical and have a dramatic effect on the world.

Gambetta, Diego, (1993). Pp. 4752.

Kendall, Kenneth, (1995, January 14). Mechanic for the scientists motor pool at the Nevada Test Site. Oral history interview conducted vi telephone by Jean Maria Arrigo, from Claremont, CA, to Portage, IN. (4 hours) Kendall also remarked on the limitations of scientists housed at the test site: "These scientists – they were brilliant but they didn't have horse sense (laughing). They didn't check the gas in the tanks and they'd drive out in the desert and run out of gas, and we'd have to take them gas.

Advertising for the Protection Industry

Gambetta remarked on the difficulty that industries face in marketing "illegal services." Exposés of the mafia function as advertisements. Far from alienating potential customers, these stories publicize its services and demonstrate its efficacy. He believed that the mafia had participated in the casting of "The Godfather" a life – in – the mafia film.

Sensationalist accounts of covert operations might also be said to advertise the efficacy of intelligence. A special "Spy Issue" of the newsstand magazine George, laid out a time line of CIA exploits with such capsules as: "June 1954 CIA Overthrows Arbenz in Guatemala, President Eisenhower orders the CIA to topple Guatemala's democratically elected leftist government...." George, in effect, advertised the CIA as an instrument for presidential mastery of foreign affairs.

Disparaging this view, Garcia wrote, so to speak, a personals ad, which he sent to Guatemala via a member of Psychologists for Social Responsibility: 24

April 2, 1998

Dear People of Guatemala,

I send this message with a broken heart and begging forgiveness for me and my country and for my American colleagues who did work as

intelligence covert operators in your country and unleashed a "demon that must surely have come from hell." As a very young man, working against my will, I participated in an assignment of implementing what was supposed to have been a democratic government in your country (at least that's what we were told) – what we really did – why should I tell you, you already know.
I just ask forgiveness in the name of "God" for the part I played in implementing this horrible act against the civilized people of this country and others....

To the tales of CIA exploits, George added a picture story of the CIA's 1959 rescue of the "Dalai Lama from Tibet," under siege from the Chinese army. According to George, when the Dalai Lama appealed to a traditional oracle for advice, the monk who served as medium "wrote explicit instructions for the Dalai Lama's escape from Tibet. Unbeknownst to the Dalai Lama, the Central Intelligence Agency, in collaboration with Tibetan armies, had scripted (the medium's) instructions down to a stop in the smallest mountain village."25 The Special Envoy of the Dalai Lama in Washington denied George's account: "It is an insult to the Tibetan freedom movement to imply we were inspired and led by the CIA. On the contrary, the Dalai Lama's fight was planned and executed by Tibetans."26

The *Protection Industry* explanation directs us to consider not the truth or falsity of the claims by

George, Ernest Garcia, or the CIA but to consider the efficacy of these claims as advertising for the CIA. "Publicity about human rights violations in clandestine scientific research can be interpreted as advertisements of research opportunities for scientists." Citizens may also see they have an economic or political advantage in intelligence operations about which they feel moral outrage, so they then prefer for the government to allocate funds for operations without close oversight. "The election of George Bush as president (19) after serving as Director of Central Intelligence (19) is consistent with Gambetta's view of the success of *Protection Industry* advertising.

Evaluation of the Explanation of Intelligence as a Necessary Evil

By Thagard's criteria of evaluation, the *Protection Industry* explanation, following Gambetta's analysis, has admirable simplicity. The premises that might be deduced from his model are: nations *must* engage in vital transactions with each other; international norms and law cannot make these transactions dependable; and, given the market forces, enterprises more or less like intelligence must arise to stabilize transactions. In regard to consilience, the *Protection Industry* explanation explains particularly well the exploits of intelligence, the liaison with science, and the expose's that expand the industry. It systematizes the case-by-case rationales for clandestine research projects with a general schema of market transactions among nations. "A moral problem becomes a market problem, and thereby becomes amenable to rational treatment." The *Protection Industry* though, explains less well than *Regressive Science* the transcendent idealism and unrewarded self-sacrifice of patriotic intelligence personnel in clandestine science, "for mafia loyalty is more self-interested and parochial."

See Appendix_ for full text of Ernest Garcia's letter (personal communication, April 2, 1998).

Roberts, John B. ll. (1997, October). The Dalai Lama's great escape. George: Not just politics as usual. 130133. Pp. 130 & 132.

George Magazine's claim CIA "Rescued" Dalai Lama Inaccurate: Envoy of Dalai Lama regrets "Misinformation," p. 9. (October, 1997). Tibet Press Watch. Washington, DC: The International Campaign for Tibet. P. 9. (1825 K St., NW. Suite #520. Washington, DC 20006).

The analogy to the mafia explains hierarchical structure, "employment by levels of trust, and in-group loyalty and pride in clandestine research" that *Cynicism* and *Regressive Science* cannot match. The structural analogy breaks down on finer points, such as "the far greater power of the mafia than intelligence relative to the entities they monitor." Conceptually, the analogy is too close to stimulate much new insight into intelligence from the mafia: Holyoak and Thagard recommended remote analogies for greater payoff. However, it does successfully guide interpretation of data and solutions to the "moral problems" of clandestine research.

Methodological Note on Theory and Analogy

Consideration of the three alternatives to the *Epistemological Explanation* exhibits the tremendous power of theory in guiding inquiry and proposing solutions to problems. *Cynicism* guides inquiry toward institutional and individual opportunities for wrongdoing. It proposes restrictions and closing of loopholes. *Regressive Science* guides inquiry to the ethics of programs of scientific research and proposes training and advances in scientific ethics. The *Protection Industry* guides inquiry toward "clandestine research" as an arm of "intelligence" in stabilizing transactions among nations and proposes development of just and public mechanisms for monitoring and "enforcing agreements."

9

U.S. ARMY AND CIA INTERROGATION MANUALS

The U.S. Army and CIA interrogation manuals are seven controversial military manuals, which were declassified by the Pentagon in 1996. In 1997, two additional CIA manuals were declassified in response to a Freedom of Information Act (FOIA) request filed by the Baltimore Sun. The manuals in question have been referred to as "the Torture Manuals" by many US media sources. (2)(3)(4)

Army manuals

These manuals were prepared by the U.S. military and used between 1987 and 1991 for intelligence training courses at the U.S. Army School of the Americas (SOA). Some of the material was similar to the older CIA manuals described below. The manuals were also distributed by Special Forces Mobile Training Teams to military personnel and intelligence schools in Colombia, Ecuador, El Salvador, Guatemala, and Peru.(5)(6)(7)(8)(9)

The Pentagon press release accompanying the release stated that a 199192 investigation into the manuals concluded that "two dozen short passages in six of the manuals, which total 1169 pages, contained material that either was not or could be interpreted not to be consistent with U.S. policy."(5)

The Latin America Working Group criticized this: "The unstated aim of the manuals is to train Latin American militaries to identify and suppress antigovernment movements. Throughout the eleven hundred pages of the manuals, there are few mentions of democracy, human rights, or the rule of law. Instead, the manuals provide detailed techniques for infiltrating social movements, interrogating suspects, surveillance, maintaining military secrecy, recruiting and retaining spies, and controlling the population. While the excerpts released by the Pentagon are a useful and not misleading selection of the most egregious passages, the ones most clearly advocating torture, execution and blackmail, they do not provide adequate insight into the manuals' highly objectionable framework. In the name of defending democracy, the manuals advocate profoundly undemocratic methods."(5)

After this 1992 investigation, the Department of Defense discontinued the use of the manuals, directed their recovery to the extent practicable, and destroyed the copies in the field. U.S. Southern Command advised governments in Latin

America that the manuals contained passages that did not represent U.S. government policy, and pursued recovery of the manuals from the governments and some individual students.(10)

CIA manuals

The first manual, "KUBARK Counterintelligence Interrogation," dated July 1963, is the source of much of the material in the second manual. KUBARK was a U.S. Central Intelligence Agency cryptonym for the CIA itself.(12) The cryptonym KUBARK appears in the title of a 1963 CIA document KUBARK *Counterintelligence Interrogation* which describes interrogation techniques, including, among other things, "coercive counterintelligence interrogation of resistant sources." This is the oldest and most abusive manual, such as two references to the use of "electric shock."(12)

The second manual, *"Human Resource Exploitation Training Manual – 1983,"* was used in at least seven U.S. training courses in Latin American countries, including Honduras, between 1982 and 1987. According to a declassified 1989 report prepared for the Senate intelligence committee, the 1983 manual was developed from notes of a CIA interrogation course in Honduras.(4)

U.S. Army and CIA interrogation manuals – Wikipedia, the free encyclopedia. Pp.16.

School of Americas Training Manual Titles (1)

Spanish Titles	No. of Pages	English Titles
Manejo de Fuente	174	Handling of Sources
Contrainteligencia	310	Counterintelligence
Guerra Revolucionaria e Ideologia Comunista	128	Revolutionary War and Communist Ideology
Terrorismo y Guerrilla Urbana	175	Terrorism and the Urban Guerrilla
Interrogacion	150	Interrogation
Inteligencia de		Combat

Combate Intelligence	172
* Analisis I Analysis I	90 *
Total Pages:	1169

No questionable or objectionable statements found.

Both manuals deal exclusively with interrogation (13) (14) both manuals have an entire chapter devoted to "coercive techniques." These manuals recommend arresting suspects early in the morning by surprise, blindfolding them, and stripping them naked. Suspects should be held incommunicado and should be deprived of any kind of normal routine in eating and sleeping. Interrogation rooms should be windowless, soundproof, dark and without toilets.

The manuals advise that torture techniques can backfire and that the threat of pain is often more effective than pain itself. The manuals describe coercive techniques to be used "to induce psychological regression in the subject by bringing a superior outside force to bear on his will to resist." These techniques include prolonged constraint, prolonged exertion, extremes of heat, cold, or moisture, deprivation of food or sleep, disrupting routines, solitary confinement, threats of pain, deprivation of sensory stimuli, hypnosis, and use of drugs of placebos.(5)(15)

Between 1984 and 1985, after congressional committees began questioning training techniques being used by the CIA in Latin America, the 1983 manual went through substantial revision. In 1985 a page advising against using coercive techniques was inserted at the front of *Human Resource Exploitation Training Manual*. Handwritten changes were also introduced haphazardly into the text. For example, "While we do not stress the use of coercive techniques, we do want to make you aware of them and the proper way to use them," has been altered to, "While we deplore the use of coercive techniques, we do want to make you aware of them so that you may avoid them." (p.A2)

But the entire chapter on coercive techniques is still provided with some items crossed out. (5)(4)

The same manual states the importance of knowing local laws regarding detention but then notes, "Illegal detention always requires prior HQS (headquarters) approval." (p.B2) (5)

The two manuals were completely declassified and released to the public in May 2004, and are now available online. (12)

The 1983 manual and Battalion 316

In 1983, the Human Resource Exploitation Training Manual – 1983 methods were used by the U.S. trained Honduran Battalion 316. (7)

On January 24, 1997, *KUBARK Counterintelligence Interrogation* and *Human Resource Exploitation Training Manual – 1983* were declassified in response to a FOIA request filed by the Baltimore Sun in 1994. The Baltimore Sun was investigating the "kidnapping, torture and murder" of the Honduran Battalion 316 death squad. The documents were released only after the Baltimore Sun had threatened to sue the CIA. (16)(4)

In June 11 to 18, 1995 four-part series, the Baltimore Sun printed excerpts of an interview with Florencio Caballero, a former member of Battalion 316. Caballero said CIA instructors taught him to discover "what his prisoners loved and what they hated."

"If a prisoner did not like cockroaches, then that person might be more cooperative if there were cockroaches running around the room."(4) The methods taught in the 1983 manual and those used by Battalion 316 in the early 1980s show unmistakable similarities. In 1983, Caballero attended a CIA "human resources exploitation or interrogation course," according to declassified testimony by Richard Stolz, who was the deputy director for operations at the time, before the June 1988 Senate Select Committee on Intelligence.

The manual advises an interrogator to "manipulate the subject's environment, to create unpleasant or intolerable situations."

The manual gives the suggestion that prisoners be deprived of sleep and food, and made to maintain rigid positions, such as standing at attention for long periods. Ines Consuelo Murillo, who spent 78 days in Battalion 316's secret jails in 1983, said she was given no food or water for days, and one of her captors entered her room every 10 minutes and poured water over her head to keep her from sleeping.(4)

The "Human Resource Exploitation Training Manual – 1983" gives the suggestion that interrogators show the prisoner letters from home to give the prisoner the impression that the prisoner's relatives are in danger or suffering. (4)

The Baltimore Sun reported that, former Battalion 316 member Jose Barrera said he was taught interrogation methods by U.S. instructors in 1983, used this technique: "The first thing we would say is that we know your mother, your younger brother. And better you cooperate, because if you don't, we're going to bring them in and rape them and torture them and kill them." (4)

Techniques discussed in School of Americas training manuals, 1987 – 1991: (11) (5) (1)
- Motivation by fear

- Payment of bounties for enemy dead

- False imprisonment
- Use of truth serum
- Torture
- Execution
- Extortion
- Kidnapping and arresting a target's family members

10

PROJECT MKULTRA

Project MK-ULTRA, or **MKULTRA,** was the code name for a covert CIA mind control and chemical interrogation research program, run by the Office of Scientific Intelligence. The program began in the early 1950s, continuing at least through the late 1960s, and "it used United States citizens as its test subjects." (1)(2)(3) The published evidence indicates that Project ML-ULTRA involved the surreptitious use of many types of drugs, as well as other methods, "to manipulate individual mental states and to alter brain function."(4)

Project MKULTRA was first brought to wide public attention in 1975 by the U.S. Congress, through investigations by the Church Committee, and by a presidential commission known as the Rockefeller Commission. Investigative efforts were hampered by the fact that CIA Director Richard Helms ordered all MKULTRA files destroyed in 1973; the Church Committee and Rockefeller Commission investigations relied on the sworn testimony of direct participants and on the relatively small number of documents that survived Helms' destruction order. (5)

Although the CIA insists that MKULTRA-type experiments have been abandoned, 14year CIA veteran Victor Marchetti has stated in various interviews that the CIA routinely conducts disinformation campaigns and that CIA mind control research continued. In a 1977 interview, Marchetti specifically called the CIA claim that MKULTRA was abandoned a "cover story." (6)(7)

On the Senate floor in 1977, Senator Ted Kennedy said:

The Deputy Director of the CIA revealed that over thirty universities and institutions were involved in an "extensive testing and experimentation" program which included covert drug test on unwitting citizens "at all social levels, high and low, native Americans and foreign." Several of these tests involved the administration of LSD to "unwitting subjects in social situations." At least one death that of Dr. Frank Olsen resulted from these activities. The Agency itself acknowledged that these tests made little scientific sense. The agents doing the monitoring were not qualified scientific observers. (8)

To this day most specific information regarding Project MKULTRA remains highly classified.

Title and origins

The project's intentionally oblique CIA cryptonym is made up of the digraph *MK*, meaning that the project was sponsored by the agency's Technical Services Division, followed by the most *ULTRA* (which had previously been used to designate the most secret classification of World War ll intelligence). Other related cryptonyms include MKNAOMI and MKDELTA.

A precursor of the MKULTRA program began in 1945 when the Joint Intelligence Objectives Agency was established and given direct responsibility for Operation Paperclip. "Operation Paperclip was a program to recruit former Nazi spies, scientists and experts in torture and brainwashing, some of whom had just identified and prosecuted as war criminals during the Nuremberg Trails."

Several secret U.S. government projects grew out of Operation Paperclip. These projects included Project CHATTER (established 1947), and Project BLUEBIRD (established 1950), which was later renamed to Project ARTICHOKE in 1951. Their purpose was to study mind control, interrogation, behavior modification and related topics.

Headed by Dr. Sidney Gottlieb, the MKULTRA project was started on the order of CIA director Allen Dulles on April 13, 1953, (9) largely in response to Soviet, Chinese, and Noth Korean use of mind control techniques on U.S. prisoners of war in Korea. (10)

Project MKULTRA – Wikipedia, the free encyclopedia. Pp. 113.

The CIA wanted to use similar methods on their own captives. The CIA was also interested in being able to manipulate foreign leaders with such techniques,(11) and would later invent several schemes to drug Fidel Castro.

Experiments were often conducted without subjects' knowledge or consent. (12) In some cases, academic researchers being funded through grants from CIA front organizations were unaware that their work was being used for these purposes. (13)

In 1964, the project was renamed MKSEARCH. The project attempted to produce a perfect truth drug for use in interrogating suspected Soviet spies during the Cold War, and generally to explore any other possibilities of mind control.

Another MKULTRA effort, Subproject 54, was the Navy's top secret "Perfect Concussion" program, which used subdural frequency blasts to erase memory. (14)

Because most MKULTRA records were deliberately destroyed in 1973 by order of then CIA Director Richard Helms, it has been difficult, if not impossible, for investigators to gain a complete understanding of the more than 150 individually funded research subprojects sponsored by MKULTRA and relate CIA programs. (15)

Aims and goals

The Agency poured millions of dollars into studies probing dozens of methods of influencing and controlling the mind.

One 1955 MKULTRA document gives an indication of the size and range of the effort; this document refers to the study of an assortment of mind-altering substances described as follows: (16)

1. Substances which will promote illogical thinking and impulsiveness to the point where the recipient would be discredited in public.
2. Substances which increase the efficiency of mentation and perception.
3. Materials which will prevent or counteract the intoxicating effect of alcohol.
4. Materials which will promote the intoxicating effect of alcohol.
5. Material which will produce the signs and symptoms of recognized diseases in a reversible way so that they may be used for malingering, etc.
6. Materials which will render the induction of hypnosis easier or otherwise enhance its usefulness.
7. Substances which will enhance the ability of individuals to withstand privation, torture and coercion during interrogation and so-called "brainwashing."
8. Materials and physical methods which will produce amnesia for events preceding and during their use.
9. Physical methods of producing shock and confusion over extended periods of time and capable of surreptitious use.

10. Substances which produce physical disablement such as paralysis of the legs, acute anemia, etc.
11. Substances which will produce "pure" euphoria with no subsequent letdown.
12. Substances which alter personality structure in such a way that the tendency of the recipient to become dependent upon another person is enhanced.
13. A material which will cause mental confusion of such a type that the individual under its influence will find it difficult to maintain a fabrication under questioning.
14. Substances which will lower the ambition and general working efficiency of men when administered in undetectable amounts.
15. Substances which promote weakness or distortion of the eyesight or hearing faculties, preferably without permanent effects.
16. A knockout pill which can surreptitiously be administered in drinks, food, cigarettes, as an aerosol, etc., which will be safe to use, provide a maximum of amnesia, and be suitable for use by agent types on an ad hoc basis.
17. A material which can be surreptitiously administered by the above routes and which in very small amounts will make it impossible for a man to perform any physical activity whatsoever.

Historians have learned that creating a "Manchurian Candidate" subject through "mind control" techniques was undoubtedly a goal of MKULTRA and related CIA projects. (17)

Budget

A secretive arrangement granted a percentage of the CIA budget. The MKULTRA director was granted six percent of the CIA operating budget in 1953, without oversight or accounting. (18) An estimated US $10m or more was spent (19).

Experiments

CIA documents suggest that "chemical, biological and radiological" means were investigated for the purpose of mind control as part of MKULTRA. (20)

Drugs
LSD

Early efforts focused on LSD, which later came to dominate many of MKULTRA's programs.

Experiments included administering LSD to CIA employees, military personnel, doctors, other government agents, prostitutes, mentally ill patients, and members of the general public in order to study their reactions, LSD and other drugs were usually administered without the subject's knowledge and informed consent, a violation of the Nuremberg Code that the U.S. agreed to follow after World War II.

Efforts to "recruit" subjects were often illegal, even discounting the fact that drugs were being administered (though actual use of LSD, for example, was legal in the United States until October 6, 1966). In Operation Midnight Climax, the CIA set up several brothels to obtain a selection of men who would be too embarrassed to talk about the events. The men were doused with LSD, and the brothels were equipped with one-way mirrors and the "sessions" were filmed for later viewing and study. (21)

Some subjects' participation was consensual, and in many of these cases, the subjects appeared to be singled out for even more extreme experiments. In one case, volunteers were given LSD for 77 consecutive days. (22)

LSD was eventually dismissed by MKULTRA's researchers as too unpredictable in its results. (1) (http://www.michaelrobinett.com/declass/c011.htm) Although useful information was sometimes obtained through questioning subjects on LSD, not uncommonly the most marked effect would be the subject's absolute and utter certainty that they were able to withstand any form of interrogation attempt, even physical torture.

Other drugs

Another technique investigated was connecting a barbiturate IV into one arm and an amphetamine IV into the other. (23) The barbiturates were released into the subject first, and as soon as the subject began to fall asleep, the amphetamines were released. The subject would begin babbling incoherently at this point, and it was sometimes possible to ask questions and get useful answers.

Other experiments involved heroin, morphine, temazepam (used under code name MKSEARCH), mescaline, psilocybin, scopolamine, marijuana, alcohol, and sodium pentothal. (24)

Hypnosis

Declassified MKULTRA documents indicate hypnosis was studied in the early 1950s. Experimental goals included: the creation of "hypnotically induced anxieties," "hypnotically increasing ability to learn and recall complex written matter," studying hypnosis and polygraph examinations, "hypnotically increasing ability to observe and recall complex arrangements of physical objects," and studying "relationship of personality to susceptibility to hypnosis." (25)
Canadian experiments

The experiments were exported to Canada when the CIA recruited Scottish physician Donald Ewen Cameron, creator of the "psychic driving" concept, which the CIA found particularly interesting. Cameron had been hoping to correct schizophrenia by erasing existing memories and reprogramming the psyche. He commuted from Albany, New York to Montreal every week to work at the Allen Memorial Institute of McGill University and was paid $69,000 from 1957 to 1964 to carry out MKULTRA experiments there. In addition to LSD, Cameron also experimented with various paralytic drugs as well as electroconvulsive therapy at thirty to forty times the normal power. His "driving" experiments consisted of putting subjects into drug induced coma for weeks at a time (up to three months in one case) while playing tape loops of noise or simple repetitive statements. His experiments were typically carried out on patients who had entered the institute for minor problems such as anxiety disorders and postpartum depression, many of whom suffered permanently from his actions. (26) His treatments resulted in victims' incontinence, amnesia, forgetting how to talk, forgetting their parents, and thinking their interrogators were their parents. (27) His work was inspired and paralleled by the British psychiatrist Dr. William Sargent at St. Thomas' Hospital, London, and Belmont Hospital, Surrey, who also experimented extensively and very damagingly on his patients without their consent and was similarly involved with the Intelligence Services. (28) Dr. Cameron and Dr. Sargent are the only two identified Canadian experimenters, but the MKULTRA file makes reference too many other unnamed physicians who were recruited by the CIA.

It was during this era that Cameron became known worldwide as the first chairman of the World Psychiatric Association as well as president of the American and Canadian psychiatric associations. Cameron had also been a member of the Nuremberg medical tribunal in 194647. (29)

Revelation

In 1973, CIA Director Richard Helms ordered all MKULTRA files "destroyed." Pursuant to this order, most CIA documents regarding the project were destroyed, "making a full investigation of MKULTRA all but impossible."

In December 1974, *The New York Times* reported that the CIA had conducted illegal domestic activities, including experiments on U.S. citizens, during the 1960s. That report prompted investigations by the U.S. Congress, in the form of the Church Committee, and by a presidential commission known as the Rockefeller Commission that looked into domestic activities of the CIA, the FBI, and intelligence related agencies of the military.

In the summer of 1975, congressional Church Committee reports and the presidential Rockefeller Commission report revealed to the public for the first time that the CIA and the Department of Defense had conducted experiments on both unwitting and cognizant human subjects as part of an extensive program to influence and control human behavior through the use of psychoactive drugs such as LSD and mescaline and other chemical, biological, and psychological means. They also revealed that at least one subject had died after administration of LSD.

Much of what the Church Committee and the Rockefeller Commission learned about MKULTRA was contained in a report, prepared by the Inspector General's office in 1963, that had survived the destruction of records ordered in 1973. (30) However, it contained little detail.

The congressional committee investigating the CIA research, chaired by Senator Frank Church, concluded that "prior consent was obviously not obtained from any of the subjects." The committee noted that the "experiments sponsored by these researchers...call into question the decision by the agencies not to fix guidelines for experiments."

Following the recommendations of the Church Committee, President Gerald Ford in 1976 issued the first Executive Order on Intelligence Activities which, among other things, prohibited "experimentation with drugs on human subjects, except with the informed consent, in writing and witnessed by a disinterested party, of each such human subject" and in accordance with the guidelines issued by the National Commission. Subsequent orders by President Carter and Reagan expanded the directive to apply to any human experimentation.

On the heels of the revelations about CIA experiments, similar stories surfaced regarding U.S. Army experiments. In 1975 the Secretary of the Army instructed the Army Inspector General to conduct an investigation. Among the findings of the Inspector General was the existence of a 1953 memorandum penned by then Secretary of Defense Charles Erwin Wilson. Documents show that the CIA participated in at least two of Department of Defense committees during 1952.

These committee findings led to the issuance of the "Wilson Memo," which mandated—in accord with Nuremberg Code protocols—that only volunteers be used for experimental operations conducted in the U.S. armed forces. In response to the Inspector General's investigation, the Wilson Memo was declassified in August 1975.

With regard to drug testing within the Army, the Inspector General found that "the evidence clearly reflected that every possible medical consideration was observed by the professional investigators at the Medical Research Laboratories." However the Inspector General also found that the mandated requirements of Wilson's 1953 memorandum had been only partially adhered to; he concluded that the "volunteers were not fully informed, as required, prior to their participation; and the methods of procuring their services, in many cases, appeared not to have been in accord with the intent of

Department of the Army policies governing use of volunteers in research."

Other branches of the U.S. armed forces, the Air Force for example, were found not to have adhered to Wilson Memo stipulations regarding voluntary drug testing.

In 1977, during a hearing held by the Senate Select Committee on Intelligence, to look further into MKULTRA, Admiral Stansfield Turner, then Director of Central Intelligence, revealed that the CIA had found a set of records, consisting of about 20,000 pages, (31) that had survived the 1973 destruction orders, due to having been stored at a records center not usually used for such documents. (32)

These files dealt with the financing of MKULTRA projects, and as such contained few details of those projects, but much more was learned from them than from the Inspector General's 1963 report.

In Canada, the issue took much longer to surface, becoming widely known in 1984 on a CBS news show, *The Fifth Estate*. It was learned that not only had the CIA funded Dr. Cameron's efforts, but perhaps even more shockingly, the Canadian government was fully aware of this, and had later provided another $500,000 in funding to continue the experiments. This revelation largely derailed efforts by the victims to sue the CIA as their U.S. counterparts had, and the Canadian government eventually settled out of court for $100,000 to each of the 127 victims. None of Dr. Cameron's personal records of his involvement with MKULTRA survive, since his family destroyed them after his death from a heart attack while mountain climbing in 1967. (33)

U.S. General Accounting Office Report

The U.S. General Accounting Office issued a report on September 28, 1994, which stated that between 1940 and 1974, DOD and other national security agencies studied thousands of human subjects in test and experiments involved hazardous substances.

The quote from the study:

... Working with the CIA, the Department of Defense gave hallucinogenic drugs to thousands of "volunteer" soldiers in the 1950's and 1960's. In addition to LSD, the Army also tested quinuclidiny 1 benzilate, a hallucinogen codenamed BZ.

(Note 37) Many of these tests were conducted under the so called MKULTRA program, established to counter perceived Soviet and Chinese advances in brainwashing techniques. Between 1953 and 1964, the program consisted of 149 projects involving drug testing and other studies on unwitting human subjects... (34)

Deaths

Harold Bluer, a professional tennis player in New York City, died as a result of a secret Army experiment involving MDA. (35)

Frank Olson, a United States Army biochemist and biological weapons researcher, was given LSD without his knowledge or consent in 1953 as part of a CIA experiment, and died under suspicious circumstances (initially labeled suicide) a week later following a severe psychotic episode. A CIA doctor assigned to monitor Olson's recovery claimed to be asleep in another bed in New York City hotel room when Olsen jumped through the window to fall ten stories to his death. (36)

Project MKULTRA – Wikipedia, the free encyclopedia. Pp. 113.

Garcia, Ernest, (2008, July 18 – August 21st). An OSS/CIA covert actions operator. Oral history interview conducted by Marcel L. Garcia Jr., Albuquerque, New Mexico. Garcia was assigned to Frank Olson as his associate. Mr. Garcia described a different occurrence to Frank Olson's death, as previously stated.

The CIA's own internal investigation, by contrast, claimed Gottlieb had conducted the experiment with Olson's prior knowledge, although neither Olson nor the other men taking part in the experiment were informed as to the exact nature of the drug until some 20 minutes after its ingestion. The report further suggested that Gottlieb was nonetheless due a reprimand, as he failed to take into account Olson's already diagnosed suicidal tendencies, which might well have been exacerbated by the LSD. (36)

Legal issues involved informed consent

The revelations about the CIA and the Army prompted a number of subjects or their survivors to file lawsuits against the federal government for conducting illegal experiments. Although the government aggressively, and sometimes successfully, sought to avoid legal liability, several plaintiffs did receive compensation through court order, out of court settlement, or acts of Congress. Frank Olson's family received $750,000 by a special act of Congress, and both President Ford and CIA director William Colby met with Olson's family to publicly apologize.

Previously, the CIA and the Army had actively and successfully sought to withhold incriminating information, even as they secretly provided compensation to the families. One subject of Army drug experimentation, James Stanley, an Army sergeant, brought an important, albeit unsuccessful, suit. The government argued that Stanley was barred from suing under a legal doctrine known as the Feres doctrine, after a 1950 Supreme Court case, *Fres v. United States* that prohibits members of the Armed Forces from suing the government for any harms that were inflicted incident to service.

In 1987, the Supreme Court affirmed this defense in a 54 decision that dismissed Stanley's case (483 U.S. 669). The majority argued that "a test for liability that depends on the extent to which particular suits would call into question military discipline and decision making would itself require judicial inquiry into, and hence intrusion upon, military matters." In dissent, Justice William Brennan argued that the need to preserve military discipline should not protect the government for liability and punishment for serious violations of constitutional rights:

> The medical trails at Nuremberg in 1947 deeply impressed upon the world that experimentation with unknowing human subjects is morally and legally unacceptable. The United States Military Tribunal established the Nuremberg Code as a standard against which to judge German scientist who experimented with human subjects... In defiance of this principle, military intelligence officials...began surreptitiously testing chemical and biological materials, including LSD.

Justice Sandra Day O'Connor, writing a separate dissent, stated:

> No judicially crafted rule should insulate from liability the involuntary and unknowing human experimentation alleged to have occurred in this case. Indeed, as Justice Brennan observes, the United States played an instrumental role in the criminal prosecution of Nazi officials who experimented with human subjects during the Second World War, and the standard that the Nuremberg Military

Tribunals developed to judge the behavior of the defendants stated that the "voluntary consent of the human subject is absolutely essential...to satisfy moral, ethical, and legal concepts." If this principle is violated, the very least that society can do is to see that the victims are compensated, as best they can be, by the perpetrators.

This is the only Supreme Court case to address the application of the Nuremberg Code to experimentation sponsored by the U.S. government. And while the suit was unsuccessful, dissenting opinions put the Army – and by association the entire government – on notice that use of individuals without their consent is unacceptable. The limited application of the Nuremberg Code in U.S. courts does not detract from the power of the principles it espouses, especially in light of stories of failure to follow these principles that appeared in the media and professional literature during the 1960s and 1970s and the policies eventually adopted in the mid1970s.

In another law suit, Wayne Ritchie, a former United States Marshall, alleged the CIA laced his food or drink with LSD at a 1957 Christmas party. While the government admitted it was, at that time, drugging people without their consent, U.S. District Judge Marilyn Hall Patel found Ritchie could not prove he was one of the victims of MKULTRA and dismissed the case in 2007. (39)

Extent of participation

Forty-four American colleges or universities, 15 research foundations or chemical or pharmaceutical companies and the like including Sandoz (currently Novartis) and Eli Lilly & Co., 12 hospitals or clinics (in addition to those associated with universities), and 3 prisons are known to have_participated in MKULTRA. (40)(41)

Project MKULTRA – Wikipedia, the free encyclopedia. Extent of participation. Page 9 of 13.

Notable subjects

A considerable amount of credible circumstantial evidence suggests that Theodore Kaczynski, also known as the Unabomber, participated in CIA sponsored MKULTRA experiments conducted at Harvard University from the fall of 1959 through the spring of 1962. During World War ll, "Henry Murray, the lead researcher" in the Harvard experiments, served with the Office of Strategic Services (OSS), which was a forerunner of the CIA. Murray applied for a grant funded by the United States Navy, and his Harvard stress experiments strongly resembled those run by the OSS. (42) Beginning at the age of sixteen, Kaczynski participated along with twenty-one other undergraduate students in the Harvard experiments, which have been described as "disturbing" and "ethically indefensible." (42)(43)

Merry Prankster Ken Kesey, author of *One Flew Over the Cuckoo's Nest,* volunteered for MKULTRA experiments while he was a student at Stanford University, Kesey's ingestion of LSD during these experiments led directly to his widespread promotion of the drug and the subsequent development oh hippie culture. (44)

Candy Jones, American fashion model and radio host, claimed to have been a victim of mind control in the '60s. (45)
Infamous Irish mob boss James "Whitey" Bulger volunteered for testing while in prison. (46)

Conspiracy theories

MKULTRA plays a part in many conspiracy theories given its nature and the destruction of most records.

Lawrence Teeter, attorney for convicted assassin Sirhan Sirhan, believed Sirhan was under the influence of hypnosis when he fired his weapon at Robert F. Kennedy in 1968. Teeter linked the CIA's MKULTRA program to "mind control techniques" that he claimed were used to "control Sirhan." (47) Teeter's assertions are generally dismissed due to lack of supporting evidence.

Jonestown, the Guyana location of the Jim Jones cult and Peoples Temple mass suicide, was thought to be a test site for MKULTRA medical and "mind control experiments" after the official end of the program. Congressman Leo Ryan, a known critic of the CIA, was assassinated after he personally visited Jonestown to investigate various reported irregularities. (48)

Additional subjects found in, Project MKULTRA – Wikipedia, the free encyclopedia, are as followed:
Popular culture; Pp. 910.
See also; Page 10.
Footnotes; Pp. 1012.
Further reading; Page 12.
External links; Page 13.

- All text is available under the terms of the GNU Free Documentation License. (See **Copyrights** for details.)
- Wikipedia® is a registered trademark of the Wikimedia Foundation, Inc., a U.S. registered 501 (c) (3) tax-deductible nonprofit charity.

11

MIND CONTROL

From Wikipedia, the free encyclopedia
(Redirected from Thought control)

Mind control is a broad range of psychological tactics able to subvert an individual's control of his own thinking, behavior, emotions, or decisions. There are a number of controversial issues regarding mind control and the methods by which "control" might be attained (either direct or more subtle) are the focus of study among psychologists, neuroscientist, and sociologists.

The question of mind control has been discussed in relation to religion, politics, prisoners of war, totalitarianism, black operations, neural cell manipulation, cults, terrorism, torture, parental alienation, and even battered person syndrome. Mind control as a legal defense tactic (see also temporary insanity) was rejected by the court in the case of Patty Hearst, and in several court cases involving New Religious Movements. Also, questions of mind control are regarding ethical questions linked to the subject of free will. Mind control theories are based on the premise that an outside source can strongly influence or even control an individual's thinking, behavior or consciousness. Such theories have ethical and legal implications. Perhaps the most frequently thought of example of mind control is hypnosis, a widely accepted practice often used for entertainment and psychological assessment.

Theoretical models and methods

Robert Lifton 's Thought Reform Model

In his 1961 book *Thought Reform and the Psychology of Totalism: A Study of "Brainwashing" in China,* psychiatrist Robert Jay Lifton, M.D., describes eight coercive methods, which, he says, are able to change the mind of individuals without their knowledge and were used with this purpose on prisoners of war in Korea and China. These include: (1)

- **Milieu Control.** This involves the control of information and communication both within the environment and, ultimately, within the individual, resulting in a significant degree of isolation from society at large.
- **Mystical Manipulation.** There is manipulation of experiences that appear spontaneous but in fact were planned and orchestrated by the group or its leaders in order to demonstrate divine authority or spiritual advancement or some special gift

or talent that will then allow the leader to reinterpret events, scripture, and experiences as he or she wishes.
- **Demand for Purity**. The world is viewing as black and white and the members are constantly exhorted to conform to the ideology of the group and strive for perfection. The induction of guilt and/or shame is a powerful control device used here.
- **Confession**. Sins, as defined by the group, are to be confessed either to a personal monitor or publicly to the group. There is no confidentiality; members' "sins," "attitudes," and "faults" are discussed and exploited by the leaders.
- **Sacred Science**. The group's doctrine or ideology is considered to be the ultimate Truth, beyond all questioning or dispute. Truth is not to be found outside the group. The leader, as the spokesperson for God or for all humanity, is likewise above criticism.
- **Loading the Language**. The group interprets or uses words and phrases in new ways so that often the outside world does not understand. This jargon consists of thought termination clichés, which serve to alter members' thought processes to conform to the group's way of thinking.
- **Doctrine over person**. Member's personal experiences are subordinated to the *"sacred science"* and any contrary

experiences must be denied or reinterpreted to fit the ideology of the group.
- **Dispensing of existence**. The group has the prerogative to decide "who has the right to exist" and "who does not." This is usually not literal but means that those in the outside world are not saved, unenlightened, unconscious and they must be converted to the group's ideology. If they do not join the group or are critical of the group, then they must be rejected by the members. Thus, the outside world loses all credibility. In conjunction, should any member leave the group, he or she must be rejected also.

In his 1999 book *Destroying the world to save it: Aum Shinrikyo, Apocalyptic Violence and the New Global Terrorism,* he concluded that thought reform was possible without violence or physical coercion.

Robert W. Ford, a British radio operator who worked in Tibet in the 50's spent 5 years in Chinese jails. He published a book entitled "Captured in Tibet," describing and analyzing thought reform to which he was harshly subjected. (2)

William Sargent's Theories on Mind Control

William Sargent connected Pavlov's findings to the ways people learned and internalized belief systems. Conditioned behavior patterns could be changed by stimulated stresses beyond a dog's capacity for response, in essence causing a breakdown. This could also be caused by intense signals, longer than normal waiting periods, rotating positive and negative signals and changing a dog's physical condition, as through illness.

Depending on the dog's initial personality, this could possibly cause a *"new belief system"* to be held tenaciously. Sargent also connected Pavlov's findings to the mechanisms of "brainwashing in religion and politics." (3)

"Though men are not dogs, they should humbly try to remember how much they resemble dogs in their brain functions, and not boast themselves as demigods. They are gifted with religious and social apprehensions, and they gifted with the power of reason; but all these faculties are physiologically entailed to the brain. Therefore the brain should not be abused by having forced upon it any religious or political mystique that stunts the reason, or any form of crud rationalism that stunts the religious sense." (p. 274) (3)

Margaret Singer's Conditions for Mind Control

Psychologist Margaret Singer describes in her book *Cult in our Midst* six conditions, which she says would create an atmosphere in which "thought reform is possible." Singer states that these conditions involve no need for physical coercion or violence. (4)

- Keep the person unaware of what is going on and how attempts to psychologically condition him or her are directed in a step-by-step manner.
- Potential new members are led, step-by-step, through a behavioral change program without being aware of the final agenda or full content of the group. "The goal may be to make them deployable agents for the leadership, to get them to buy more courses, or get them to make a deeper commitment, depending on the leader's aim and desires."
- Control the person's social and/or physical environment; especially control the person's time.
- Through various methods, newer members are kept busy and led to think about the group and its content during as much of their waking time as possible.
- Systematically create a sense of powerlessness in the person.
- This is accomplished by getting members away from their normal social support group for a period of time and into an environment where the majority of people are already group members.
- The members serve as models of the attitudes and behaviors of the group and speak an in-group language.

- Strip members of their main occupation (quit jobs, drop out of school) or source of income or have them turn over their income (or the majority of) to the group.
- Once the target is stripped of their usual support network, their confidence in their own perception erodes.
- "As the target's sense of powerlessness increase, their good judgment and understanding of the world are diminished." (Ordinary view of reality is destabilized).
- As the group attacks the target's previous worldview, it causes the target distress and inner confusion; yet they are not allowed to speak about this confusion or object to it – leadership suppresses questions and counters resistance.
- This process is sped up if the targeted individual or individuals are kept tired – the cult will take deliberate actions to keep the target constantly busy.
- Manipulate a system of rewards, punishments and experiences in such a way as to inhibit behavior that reflects the person's former social identity.
- Manipulation of experience can be accomplished through various methods of trance induction, including leaders using such techniques as paced speaking patterns, guided imagery, chanting, long prayer sessions or lectures, lengthy meditation sessions.

- The target's old beliefs and patterns of behavior are defined as irrelevant or evil. Leadership wants these old patterns eliminated, so the member must suppress them.
- Members get positive feedback for conforming to the group's beliefs and behaviors and negative feedback for old beliefs and behavior.
- The group manipulates a system of rewards, punishments, and experiences in order to promote learning the group's ideology or belief system and group approved behaviors.
- Good behavior, demonstrating an understanding and acceptance of the group's beliefs, and compliance are rewarded while questioning, expressing doubts or criticizing are met with disapproval, redress and possible rejection. If one expresses a question, he or she is made to feel that there is something inherently disordered about them to be questioning.
- The only feedback members get is from the group; they become totally dependent upon the rewards given by *"those who control the environment."*
- Members must learn varying amounts of new information about the beliefs of the group and the behaviors expected by the group.

- The more complicated and filled with contradictions the new system is and the more difficult it is to learn, the more effective the conversion process will be.
- Esteem and affection from peers is very important to new recruits. Approval comes from having the new member's behaviors and thought patterns conform to the models (members). Members' relationship with peers is threatened whenever they fail to learn or display new behaviors. Over time, the easy solution to the insecurity generated by the difficulties of learning the new system is to inhibit any display of doubts – new recruits simply acquiesce, affirm and act as if they do understand and accept the new ideology.
- Put forth a closed system of logic and an authoritarian structure that permits no feedback and refuses to be modified except by leadership approval or executive order.
- The group has a top down, pyramid structure. "The leaders must have verbal ways of never losing."
- Members are not allowed to question, criticize or complain – if they do, the leaders allege that the member is defective – not the organization or the beliefs.
- The targeted individual is treated as if he or she is always intellectually incorrect or unjust, while conversely the system, "*its leaders*" and its beliefs are always

automatically, and by default, considered as "absolutely just."
- Conversion or remolding of the individual member happens in a closed system. As members learn to modify their behavior in order to be accepted in this closed system, they change – begin to speak the language – which serves to further isolate them from their prior beliefs and behaviors.

A report on brainwashing and mind control presented by an American Psychological Association (APA) task force known as the APA Taskforce on Deceptive and Indirect Techniques of Persuasion and Control (DIMPAC), chaired by Singer, was rejected in 1987 by the APA's Board of Social and Ethical Responsibility for Psychology (BSERP) as lacking "the scientific rigor and evenhanded critical approach necessary for APA imprimatur," and cautioned the task force members to "not distribute or publicize the report without indicating that the report was unacceptable to the Board." (5)

In 2001, Alberto Amitrani and Raffaella Di Marzio, from the Roman seat of the Group for Research and Information about Sects (GRIS) published an article in which they assert that the rejection of the report "should not" be construed as a rejection of the theories of thought reform and mind control as applied to New Religious Movements, and that the rejection by one division of the APA "does not represent the whole association." They quote a personal email from Benjamin Zablocki, professor of sociology, from 1997 in which Zablocki told the authors "many people have been misled about the true position of the APA and the ASA with regard to brainwashing," and that the APA urged scholars to do more research on the matter.

They also write that they have reason to believe that the APA still considers "psychological coercion" to be a phenomenon worth investigating, and not a notion rejected by the scientific community. They also write "Otherwise, why would people such as Margaret Singer, Michael Langone, and others considered to be 'anticultists' contribute to APA Conventions and be respected in other prestigious professional bodies as well?" (6)

Writing in 1999, research and forensic psychologist Dick Anthony noted that the removal of Singer's brainwashing concept from the most recent edition of the Diagnostic and Statistical Manual of Mental Disorders (DSM IV) "would seem to indicate that the American Psychiatric Association, like the American Psychological Association, and the Society for the Scientific Study of Religion, has repudiated Singer's cultic brainwashing theory because of its unscientific character." Anthony also noted that Singer's testimony had also been repeatedly excluded from American legal trials. (7)

Benjamin Zablocki points out the limitations of Dick Anthony's characterization of Singer's cultic brainwashing theory as 'unscientific,' in passing in a paper titled 'Methodological Fallacies In Anthony's Critique Of Exit Cost Analysis' (2) In this paper, Zablocki attempts to rebutt Anthony's criticisms of his theoretical work on brainwashing in a chapter of the book 'Misunderstanding Cults' (University of Toronto Press 2001). Zablocki writes:

> There is one error that Anthony makes so persistently that it runs through fully one third of all his 98 propositions.

This is the error that assuming that my theory asserts that the influence mechanism I am describing involves the destruction of the target's free will. (...) It is true that various anti-cult writers, drawn mostly from the ranks of mental health professionals rather than social sciences, have alleged that cults take away the free will of their members, not realizing or not caring – that the overthrow of free will is an un-falsifiable (and therefore unscientific) phenomenon. It is also true that Anthony has been successful in the past in exposing the nonscientific nature of these cultic loss – of – free will arguments. He senses correctly that if he could only map an isomorphism between my theory and theirs, his work would be mostly done and he could tar me with the same brush he has used successfully in the past on these hapless clinicians (of which Margaret Singer is the most notorious example), (...) Anthony does not seem to grasp that one can discuss socially imposed constraints without declaring the overthrow of free will.

Steven Hassan's BITE model

In his book *Releasing the Bonds: Empowering People to Think for Themselves,* mental health counselor and exit counselor Steven Hassan describes his mind-control model, "BITE." "BITE" stands for "Behavior, Information, Thoughts, and Emotions." The model has a basis in the works of Singer and Lifton, and in the cognitive dissonance theory of Leon Festinger. (8)

In the book, Hassan describes the components of the BITE model: (8)

Behavior Control
- Regulation of individual's physical reality.
- Major time commitment required for indoctrination sessions and group rituals.
- Need to ask permission for major decisions.
- Need to report thoughts, feelings, and activities to superiors.
- Reward and punishments (behavior modification techniques positive and negative).
- Individualism discouraged; "group think" prevails.
- Rigid rules and regulations.
- Need for obedience and dependency.

Information Control
- Use of deception.
- Access to non-cult sources of information minimized or discouraged.
- Compartmentalization of information; Outsider vs. Insider doctrines.
- Spying on other members is encouraged.

- Extensive use of cult generated information and propaganda.
- Unethical use of confession.

Thought Control
- Need to internalize the group's doctrine as "Truth."
- Use of "loaded" language (for example, "thought terminating clichés"). Words are the tools we use to think with. These "special" words constrict rather than expand understanding, and can even stop thoughts altogether. They function to reduce complexities of experience into trite, platitudinous "buzz words."
- Only "good" and "proper" thoughts are encouraged.
- Use of hypnotic techniques to induce altered mental states.
- Manipulation of memories and implantation of false memories.
- Use of thought stopping techniques, which shut down "reality testing" by stopping "negative" thoughts and allowing only "good" thoughts.
- Rejection of rational analysis, critical thinking, constructive criticism. No critical questions about leader, doctrine, or policy seen as legitimate.
- No alternative belief systems viewed as legitimate, good, or useful.

Emotional Control
- Manipulate and narrow the range of a person's feelings.

- Make the person feel that if there are ever any problems, it is always their fault, never the leader's or the groups.
- Excessive use of guilt.
- Excessive use of fear.
- Extremes of emotional highs and lows.
- Ritual and often public confession of "sins."
- Phobia indoctrination: inculcating irrational fears about ever leaving the group or even questioning the leader's authority. The person under mind control cannot visualize a positive, fulfilled future without being in the group.

Hassan writes that cults recruit and retain members through a three step process which he refers to as "unfreezing," "changing," and "refreezing." This involves the use of an extensive array of various techniques, including systematic deception, behavior modification, withholding of information, and emotionally intense persuasion techniques (such as the induction of phobias), which he collectively terms mind control. He describes these steps as follows: (9)

- Unfreezing: the process of "breaking a person" down.
- Changing: the indoctrination process.
- Refreezing: the process of reinforcing the new identity.

In *Releasing the Bonds* he also writes "I suspect that most cult groups use informal hypnotic techniques to induce trance states. They tend to use what are called "naturalistic" hypnotic techniques. Practicing meditation to shut down thinking, chanting a phrase repetitively for hours, or reciting affirmation are all-powerful ways to promote spiritual growth. But they can also be used unethically, as methods for mind control indoctrination." (8)

Hassan, after taking part in a number of deprogramming in the late 1970s, states that he is no longer involved in this practice, (10) and which eventually became completely illegal except in the case of minors.

In *Releasing the Bonds,* Hassan describes an approach that he calls the "Strategic Interaction Approach" (SIA) in order to help cult members leave their groups, and in order to help them recover from the psychological damage that they have incurred. The approach is non-coercive and the person being treated is free to discontinue it at any time. He writes: "The goal of the SIA is to help the loved one recover his full faculties; to restore the creative, interdependent adult who fully understands what has happened to him; who has digested and integrated the experience and is better and stronger from the experience." (11)

In 1998 the Enquete Commission issued its report on "So called Sects and Psycho groups" in

Germany. Reviewing Hassan's BITE model, the report said that: (12)

> Thus, the milieu control identified by Hassan, consisting of behavioral control, mental control, emotional control and information control cannot, in every case and as a matter of principle, be characterized as "manipulative." Control of these areas of action is an inevitable component of social interactions in a group or community. The social control that is always associated with intense commitment to a group must therefore be clearly distinguished from the exertion of intentional, methodical influence for the express purpose of manipulation.

Mind Control and the Battered Person Syndrome

A very different explanation of the control some groups have over their members is by associating it with Battered person syndrome and Stockholm syndrome. This has been done by psychologists Teresa Ramirez Boulette, Ph.D. and Susan M. Andersen, Ph.D.

Social Psychology Tactics

A contemporary view of mind control sees it as an intensified and persistent use of well researched social psychology principles like compliance, conformity, persuasion, dissonance, reactance, framing or emotional manipulation.

One of the most notable proponents of such theories is social psychologist Philip Zimbardo, former president of the American Psychological Association:

I conceive of mind control as a phenomenon (sic) encompassing all the ways in which personal, social and institutional forces are exerted to induce compliance, conformity, belief, attitude, and value change in others. (13)

"Mind control is the process by which individual or collective freedom of choice and action is compromised by agents or agencies that modify or distort perception, motivation, affect, cognition and/or behavioral outcomes. It is neither magical nor mystical, but a process that involves a set of basic social psychological principles."

In *Influence, Science and Practice,* social psychologist Robert Cialdini argues that mind control is possible through the covert exploitation of the unconscious rules that underlie and facilitate healthy human social interactions. He states that common social rules can be used to prey upon the unwary, and he titles them as follows:

- "Reciprocation: The Old Give and Take...and Take."
- "Commitment and Consistency: Hobgoblins of the Mind."
- "Social Proof: Truths are Us."
- "Liking: The Friendly Thief."
- "Authority: Directed Deference."
- "Scarcity: The Rule of the Few."

Using these six broad categories, he offers specific examples of both mild and extreme mind control (both one on one and in groups), notes the conditions under which each social rule is most easily exploited for false ends, and offers suggestions on how to resist such methods.

Social Psychological Conditioning by Stahelski

Writing in the *Journal of Homeland Security,* a publication of the ANSER Institute for Homeland Security, Anthony Stahelski identifies five phases of social psychological conditioning which he calls cult-like_conditioning techniques employed by terrorist groups: (Stahelski, 2004):

1. Depluralization: stripping away all other group member identities.
2. Self-DE individuation: Stripping away each member's personal identity.
3. Other DE individuation: stripping away the personal identities of enemies.
4. Dehumanization: identifying enemies as subhuman or nonhuman.
5. Demonization: identifying enemies as evil.

Subliminal Advertising

Subliminal advertising was proposed around 1960 as a means for organized mass control of human behavior. The allegations has since then fallen out of the common debate, because there are few reports that subliminal advertising has any real effect in the way advertisers may wish.

Cults and Mind Control Controversies

Some of the mind control models discussed above have been related to religious and nonreligious cults (for debates regarding what is a cult, see the article). There is debate among scholars, members of new religious movements, and cult critics whether or not mind control is applied either in general or by any particular group.

Scholarly points of view

While the majority of scholars in the study of religion reject theories of mind control (e.g., Massimo Introvigne and J. Gordon Melton), it is often accepted in psychology and psychiatry (e.g., Margaret Singer, Michael Langone, and Philip Zimbardo) and in sociology the opinions are divided (e.g., David G. Bromley and Anson Shupe contra, Stephen A. Kent and Benjamin Zablocki pro). Most scholars have either a decided contra or a decided pro opinion; there are few who advocate a moderate point of view.

James T. (Jim) Richardson, professor of Sociology and Judicial Studies at the University of Nevada, writes in his *"Brainwashing" Claims and Minority Religions Outside the United States: Cultural Diffusion of a Questionable Concept in the Legal Arena* that, while heavy on theory, the mind control model is light on evidence:

> "The CCM movement has collected some information to support its belief that religious groups successfully employ mind control techniques. But the data is unreliable. The information typically represents a very small size. It is not practical to obtain information before, during and after an individual has been in a new religious movement (NRM). Often, their data is disproportionately obtained from former members of a religious organization who have been convinced during CCM counseling that they have been victims of mind control." (14)

James Richardson, also states that if the NRMs had access to powerful brainwashing techniques, one would expect that NRMs would have high growth rates, while in fact most have not had notable success in recruitment. Most adherents participate for only a short time, and the success in retaining members has been limited.

In addition, Thomas Robbins, Eileen Barker, Newton Maloney, Massimo Introvigne, John Hall, Lorne Dawson, Anson Shupe, David G. Bromley, Gordon Melton, Marc Galanter, Saul Levine and other scholars researching NRMs have argued and established to the satisfaction of courts and relevant professional associations and scientific communities that there exists no scientific theory, generally accepted and based upon methodologically sound research, that supports the brainwashing theories as advanced by the anticult movement. (15)

Sociologist Benjamin Zablocki sees strong indicators of mind control in some NRMs and suggests that the concept should be researched without bias:

> *"I am not personally opposed to the existence of NRMs and still less to the free exercise of religious conscience. I would fight actively against any governmental attempt to limit freedom of religious expression. Nor do I believe it is within the competence of secular scholars such as myself to evaluate or judge the cultural worth of spiritual beliefs or spiritual actions. However, I am convinced, based on more than three decades of studying NRMs through participant observation and through interviews with both members and ex-members, that these movements have unleashed social and psychological forces of truly awesome power. These forces have wreaked havoc in many lives – in both adults and in "children." It is these social and psychological influence processes that the social scientist has both the right and the duty to try to understand, regardless of whether such understanding will ultimately prove helpful or harmful to the cause of religious liberty." (Zablocki, 1997)*

Sociologists David Bromley and Anson Shupe consider the idea that "cult" *are brainwashing American youth* to be "implausible".. (14) Sociology professor Stephen A. Kent published several articles where he discusses practices of NRMs as regards to brainwashing. (16)(17)

In 1984 the American Psychological Association (APA) requested Margaret Singer, the main proponent of mind control theories, to set up a working group called the APA taskforce on Deceptive and Indirect Techniques of Persuasion and Control (DIMPAC).

In 1987 the DIMPAC committee submitted its final report to the Board of Social and Ethical Responsibility for Psychology of the APA. On May 11, 1987 the Board rejected the report. In the rejection memo (18) it is stated: *"Finally, after much consideration, BSERP does not believe that we have sufficient information available to guide us in taking a position on this issue."*

These are two interpretations of this rejection: one side (e.g. Amitrani and di Marzio 2000 and Zablocki 2001) see it as no position on the issue of brainwashing, the other (e.g. Introvigne 1997) sees it as rejecting all brainwashing theories. Philip Zimbardo, who teaches a course on the "The psychology of mind control" at Stanford University, wrote that "Several participants (in a presentation called 'Cult of Hatred') challenged our profession to form a task force on extreme forms of influence, asserting that the underlying issues inform discourses on terrorist recruiting, on destructive cults versus new religious movements, on socialpolitical'therapy' cults and on human malleability or resiliency when confronted by authority power." (19)

Recently, there are indications that some members of both sides are willing to start a dialog as, for example, in the 2001 book *"Misunderstanding Cults: Searching for Objectivity in a Controversial Field."*

Additionally, professor of Sociology Eileen Barker was invited to speak at the 2002 yearly conference of the International Cultic Studies Association. And J. Gordon Melton and Douglas Cowan were invited to speak at a conference sponsored by the Evangelical Ministries to New Religions.

Mind Control, Exit Counseling, and Deprogramming

Opponents of some new religious movements have accused them of being cults that coerce recruits to join (and members to remain) by using strong influence over members that is instilled and maintained by manipulation (see also Anti-cult movement, Opposition to cults and new religious movements and Christian counter-cult movement). Such opponents frequently advocate exit counseling as necessary to free the cult member from mind control. The practice of coercive deprogramming has practically ceased. (Kent & Szimhart, 2002)

Opponents of deprogramming generally regard it as an even worse violation of personal autonomy than any loss of free will attributable to the recruiting tactics of new religious movements. These people complain that targets of deprogramming are being deceived, denied due process, and forced to endure more intense manipulation than that encountered during their previous group membership.

Steven Hassan, who began his career as a deprogrammer, criticizes deprogramming in his book *Releasing the Bonds: Empowering People to Think for Themselves*. He writes that "Deprogramming has many drawbacks.

I have met dozens of people who were successfully deprogrammed but, to this day, experience psychological trauma as a result of the method. These people were glad to be released from the grip of cult programming but were not happy about the method used to help them." (20)

Mind Control and Recruitment Rates

Eileen Barker states that out of one thousand people persuaded by the Unification Church to attend one of their overnight programs in 1979, 90% had no further involvement. Only 8% joined for more than one week and less than 4% remained members by 1981, two years later. (14)

Tyler Hendricks, former president of the Unification Church, estimates that approximately 100,000 people "moved into" the Unification Church as fulltime members from the 1970s to the 1990s. Membership in the church was 8,600 in 2004 (counting only those who joined as adults and excluding the children of members). This is an attrition rate of 93%.

Billy Graham, one of the most prominent evangelists of the last century had only an average of 1% of the attendants of his evangelizations heed the altar call at all. Follow-up work after evangelizations show that only 10% of the people responding to an alter call actually do join a church. Therefore successful Christian evangelizations resulted in a long-term success rate of 0.1% as compared to the 4% of Barker's observation. And this 0.1% do not become fulltime missionaries as in the Unification Church. (Langone, 1993).

Mind Control and Faith

The American Civil Liberties Union (ACLU) published a statement in 1977 related to brainwashing and mind control. In this statement the ACLU opposed certain methods "depriving people of the free exercise of religion." The ACLU also rejected (under certain conditions) the idea that claims of the use of "brainwashing" or of "mind control" should overcome the free exercise of religion. (21)

Leon Festinger based his theory of the cognitive dissonance, a component of Hassan's Mind Control model, on his observation that the faith of most members of a UFO cult was unshattered by failed prophecy. (22)

Barrett who is affiliated with CESNUR and Eileen Barker, whom some anti-cult activists consider *cult apologists,* wrote that logical arguments are irrelevant when trying to persuade some members to leave a movement due to the certainty that they have about their faith, which he sees as not confined to cults, but also occurring in some forms of mainstream religion. He also wrote that some members do not leave the movement even though they realize that things are wrong. See also leaving a cult.

Counter-cult Movement and Mind Control

In the Christian counter-cult movement there are several commentators who reject mind control as a factor in cult membership, and membership in both Christian and non-Christian cults as a spiritual or theological issue.

In an article by the evangelical Christian writers Bob and Gretchen Passantino, first appearing in Cornerstone magazine, titled *Overcoming The Bondage Of Victimization: A Critical Evaluation of Cult Mind Control Theories* they challenge the validity of mind control theories and the alleged "victimization" by mind-control, and assert in their conclusion:

> *(...) the Bogey Man of cult mind control is nothing but a ghost story, good for inducing an adrenaline high and maintaining a crusade, but irrelevant to reality. The reality is that people who have very real spiritual, emotional, and social needs are looking for fulfillment and significance for their lives. Ill-equipped to test the false gospels of this world, they make poor decisions about their religious affiliations. Poor decisions, yes, but decisions for which they are personally responsible nonetheless. As Christians who believe in an absolute standard of truth_and religious*

reality, we cannot ignore the spiritual threat of the cults. We must promote critical thinking, responsible education, biblical apologetics, and Christian evangelism. We must recognize that those who join the cults, while morally responsible, are also spiritually ignorant. (23)

In a rebuttal to the Passantino's article, a protagonist of the counter-cult movement, Paul R. Martin, Ph. D. et al. in his *Overcoming the Bondage of Revictimization: A Rational/Empirical Defense of Thought Reform,* (first appeared in Cultic Studies Journal 15/2 1998), writes:

"The Passantinos are well known and respected evangelical writers. Consequently, their critique, which is rife with errors and misinterpretations, disturbs us very much and calls for a detailed rebuttal. (...) For us, theological considerations inform our understanding of the sociological and psychological destruction caused by cults, although others hold similar positions without considering theological issues. Cults distort one's perceptions both of natural reality (sociological and psychological) and spiritual reality. In the Christian tradition, the former is supposed to reveal the latter;

Therefore, those interested in spiritual issues must address both sides in order to minister adequately to former cult members. (24)

Legal issues

Some persons have claimed a "brainwashing defense" for crimes committed while purportedly under mind control. In the cases of Patty Hearst, Steven Fishman and Lee Boyd Malvo the court rejected such defenses.

Also in the court cases against members of Aum Shinrikyo regarding the 1995 sarin gas attack on the Tokyo subway system the mind control defense was not a mitigating factor.

Starting from the Fishman case (1990) (where a defendant accused of commercial fraud raised as a defense that he was not fully responsible since he was under mind control of Scientology) American courts consistently rejected testimonies about mind control and manipulation, stating that these were not part of accepted mainline science according to the Frye Standard (Anthony & Robbins 1992: 529). Margaret Singer and her associate Richard Ofshe filed suits against the American Psychological Association) (APA) and the American Sociological Association (ASA) (who had supported APA's 1987 statement) but they lost in 1993 and 1994. (25)

The Frye standard has since been replaced by the Daubert standard and there have been two court cases where testimonies about mind control have been examined according to the Daubert standard.

Some Civil suits where mind control was an issue, were, though, more effective:

In the case of Wollersheim v. Church of Scientology of California the court states church practices had been conducted in a coercive environment and so *were not protected by religious freedom guarantees.* Wollershiem was finally awarded $8 million in damages. (California appellate court, 2nd district, 7th division, Wollershiem v. Church of Scientology of California, Civ. No. B023193 Cal. Super. (1986)

"During trial, Wollersheim's expert testified Scientology's "auditing" and "disconnect" practices constituted "<u>brainwashing</u>" and "<u>thought reform</u>" akin to what the Chinese and North Koreans practiced on American prisoners of war. A religious practice which takes place in the context of this level of coercion has less religious value than the one the recipient engages in voluntarily. <u>Even more significantly, it poses a greater threat to society to have coerced religious practices inflicted on its citizens.</u>" "Using its position as religious leader, the 'church' and its agents coerced Wollersheim into continuing auditing even though his sanity was repeatedly threatened by this practice…Thus there is adequate proof the religious practice in this instance caused real harm to the individual and the appellant's outrageous conduct caused that harm… 'Church' practices conducted in a coercive environment are not qualified to be voluntary religious practices entitled to first amendment religious freedom guarantees." (26)

In 1993 the European Court of Human Rights upheld the right of a Greek Jehovah's Witness Minos Kokkinakis, who had been sentenced to prison and a fine for proselytizing, to spread his faith, though the court sought to define what it regarded as acceptable ways of sharing one's faith. However, in a dissenting judgment, two judges argued that Kokkinakis and his wife had applied "unacceptable psychological techniques" akin to brainwashing. KOKKINAKIS v. GREECE (14307/88) (1993) ECHR 20 (25 May 1993)(27)

All text is available under the terms of the GNU Free Documentation License. (See Copyrights for details.)
Wikipedia® is a registered trademark of the Wikimedia Foundation, Inc., a U.S. registered 501 (C) (3) tax-deductible nonprofit charity.
Mind Control. Pp. 116.

All research and documentation was brought forward by the author, Marcel L. Garcia Jr., Albuquerque, New Mexico.

12

BRAINWASHING

Brainwashing (also known as **thought reform** or **reeducation**) consists of any effort aimed at instilling certain attitudes and beliefs in a person – beliefs sometimes unwelcome or in conflict with the person's prior beliefs and knowledge, in order to affect that individual's value system and subsequent thought patterns and behaviors. In 1987, the American Psychological Association (APA) Board of Social and Ethical Responsibility for Psychology (BSERP) provisionally declined to endorse one particular approach to brainwashing as "lacking the scientific rigor and evenhanded critical approach necessary for APA imprimatur." The debate amongst APA members on this subject continues. (1)

Terminology

The English words "reeducate" and "reeducation," which the Oxford English Dictionary attests in general senses from 1808, began in the 1940s to express specifically political connotations. George Orwell mentioned in *Animal Farm*. (1945) "the Wild Comrades' Reeducation Committee (the object of this was to tame the rats and rabbits)"; and Arthur Koestler in *The Age of Longing* (1951) wrote of "revolutionary vigilance,...and discipline, and reeducation camps."

The term *"brainwashing"* first came into use in the English language in the 1950s. The OED records its earliest known English language usage of "brainwashing" by E. Hunter in *New Leader* on 7 October 1950. John D. Marks claimed that Edward Hunter was "later revealed" to have worked undercover for the Central Intelligence Agency (CIA). (2)

Earlier forms of coercive persuasion occurred for example during the Inquisition and in the course of show trials against "enemies of the state" in the Soviet Union; but no specific term emerged until the methodologies of these earlier movements became systematized during the early decades of the People's Republic of China for use in struggles against class enemies and foreign invaders. Until that time, presentations of the phenomenon described only concrete specific techniques.

The Chinese term (xi nao, literally "wash brain") originally referred to methodologies of coercive persuasion used in the (gai zao, reconstruction, change, alter).

Of the so-called feudal (feng jian) thought patterns of Chinese citizens raised under prerevolutionary regimes; the term punned on the Taoist custom of "cleansing/washing the heart" (xi xin) prior to conducting certain ceremonies or entering certain holy places, and in Chinese, the word "zin" also refers to the soul or the mind, contrasting with the brain. The term first came into general use in the United States in the 1950s during the Korean War (19501953) to describe those same methods as applied by the Chinese communists to attempt deep and permanent behavioral changes in foreign prisoners, and especially during the Korean War to disrupt the ability of captured United Nations troops to effectively organize and resist their imprisonment. (3)

The word *brainwashing* consequently came into use in the United States of America to explain why, unlike in earlier wars, a relatively high percentage of American GI's defected to the enemy side after becoming prisoners of war in Korea. Later analysis determined that some of the primary methodologies employed on them during their imprisonment included sleep deprivation and other intense psychological manipulations *designed to break down the autonomy of individuals*. American alarm at the new phenomenon of substantial numbers of U.S. troops switching their allegiance to support foreign Communists lessened after the repatriation of prisoners, when it emerged that few of them retained allegiance to the Marxist and "anti-American" doctrines inculcated during their incarcerations. When rigid control of information ceased and the former prisoners' "natural" cultural methods of reality testing could resume functioning, the superimposed values and judgments rapidly decreased.

Although the use of brainwashing on United Nations prisoners during the Korean War produced some propaganda benefits to the forces opposing the United Nations, its main utility to the Chinese lay in the fact that it significantly increased the maximum number of prisoners that one guard could control, thus freeing other Chinese soldiers for frontline battlefield duties.

After the Korean War the term "brainwashing" came to apply to other methods of coercive persuasion and even to the effective use of ordinary propaganda and indoctrination. Formal discourses of the Chinese Communist Party came to prefer the more clinical sounding term *si xiang gai zoo* ("thought reform"). Metaphorical uses of "brainwashing" extended as far as the memes of fashion following.

Political

Korean War (19501953)

The Communist Party of China used the phrase "xi nao" ("wash brain,") to describe its methods of persuading into orthodoxy those members who did not conform to the Party message. The phrase played on xi xin (wash heart), an admonition – found in many Taoist temples – which exhorted the faithful to cleanse their hearts of impure desires before entering.

In September 1950, the *Miami Daily News* published an article by Edward Hunter titled "Brainwashing Tactics Force Chinese into Ranks of Communist Party."

It contained the first printed use of the English language term "brainwashing," which quickly became a stock phrase in Cold War headlines. Hunter, identified by some as "a CIA propaganda operator," turned out a steady stream of books and articles on the theme. (4) An additional article by Hunter on the same subject appeared in *New Leader* magazine in 1951. (5) In 1953 Allen Welsh Dulles, the CIA director at that time explained that "the brain under (Communist influence) becomes a phonograph playing a disc put on its spindle by an outside genius over which it has no control."

In his 1956 book *Brainwashing: The Story of Men Who Defied It* (Pyramid Books), Hunter described "a system of befogging the brain so a person can be seduced into acceptance of what otherwise would be abhorrent to him." According to Hunter, the process became so destructive of physical and mental health that many of his interviewees had not fully recovered after several years of freedom from Chinese captivity.

In 1954 and 1956, two studies of the Korean War defections by Robert Lifton (6) and by Edgar Schein (7) concluded that brainwashing had a transient effect when used on prisoners of war. Lifton and Schein found that the Chinese did not engage in any systematic reeducation of prisoners, but generally used their techniques of coercive persuasion to disrupt the ability of the prisoners to organize to maintain their morale and to try to escape. The Chinese did, however, succeed in getting some of the prisoners to make anti-American statements by placing the prisoners under harsh conditions of physical and social deprivation and disruption, and then by offering them more comfortable situations such as better sleeping quarters, quality food, ext..

Nevertheless, the psychiatrists noted that even these measures of coercion proved quite ineffective at changing basic attitudes for most people. In essence, the prisoners did not actually adopt Communist beliefs. Rather, many of them behaved as though they did in order to avoid the plausible threat of extreme physical abuse. Moreover, the few prisoners influenced by Communist indoctrination apparently succumbed as a result of the confluence of the coercive persuasion, and of the motives and personality characteristics of the prisoners that already existed before imprisonment. In particular, individuals with very rigid systems of belief tended to snap and realign, whereas individuals with more flexible systems of belief tended to bend under pressure and then restore themselves after the removal of external pressures.

Working individually, Lifton and Schein discussed coercive persuasion in their published analyses of the treatment of Korean War POWs. They define coercive persuasion as a mixture of social, psychological and physical pressures applied to produce changes in an individual's beliefs, attitudes, and behaviors. Lifton and Schein both concluded that such "coercive persuasion can succeed" in the presence of a physical element of confinement, "forcing the individual into a situation in which he must, in order to survive physically and psychologically, expose himself to persuasive attempts." They also concluded that such coercive persuasion succeeded only on a minority of POWs, and that the end result of such coercion remained very unstable, as most of the individuals reverted to their previous condition soon after they left the coercive environment.

Following the armistice that interrupted hostilities in the Korean War (July 1953), a large group of intelligence officers, psychiatrists, and psychologists received assignments to debrief United Nations soldiers in the process of repatriation. The government of the United States wanted to understand the unprecedented level of collaboration, the breakdown of trust among prisoners, and other such indications that the Chinese had achieved something new and effective in their handling of prisoners of war. Formal studies in academic journals began to appear in the mid1950s, as well as some first person reports from former prisoners. In 1961, two specialists in the field published books which synthesized these studies for the non-specialists concerned with issues of national security and social policy. Edgar H. Schein wrote on *Coercive Persuasion* and Robert J. Lifton wrote on *Thought Control and the Psychology of Totalism.* Both books focused primarily on the techniques called xi nao, or more formally si xiang gai zao (reconstructing or remodeling thought). The following discussion largely builds on their studies.

Although the attention of Americans came to bear on thought reconstruction or brainwashing as one result of the Korean War (19501953), the techniques had operated on ordinary Chinese citizens after the establishment of the People's Republic of China (PRC) in October 1949. The PRC had refined and extended techniques earlier used in the Soviet Union to prepare prisoners for show trials, and they in turn had learned much from the Inquisition. In the Chinese context, these techniques had multiple goals that went far beyond the "simple control of subjects" in the prison camps of North Korea.

They aim to produce confessions, to convince the accused that they had indeed perpetrated antisocial acts, to make them feel guilty of these crimes against the state, to make them desirous of a fundamental change in outlook toward the institutions of the new communist society, and, finally, to actually accomplish these desired changes in the recipients of the brainwashing/thought reform. To the end, brainwashers desired techniques that would break down the psychic integrity of the individual with regard to information processing, with regard to information retained in the mind, and with regard to values. Chosen techniques included:

- dehumanizing of individuals by keeping them in filth
- sleep deprivation
- partial sensory deprivation
- psychological harassment
- inculcation of guilt
- group social pressure

The ultimate goal that drove these extreme efforts consisted of the transformation of an individual with an ostensible "feudal" or capitalist mindset into a "right-thinking" member of the new social system, or, in other words, to transform what the state regarded as a criminal mind into what the state could regard as a noncriminal mind.

The methods of *thought control* "proved extremely useful" when deployed for gaining the compliance of prisoners of war. Key elements in their success included tight *control* of the information available to the individual and tight *control* over the behavior of the individual.

When, after repatriation, close control of information ceased and "reality" testing could resume, former prisoners fairly quickly regained a close approximation of their original picture of the world and of the societies from which they had come. Furthermore, prisoners subject to thought control often had simply behaved in ways that pleased their captors, without changing their fundamental beliefs. So the fear of brainwashed sleeper agents, such as that dramatized in the novel and in the two films called *The Manchurian Candidate,* never materialized.

Terrible though the process frequently seemed to individuals imprisoned by the Chinese Communist Party, these attempts at extreme coercive persuasion ended with a reassuring result: they showed that the human mind has enormous ability to adapt to stress (not a recognized term in common use with reference to psychology in the early 1950s) and also a powerful homeostatic capacity. John Clifford, S.J. gives an account of one man's adamant resistance to brainwashing in *"In the Presence of My Enemies"* (8) that substantiates the picture drawn from studies of large groups reported by Lifton and Schein. Allyn and Adele Rickett (9) wrote a more penitent account of their imprisonment (Allyn Rickett had by his own admission broken PRC laws against espionage) in "Prisoners of the

Liberation," (10) but it too details techniques such as the "struggle groups" described in other accounts. Between these opposite reactions to attempts by the state to reform them, experience showed that most people would change under pressure and would change back following the removal of that pressure.

Interestingly, some individuals derived benefit from these coercive procedures due to the fact that the interactions, perhaps as an unintended side effect, actually promoted insight into dysfunctional behaviors that the subjects then abandoned.

In Tibet in the 1950s the invading Chinese army arrested Robert W. Ford, a British radio operator working there. Ford spent nearly 5 years in jail, in constant fear of execution, and experienced interrogation and thought reform. He published a book, *Captured in Tibet,* about his experience in Tibet, describing and analyzing thought reform in practice. (11)

Criticism of claims

According to forensic psychologist Dick Anthony, the CIA invented the concept of "brainwashing" as a propaganda strategy to undercut communist claims that American POWs in Korean communist camps had voluntarily expressed sympathy for communism. Anthony stated that definitive research demonstrated that fear and duress, not brainwashing, caused western POWs to collaborate. He argued that the books of Edward Hunter (whom he identified as a secret CIA "psychological warfare specialist" passing as a journalist) pushed the CIA brainwashing theory onto the general public. He further asserted that for twenty years, starting in the early 1950s, the CIA and the Defense Department conducted secret research (notably including Project MKULTRA) in an attempt to develop brainwashing techniques, and that their attempt failed.

Cults

Frequent disputes regarding brainwashing take place in discussion of cults and of new religious movement (NRMs). The controversy about the existence of cultic brainwashing has become one of the most polarizing issues among cult followers, academic researchers of cults, and cult critics. Parties disagree about the existence of a social process attempting coercive influence, and also disagree about the existence of the social outcome – that people become influenced against their will.

The issue gets even more complicated due to the existence of several definitions of the term "brainwashing" (some of them almost straw man caricature metaphors of the original Korean War era concept (12) and through the introduction of the similarly controversial concept of "mind control" in the 1990s. (13) (In some usages "mind control" and "brainwashing" serve as exact synonyms; other usages differentiate the two terms.) Additionally, some authors refer to brainwashing as a recruitment method (Baker) while others refer to brainwashing as a method of retaining existing members (Kent 1997; Zablocki 2001).

Theories on brainwashing have also become the subject of discussions in legal courts, where experts have had to pronounce their views before juries in simpler terms than those used in academic publications and where the issue became presented in rather black and white terms in order to make a point in a case. The media have taken up some such cases – including their black and white colorings.

Proponents of negative proof can quote Eileen Barker: in 1984 the British sociologist wrote in her book *The Making of a Moonie: Choice or Brainwashing?* (Based on her firsthand studies of British members of the Unification Church) that she had found no extraordinary persuasion techniques used to recruit or retain members.

Charlotte Allen reported that:

"(i)n his article in *Nova Religio,* Zablocki was worried less about those academics who may stretch the brainwashing concept than about those, like Bromley, who reject it altogether. And in advancing his case, he took a hard look at such scholars' intentions and tactics. (His title is deliberately provocative: 'The Blacklisting of a Concept: The Strange History of the Brainwashing Conjecture in the Sociology of Religion.')" (14)

In his book *Combating Cult Mind Control* Steven Hassan describes the extraordinary persuasion technique that (in his opinion) members of the Unification Church used to accomplish his own recruitment and retention.

Philip Zimbardo writes that "(mind control is the process by which individual or collective freedom of choice and action is compromised by agents or agencies that modify or distort perception, motivation, affect, cognition and/or behavioral outcomes. It is neither magical nor mystical, but a process that involves a set of basic social psychological principles."(15)

Some people have come to use the terms "brainwashing" or "mind control" to explain the otherwise intuitively puzzling success of some fast acting episodes of religious conversion or of recruitment of inductees into groups known variously as *"new religious movements or as cults."* (16)

One of the first published uses of the term *thought reform* (17) occurred in the title of the book by Robert Jay Lifton: *Thought Reform and the Psychology of Totalism: A Study of 'Brainwashing' in China* (1961). (Lifton also testified on behavioral change methodologies at the 1976 trial of Patty Hearst.) In his book Lifton used the term "thought reform" as a synonym for "brainwashing," though he preferred the first term. The elements of thought reform as published in that book sometimes serve as a bases for cult checklist, and read as follows: (18)(19)

- Milieu Control
- Mystical Manipulation
- The Demand For Purity
- Confession
- Sacred Science
- Loading the Language
- Doctrine Over Person
- Dispensing of Existence

Benjamin Zablocki sees brainwashing as a "term for a concept that stands for a form of influence manifested in a deliberately and systematically applied traumatizing and obedience producing process of ideological re-socializations." Zablocki states that this same concept, historically, also bore the names "thought reform" and "coercive persuasion."

Proto-brainwashing

Before the popularization of the name and concept of "brainwashing" in the 1950s, popular lore often associated the enthusiasm and commitment of recruits joining cults to witchcraft or to mesmerism/hypnotism. (20)

The APA, DIMPAC, and Theories of Brainwashing

In the early 1980s some mental health professionals in the United States became prominent figures due to their involvement as expert witnesses in court cases involving new religious movements. In their court testimony they presented certain theories involving brainwashing, mind control, or coercive persuasion as concepts generally accepted within the scientific community. The American Psychological Association (APA) in 1983 asked Margaret Singer, one of the leading proponents of coercive persuasion theories, to chair a taskforce called the APA Task Force on Deceptive and Indirect Techniques of Persuasion and Control (DIMPAC) to investigate whether brainwashing or "coercive persuasion" did indeed play a role in recruitment by such movements. Before the taskforce had submitted its final report, the APA submitted on February 10, 1987 an *amicus curiae* brief in an ongoing case. The brief stated that:

> (t)he methodology of Drs. Singer and Benson has been repudiated by the scientific community (...the hypotheses advanced by Singer comprised) little more than uninformed speculation, based on skewed data (...) (t)he coercive persuasion theory ... is not a meaningful scientific concept. (...) The theories of Drs. Singer and Benson are not new to the scientific community. After searching scrutiny, the scientific community has repudiated the assumptions, methodologies, and conclusions of Drs. Singer and Benson. The validity of the claim that, absent physical force or threats, "systematic manipulation of the social influences"

can coercively deprive individuals of free will lacks any empirical foundation and has never been confirmed by other research. The specific methods by which Drs. Singer and Benson have arrived at their conclusions have also been rejected by all serious scholars in the field. (21)

The brief characterized the theory of brainwashing as not scientifically proven and suggested the hypothesis that cult recruitment techniques might prove coercive for certain sub groups, while not affecting others coercively. On March 24, 1987, the APA filed a motion to withdraw its signature from this brief, as it considered the conclusion premature, in view of the ongoing work of the DIMPAC taskforce. (22) The *amicus* as such remained, as only the APA withdraw the signature, but not the cosigned scholars (including Jeffrey Hadden, Eileen Barker, David Bromley and J. Gordon Melton). On May 11, 1987, the APA's Board of Social and Ethical Responsibility for Psychology (BSERP) rejected the DIMPAC report because the brainwashing theory espoused "lacks the scientific rigor and evenhanded critical approach necessary for APA imprimatur," and concluded "Finally, after much consideration, BSERP does not believe that we have sufficient information available to guide us in taking a position on this issue."

With the rejection memo came two letters from external advisers to the APA who reviewed the report. One of the letters, from Professor Benjamin Beit-Hallahmi of the University of

Haifa, stated amongst other comments that "lacking psychological theory, the report resorts to sensationalism in the style of certain tabloids" and that "the term 'brainwashing' is not a recognized theoretical concept, and is just a sensationalist 'explanation' more suitable to 'cultists' and revival preachers.

It should not be used by psychologists, since it does not explain anything." Professor Beit-Hallahmi asked that the report not be made public. The second letter, from Professor of Psychology Jeffrey D. Fisher, Ph. D., said that the report "(...) seems to be unscientific in tone, and biased in nature. It draws conclusions, which in many cases do not mesh well with the evidence presented. At times, the reasoning seems flawed to the point of being almost ridiculous. In fact, the report sometimes seems to be characterized by the use of deceptive, indirect techniques of persuasion and control – the very thing it is investigating." (23)

When the APA's BSERP rejected her findings, Singer sued the APA in 1992 for "defamation, frauds, aiding and abetting and conspiracy"; and lost in 1994. (24)

Zablocki (1997) and Amitrani (2001) cite APA boards and scholars on the subject and conclude that the APA has made no unanimous decision regarding this issue. They also write that Margaret Singer, despite the rejection of the

DIMPAC report, continued her work and retained respect in the psychological community, which they corroborate by mentioning that in the 1987 edition of the peer reviewed Merck Manual, Margaret Singer wrote the article "Group Psychodynamics and Cults" (Singer, 1987).

Benjamin Zablocki, professor of sociology and one of the reviewers of the rejected DIMPAC report wrote in 1997:

"Many people have been misled about the true position of the APA and the ASA with regard to brainwashing. Like so many other theories in the behavioral sciences, the jury is still out on this one. The APA and the ASA acknowledge that some scholars believe that brainwashing exists but others believe that it does not exist.

The ASA and the APA acknowledge that nobody is currently in a position to make a Solomonic decision as to which group is right and which group is wrong. Instead they urge scholars to do further research to throw more light on this matter. I think this is a reasonable position to take."

APA Division 36 (then "Psychologists Interested in Religious Issues," today "Psychology of Religion") in its 1990 annual convention approved the following resolution:

"The Executive Committee of the Division of Psychologist Interested in Religious Issues supports the conclusion that, at this time, there is no consensus that sufficient psychological research exists to scientifically equate undue nonphysical persuasion (otherwise known as

"coercive persuasion," "mind control" or "brainwashing") with techniques of influence as typically practiced by one or more religious groups. Further, the Executive Committee invites those with research on this topic to submit proposals to present their work at Divisional programs." (PIRI Executive Committee Adopts Position on Non-Physical Persuasion Winter, 1991, in Amitrano and Di Marzio, 2001)

In 2002, APA's then president, Philip Zimbardo wrote in *Psychology Monitor*:

"A body of social science " evidence shows" that when systematically practiced by state sanctioned police, military or destructive cults, mind control can induce false confessions, create converts who willingly torture or kill "invented enemies," engage indoctrinated members to work tirelessly, give up their money – and even their lives – for "the cause." (Zimbardo, 2002)

Other views

Two months after her kidnapping by the Symbionese Liberation Army in 1974, Patty Hearst, an American newspaper heiress, participated in a bank robbery with her kidnappers.

In her trial, the defense postulated a concerted brainwashing program as central. Despite this claim, the court convicted her of bank robbery.

In the 1990 U.S. V. Fishman Case, Steven Fishman offered a "brainwashing" defense to charges of embezzlement. Margaret Singer and Richard Ofshe would have appeared as expert witnesses for him. The court disallowed the introduction of Singer and Ofshe's testimony: (25) The evidence before the Court, which is detailed below, shows that neither the APA nor the ASA has endorsed the views of Dr. Singer and Dr. Ofshe on thought reform...At best, the evidence establishes that psychiatrists, psychologists and sociologists disagree as to whether or not there is agreement regarding the Singer-Ofshe thesis. The Court therefore excludes defendants' proffered testimony *(U.S. vs. Fishman, 1989)*

New religious movements

The Association of World Academics for Religious Education states that "... without the legitimating umbrella of brainwashing ideology, deprogramming – the practice of kidnapping members of NRMs and destroying their religious faith – cannot be justified, either legally or morally." F.A.C.T. net states that "Forced deprogramming was sometimes successful and sometimes unsuccessful, but is not considered an acceptable, legal, or ethical method of rescuing a person from a cult." (26) The American Civil Liberties Union (ACLU) published a statement in 1977 related to brainwashing and mind control.

In this statement the ACLU opposed certain methods "depriving people of the free exercise of religion." The ACLU also rejected (under certain conditions) the idea that claims of the use of "brainwashing" or of "mind control" should overcome the free exercise of religion. (See quote) (http://en.wikiquote.org/wiki/Brainwashing).

In the 1960s, after coming into contact with new religious movements (NRMs, a subset of which have gained the popular designation of "cults"), some young people suddenly adopted faiths, beliefs, and behavior that differed markedly from their previous lifestyles and seemed at variance with their upbringings. In some cases, these people neglected or even broke contact with their families. Such changes appeared strange and upsetting to their families. To explain these phenomena, some postulated brainwashing on the part of new religious movements. Observers quoted practices such as isolating recruits from their family and friends (inviting them to an end-of-term camp after university for example), arranging a sleep deprivation program (3 a.m. prayer meetings) and exposing them to loud and repetitive chanting. Another alleged technique of religious brainwashing "involved love bombing" rather than torture. "

James Richardson, a professor of Sociology and Judicial Studies at the University of Nevada, states that if the NRMs had access to powerful brainwashing techniques, one would expect that NRMs would have high growth rates, while in fact most have not had notable success in recruitment, most adherents participate for only a short time, and such groups have limited success in retaining members. (27)

Langone has rejected this claim, comparing the figures of various movements, some of which do (by common consent) not use brainwashing and others of which some authors report as using brainwashing. (Langone, 1993)

In their *Handbook of Cults and Sects in America,* Bromley and Hadden present one possible ideological foundation of brainwashing theories that they state demonstrates the lack of scientific support: they argue that a simplistic perspective (one they see as inherent in the brainwashing metaphor) appeals to those attempting to locate an effective social weapon to use against disfavored groups, and that any relative success of such efforts at *social control* should not detract from any lack of scientific basis for such opinions.

Philip Zimbardo, professor emeritus of Psychology at Stanford University, writes: "Whatever any member of a cult has done, you and I could be recruited or seduced into doing – under the right or wrong conditions. The majority of 'normal, average, intelligent' individuals can be led to engage in immoral, illegal, irrational, aggressive and self-destructive actions that are contrary to their values or personality – when manipulated situational conditions exert their power over individual dispositions." (Zimbardo, 1997)

Some religious groups, especially those of Hindu and Buddhist origin, openly state that they seek to improve what they call the "natural" human mind by "spiritual exercises." "Intense spiritual exercises have an effect on the mind," for example by leading to an altered state of consciousness. These groups also state that they do not (condone the) use (of) coercive techniques to acquire or to retain converts.

On the other hand, several scholars in sociology and psychology have in recent years stated that many scholars of NRMs express a bias to deny any possibility of brainwashing and to disregard actual evidence. (Zablocki 1997, Amitrani 1998, Kent 1998, Beit-Hallahmi 2001)

Steven Hassan, author of the book *Combating Cult Mind Control,* has suggested that the influence of sincere but misled people can provide a significant factor in the process of thought reform. (Many scholars in the field of new religious movements do not accept Hassan's BITE model).

Truth Drug

A **truth drug** (or *truth serum*) is a psychoactive drug used to attempt to obtain information from an unwilling subject, most often by a police, intelligence, or military organization. "The use of truth drugs is classified as a form of torture according to international law." (1) It has been reported that "truth drugs" have been used by Russian secret services, successors of the KGB, (2)(3).

Substances

So-called truth drugs have included ethanol, scopolamine, temazepam, and various barbiturates including the anesthetic induction agent sodium thiopental (commonly known as sodium pentothal): all are sedatives that interfere particularly with judgment and higher cognitive function.
A book by the former Soviet KGB officer Yuri Shvets based in Washington details the use of near pure ethanol to verify that a Soviet agent was not compromised by U.S. counterintelligence service. (4) Cisatracurium, invented by JJ Savarese, has been used by Japanese torture squads as a truth drug.

Applications

Russian secret services

A defector from the biological weapons department 12 of the KGB "illegals" (S) directorate (part of Russian SVR service) claimed that a truth drug codenamed SP17 is "highly effective" and has been widely used. "The 'remedy which loosens the tongue' has no taste, no smell, no color, and no immediate side effects. And, most important, a person has no recollection of having the 'heart-to-heart talk'" (the subject feels afterwards as if they had suddenly fallen asleep). Officers of the S directorate used the drug primarily to determine the trustworthiness of their own illegal agents who operate overseas. (3) The assassinated ex-FSB officer Alexander Litvinenko suggested that Russian president candidate Ivan Rybkin "was drugged" with the same substance (identified as SP117) by FSB agents during the 2004 Russian presidential election (he dropped out of the presidential race due to the alleged kidnapping and drugging by FSB agents). (2)

CIA

There are several documented CIA operations such as Edgewood Arsenal experiments and Projects MKNAOMI. MKULTRA, MKDELTA, BLUEBIRD, ARTICHOKE and CHATTER.

CBI

Allegedly India's Central Bureau of Investigation "use this drug regularly" for interrogation, but it was not proven until plans were announced for its use on the terrorist captured during the November 2008 Mumbai Attacks. (3)

Reliability

According to information obtained by public disclosure, sodium Amytal can be highly unreliable, with subjects apparently freely mixing fact and fantasy. Much of the claimed effect relies on the *belief* of the subject that they cannot tell a lie while under the influence of the drug. It has also been said that the use of sodium amobarbital does not increase truth telling, but merely increases talking; therefore, truth is more likely to be revealed, but so are lies. (6)

Retrieved from: http://en.wikipedia.org/wiki/Brainwashing
Freedom of information legislation, also described as **open records** or (especially in the United States) sunshine laws, are laws which set rules on access to information or records held by government bodies. A basic principle behind most freedom of information legislation is that the burden of proof falls on the body *asked* for information, not the person *asking* for it.

13

HUMAN SUBJECT RESEARCH

Human subject research (HSR), or **human subject use** (HSU) involves the use of *human beings as research subjects*. It is an important part of medical research, and many people volunteer for clinical trials of medical treatments. People also volunteer to be subjects for experiments in basic medical science and biology, as well as social and behavioral (psychological) research.

There are many examples throughout history of human research subjects being treated "unethically" and there are therefore many requirements, guidelines, and procedures in place today to ensure similar events are not repeated. Requirements and guidelines exist at the national, academic, and scientific community levels.

Some experiments involve the testing of cosmetic products or ingredients on "humans" instead of animals.

Research subject

In biostatistics or psychological statistics, a **research subject** is any object or phenomenon that is observed for purposes of research. In survey research and opinion polling, the subject is often called a *respondent.*

In human participant research, one highly important topic is informed consent and human participant protection. There are many guidelines, all to insure that the participant is clearly informed of what the study will be, their participation, any possible consequences that they can quit ant time without consequences, who to contact with questions, and so forth. All research involving human participant should include some aspect of human participant protection. (1)

History

Human experimentation and research ethics evolved over time. This section depicts past atrocities that led to the strict policies that are in place today.

On occasion, the subjects of human experimentation have been prisoners, slaves, or even "family members. In some notable cases, doctors have performed experiments on themselves when they have been unwilling to risk the lives of others. This is known as self-experimentation.

Ancient History

Herophilos of Chalcedon was reputed by Celcus, amongst others, to have vivisected prisoners received from the Ptolemaic kings.

Middle Ages

Systematic experimentation and quantification were introduced into the study of physiology in 1025, by the influential Persian Muslim physician, Avicenna (Ibn Sina), in *The Canon of Medicine (Alqanun fialtibb)*. (2) He also introduced the use of biomedical research,(3) clinical trails, (4) randomized controlled trails, (5)(6) drug test (3) and efficacy tests (7)(8) on human subjects.

Human dissections were carried out by Iban Zuhr (Avenzoar), (9) who introduced the use of experimentation in surgery during the 12th century, (10) (11) as well as Ibn Tufail (12) and Saladin's physician Ibn Jumay in the 12th century, Abdellatif in 1200, (13) and Ibn alNafis in the 13th century. (14)

Early Modern Times

HSR experiments were recorded during vaccination trials in the 1700s. In these early trials, physicians used themselves or their slaves as test subjects. *Experiments on others were often* conducted without informing the subjects of dangers associated with such experiments.

A famous example of such research was the Edward Jenner experiments, in which he first tested smallpox vaccines on his son and neighborhood *children*. In an instance of self-experimentation, Johann Jorg swallowed 17 drugs in various doses to record their properties. Conversely, the famous scientist Louis Pasteur "agonized over treating humans," though he was confident of previous results obtained through animal trails. He consented to treat a human only when he was convinced that the death of his first test subject, the child Joseph Meister, "appeared inevitable." (Rothman 1993)

Early 20th Century

In the 1900s, as the progress of medicine began to accelerate, the concept of the various codes of ethics of scientific disciplines changed dramatically, and the treatment of research subjects along with it.

Walter Reed's well-known experiments to develop an inoculation for yellow fever led these advances. Reed's vaccine experiments were carefully scrutinized, however, unlike earlier trials. (Brady 1982)

HSR has also been performed on subjects without informed consent, both covertly and under coercion. The pretext of medical experimentation has been used as a justification for some atrocities. From 1932 until the 1970s, in the United States, citizens were experimented upon in the Tuskegee Study of Untreated Syphilis in the Negro Male.

Declassified documents of the National Archives revealed that during the 1930s and 1940s, the British Army allegedly used hundreds of British and native British Indian Army soldiers as "guinea pigs" in their experiments to determine if mustard gas inflicted greater damage on Indian skin compared to British skin. It is unclear whether the trial subjects, some of whom were hospitalized by their injuries, were all volunteers. (15)(16)(17)(18)

Second Sino-Japanese War and World War II

In Japan, Unit 731, located near Harbin (Manchukuo), experimented with prisoner vivisection, *dismemberment* and induced epidemics *on a very large scale* from 1932 onward through the Second Sino-Japanese war. With the expansion of the empire during World War II, many other units were implemented in conquered cities such as Nanking (Unit 1644), Beijing (Unit 1855), Guangzhou (Unit 8604) and Singapore (Unit 9420). After the war, Supreme commander of occupation Douglas MacArthur gave immunity in the name of the United States to all members of the units in exchange for a tiny part of the results, so that in postwar Japan, Shiro

Ishii and others continued to hold honored positions.

The United States blocked Soviet access to this information. However, some unit members were judged by the Soviets during the Khabarovsk War Crime Trials. The effects were lasting and China is still working to counteract the effects of buried pathogen caches.

During the Second World War, Nazi *human experimentation* occurred in Germany with particular bias towards euthanasia. At the war's conclusion, 23 Nazi doctors and scientists were tried for the murder of concentration camp inmates who were used as research subjects. Of the 23 professionals tried at Nuremberg, 15 were convicted. Seven of them were condemned to death by hanging and eight received prison sentences from 10 years to life. Eight professionals were acquitted. (Mitscherlich 1992).

The results of these proceedings were the Nuremberg Code. It includes the following guidelines, among others, for researchers:

- Informed consent is essential.
- Research should be based on prior animal work.
- The risks should be justified by the anticipated benefits.
- Research must be conducted by qualified scientists.

- Physical and mental suffering must be avoided.
- Research in which death or disabling injury is expected should not be conducted.

In 1940 in the United States, four hundred prisoners in Chicago were infected with malaria to study the effects of new and experimental drugs for the disease.

Beginning in 1942, mustard gas experiments were conducted on 4,000 United States servicemen in order to study the effects on the human nervous system. These test concluded in 1945.

Fort Detrick in Maryland was the headquarters of US biological warfare experiments. Operation White Coat involved the injection of infectious agents to observe their effects in human subjects. (19)

After World War II

- Sweden: Vipeholm experiments, where <u>retarded test subjects</u> were exposed to large amounts of sugar to induce dental cares.
- United States: MKULTRA, Tuskegee syphilis experiment (The Public Health Service Syphilis Study), hepatitis experiments on children at Willowbrook State School, Jewish Chronic Disease

Study (1963), San Antonio Contraception Study (1971), Tea Room Trade Study, Obedience to Authority Study (Milgram Study), dermatological experiments on prisoners at Holmesburg Prison in Philadelphia (see Hornblum 1998), and human radiation experiments.
- United Kingdom: (voluntary) human experimentation at Porton Down in the 1950s, leading to the death of Ronald Maddison.
- Pharmaceutical giant Pfizer came under fire in 2001 for allegedly testing meningitis drugs on African children. (20)

In the United States

Numerous experiments were done on prisoners throughout the US. Many prisoners eventually filed lawsuits and these actions brought about many more investigations and suits against doctors, hospitals and pharmaceutical companies. (1)

Experiments included high-risk cancer treatments, the application of strong skin creams, new cosmetics, dioxin and high doses of LSD. Many incidents were documented in government reports, ACLU findings and various books including Acres of Skin by Allen M. Hornblum. The Stateville Penitentiary Malaria Study is one of many examples. *The Plutonium Files,* for which Eileen Welsome won a Pulitzer Prize, documents the early human tests of the toxicity of plutonium and uranium on people. (21)

The CIA ran an extensive toxicology and chemical/biological warfare program in cooperation with the US military. The Edgewood Arsenal and US Army Medical Research Institute for Infectious Diseases at Fort Detrick in Maryland were the main headquarters for such studies. At such centers, the agency developed many toxins, incapacitates, mind-altering substances and carcinogens. Mind control substances were studied to facilitate interrogation and toxins were used as weapons in assassination. One of the toxins that the CIA studied extensively was derived from red algae called din flagellate which produced the red tide.

The MKULTRA project was "a CIA run *human experiment* program" where prisoners and "unwitting subjects" were administered hallucinogenic drugs in attempt to develop incapacitating substances and "chemical mind control agents," in an operation run by Sidney Gottlieb. Biological weapons specialist Frank Olson's drink was spiked with LSD by "Sidney Gottlieb" in November 1953. He became psychotic and chronically depressed and committed suicide by jumping from the roof of his hotel ten "days later. (22)

Human vivisection

Vivisection has long been practiced on human beings. Herophilos, the "father of anatomy" and founder of the first medical school in Alexandria, was described by the church leader Tertullian as having *vivisected at least 600 live prisoners*. In recent times, the wartime programs of Nazi Dr. Josef Mengele, Shiro Ishii, founder of the Japanese military Unit 731, and Dr. Fukujiro Ishiyama at Kyushu Imperial University Hospital, conducted human vivisections on concentration camp prisoners in their respective counties during World War II. (23)

In November 2006, Doctor Akira Makino confessed to Kyodo news having performed surgery and amputations on condemned prisoners, including "women and *children*" in 1944 and 1945 while he was stationed on Mindanao. (24) In 2007, Doctor Ken Yuasa testified to the *Japan Times* that he believes at least 1,000 persons working for the Showa regime, including surgeons, were involved in vivisections over mainland China. (25)

Human volunteers can consent to be subjects for invasive experiments which may involve, for example, the taking of tissue samples (biopsies), or other procedures which require surgery on the volunteer. These procedures must be approved by ethical review, and carried out in an approved manner that minimizes pain and long-term health risks to the subject. (26) Despite this, the term is generally recognized as pejorative: one would never refer to lifesaving surgery, for example, as "vivisection." The use of the term vivisection when referring to procedures performed on humans almost always implies a lack of consent.

Ongoing Issues

- North Korea: Alleged North Korean human experimentation.

Questionable Psychological Experiments

Several experiments have been conducted on consenting volunteers whose ethical nature is now considered questionable. Following exposure of these experiments, rules regarding informed consent have been tightened.
- The Milgram experiment, in which many subjects were shown they were capable of inflicting discomfort (by electric shock) on other humans if under orders to do so.
- The Stanford prison experiment, in which many participants became violent and abusive of each other.
- The Monster Study that was conducted on orphans in 1939 in an attempt to induce stuttering.

Human Radiation Experiments

Since the discovery of ionizing radiation, a number of human radiation experiments have been performed to understand the effects of ionizing radiation and radioactive contamination on the human body.

Experiments performed in the United States

Radioactive Iodine Experiments

In 1953, the U.S. *Atomic Energy Commission* (AEC) ran several studies on the health effects of "radioactive iodine in *newborns and pregnant women*" at the University of Iowa. In one study, researchers gave pregnant women from 100 to 200 micro curies of iodine131, in order to study the women's "aborted" embryos in an attempt to discover at what stage, and to what extent radioactive iodine crosses the placental barrier. In another study, *"they gave 25 newborn babies* (who were under 36 hours old and weighed from 5.58.5 lbs.) iodine131," either by oral administration or through an injection, so that they could measure the amount of iodine in their thyroid glands. (1)

In another AEC study, researchers at the University of Nebraska College of Medicine fed iodine131 to 28 "healthy infants," through a gastric tube to test the concentration of iodine in the infants' thyroid glands. (1) In 1953 operation called "Green Run," the AEC dropped "radio dine 131 and xenon" over a 500,000 acre area which contained three small towns near the Hanford site in Washington. (2)

In 1953, the AEC sponsored a study to discover if radioactive iodine affected "premature babies" differently from "full-term babies." In the experiment, researchers from "Harper Hospital in Detroit" orally administered iodine131 "to 65 premature and full-term infants" who weighed from 2.15.5 lbs. (1)

Uranium Experiments

Between 1953 and 1957, "eleven patients" at "Massachusetts General Hospital" were injected with uranium as part of research funded by the "Manhattan Project." (2)

Plutonium Experiments

During and after the end of World War II, scientists working on the Manhattan Project and other nuclear weapons research projects conducted studies of the effects of plutonium on laboratory animals and "human subjects." In the case of human subjects, this involved injecting solutions containing (typically) five micrograms of plutonium into hospital patients who were thought either to be terminally ill or to have a life expectancy of less than ten years due either to age or chronic disease condition. The injections were made "without the informed consent of those patients." (3)

In her book, *The Plutonium Files: America's Secret Medical Experiments in the Cold War*, Eileen Welsome, Pulitzer Prizewinning journalist for *The Albuquerque Tribune,* revealed the extent of the experiments conducted on unwitting participants. (4)

At the "Fernald School in Massachusetts," an institution for "feebleminded" boys, 73 "disabled children" were fed oatmeal containing radioactive calcium and other radioisotopes. The radioactive tracers allowed scientists to track how the nutrients were digested. Immediately after World War II, *829 pregnant mothers* in Tennessee received what they were told were "vitamin drinks" that would improve the health of their babies, but were, in fact, mixtures containing radioactive iron, to determine how fast the radioisotope crossed into the placenta. Other incidents included an eighteen year old woman at an upstate New York hospital, expecting to be treated for a pituitary gland disorder, who was injected with plutonium. (5) Such experiments are now considered to be serious breach of medical ethics.

Fallout Research

In 1954, "American scientists" conducted fallout exposure on the citizens of the Marshall Islands after the Castle Bravo nuclear test in Project 4.1. The Bravo test was detonated upwind of Rongelap Atoll and the residents were exposed to serious radiation levels, up to 180 rads. 236 Marshallese were exposed, some developed severe radiation sickness and one died, long term effects included birth defects, "jellyfish" *babies*, and thyroid problems. (6)

The decision to explode the Bravo slide under the prevailing winds was made by Dr. Alvin C. Graves (19121966), the Scientific Director of Operation Castle. "Dr Graves had total authority over firing the weapon," above that of the military Commander of Operation Castle.

Dr. Graves had himself received an exposure of 200 Roentgens in the 1946 Los Alamos accident in which his personal friend, Dr. Louis Slotin, died from radiation exposure. Dr. Graves appears in the widely available film of the earlier 1952 test Mike, which examines the last minute fallout decisions. (7) The narrator (Western actor Reed Hadley) is filmed aboard the control ship in that film which shows the final conference. Hadley points out that 20,000 people live in the potential area of the fallout. He asks the control panel scientist if the test can be aborted and is told yes but it would ruin all their preparations in setting up timed measuring instruments in "the race against the Russians." In Mike the fallout correctly landed north of the inhabited area, but in the 1954 Bravo test, there was a lot of wind shear and the wind which was blowing north the day before the test steadily veered towards the east.

In addition, the yield of Bravo, the first ever American "lithium deuteride" ("solid fusion fuel") bomb, was twice the maximum expected figure (because lithum7 was unexpectedly split to give fusion able tritium, in addition to the predicted effect of lithium6). The combination of unexpectedly high yield plus the wind veering (which was already in progress even before Bravo was fired) contaminated the inhabited "islands" to the east of the detonation. It was not a deliberate radiation experiment, "although questions do remain" over the reason the emergency messages from US weather personnel, who were contaminated on Rongerik like the Marshallese, were "ignored for two days" after the test. Once the heavy fallout on the inhabited islands was discovered, all of the people were evacuated promptly and regularly checked for signs of injury.

Strontium

Strontium is a chemical element with the symbol **Sr** and the atomic number 38. An alkaline earth metal, strontium is a soft silver white or yellowish metallic element that is highly reactive chemically. The metal turns yellow when exposed to air. It occurs naturally in the minerals Celestine and Strontianite. The 90 Sr isotopes is present in radioactive fallout and has a half-life of 29.10 years. It is named for Strontiana village in Scotlandas it was found nearby in the lead mines there in 1787.

Since Strontium is so similar to calcium, it is incorporated in the bone. All four isotopes are incorporated, in roughly similar proportions as they are found in nature. However the actual distribution of the isotopes tends to vary greatly from one geographical location to another. Thus "analyzing the bone of an individual" can help determine the region it came from. This approach helps to identify the ancient migration patterns as well as the origin of commingled human remains in battlefield burial sites.

The human body absorbs strontium as if it were calcium. The radioactive 90Sr *can lead to various bone disorders and diseases, including bone cancer.*

In 2005, China was the top producer of strontium with almost two thirds world share followed by Spain and Mexico, reports the British Geological Survey. The largest commercially exploited deposits are found in England.

90Sr is a byproduct of nuclear fission, which is found in nuclear fallout and presents a health problem since it substitutes for "calcium in bone," preventing expulsion from the body. This isotope is one of the best long-lived-high-energy beta emitters known, and is used in SNAP (Systems for Nuclear Auxiliary Power) devices.

This page was last modified on 23 March 2009, at 20:05, by Wikipedia, the free encyclopedia.

The personal research and information given by Marcel L. Garcia Jr., supports the testimony given by Ernest Garcia, former O.S.S./C.I.A. Covert Actions Operator, through a personal interview with Marcel L. Garcia Jr., his cousin.

14

PROJECT SUNSHINE

Early in the Cold War, researchers in the United States, the United Kingdom, and Australia "attempted to determine just *how much nuclear fallout would be required to make the Earth uninhabitable.*"

They realized that atmospheric nuclear testing had provided them an opportunity to investigate this. Such tests had dispersed radioactive contamination "worldwide," and *"examination of human bodies"* could reveal how readily it was taken up and hence how much damage it caused.

Of particular interest was strontium90 in the bones. *"Infants were the primary focus,"* as they would have had a full opportunity to absorb the new contaminants.

As a result of this conclusion, researchers began a program to *"collect human bodies"* and *"bones"* from *"all over the world,"* *"with a particular focus on infants."* The "bones were cremated and the ashes analyzed for radioisotopes." "This project was kept secret" primarily because it would be a *"public relations disaster"*; as a result parents and family "were not told" what was being done with the "body parts" of their relatives. (8) (Wikipedia, the free encyclopedia).

The Advisory Committee on Human Radiation Experiments

The human radiation experiments of the Cold War era have come before the American public as a sort of modern morality play with *"evildoers"* and "innocents." The Albuquerque Tribune's November 1993 expose' of "The Plutonium Experiments." First roused public attention. Under the auspices of the "Manhattan Project." 18 (supposedly) terminal "patients were injected with large doses" of what one researcher called *"the most poisonous_chemical known."* 1 The purpose of the experiment was to assess the health risk from plutonium to bomb production workers. A couple of months after the expose', the initiative of Secretary of Energy Hazel O'Leary, and public clamor, led President Clinton to appoint a committee of experts to "tell the full story to the American public," 2 From government documents, the President's Advisory Committee identified "almost 4,000 human radiation experiments in the 30 years after the war."

The Committee focused inquiry on eight themes, including no therapeutic research on children, observational studies of uranium miners and Marshall Islanders, and *"human experimentation in nuclear weapons testing."* In its ethical appraisals of the experiments, the Advisory Committee chiefly represented the views of the biomedical community. The Committee's October 1995 Final Report recommended first, redress to victims and second, institution of rules and procedures for ethical conduct in future research.

My (Jean Maria Arrigo) thesis is that these rules and procedures cannot be implemented in clandestine research because they run counter to the ethics and epistemology of military and political intelligence, (3) as I will elaborate. It would be necessary to engage the intelligence community in the moral enterprise. My oral history of a *"CIA covert actions operator" who worked with scientists, "Ernest Garcia,"(4) illustrates this claim in the context of "Project Sunshine,"* one of the experiments condemned by the Advisory Committee. This case also generates much appreciation for the Committee's path breaking exploration of *"clandestine human experimentation."*

The Story according to the Advisory Committee on Human Radiation Experiment

---

Welcome, E. (1993, November 1517). The plutonium experiment. A special reprint of a three-day report published Nov. 1517, 1993. The Albuquerque Tribune. P. 2.

Advisory Committee on Human Radiation Experiments. (1993). Final Report, Advisory Committee on Human Radiation Experiments. P. 1. Washington, DC: U.S. Government Printing Office. (Final Report).

I (Jean Maria Arrigo) begin with the story of the *"human radiation experiments"* as told by the Advisory Committee. Its 1995 Final Report framed the story in the history of radiation medicine, from the discovery of x-rays in 1885, to the use of radioisotopes as tracers in 1913, to health risks surrounding the developments of nuclear weapons in the 1940s, to the past war program of biomedical research. To determine the ethical standards of the era from World War II to 1974, 5 the Committee studied the development of ethical codes and conducted oral histories with eminent medical researchers from the forties and fifties. Apparently some medical researchers perceived the Nuremberg Code as applying only to barbarians. The Committee made a stupendous search of records in "agencies that had sponsored human subjects experiments" in the 1940s and 1950s: the Atomic Energy Commission, Department of Defense, Public Health Service, National Institute of Health, and Veterans Administration – *only* the Central Intelligence Agency denied all access.

In this paper, intelligence refers not to agencies but to function: the collection analysis, and dissemination of information that bears on national security, together with related covert actions.

In a telephone conversation on October 21, 1996, Ernest Garcia granted permission for this presentation of his oral history.

In 1974 the Department of Health, Education, and Welfare promulgated regulations for the protection of human research subjects. The <u>Final Report</u> did not fully justify this bound on their investigations.
"It took public testimony from *over 200 witnesses, including 'Ernest Garcia,' at hearings across the country.*" Ultimately, it produced rich documentation of experimental programs on atomic veterans, uranium miners, Marshall Islanders, prisoners, "*children*" in non-therapeutic treatments, and so on. The Committee recommended formal apologies from the government for some and financial compensation for others.

Regarding that "wrong things happened in the past," the Committee also sought to determine policies that would ensure that "they could not happen again." 6 To assess current medical research practices, the Committee examined contemporary ethical codes and subject consent forms and interviewed 1900 patients in waiting rooms at civilian and military hospitals. As safeguards on future *classified* medical experimentation, the Committee recommended such measures as: review of "proposed experiments by nongovernmental experts with security clearances": clear distinctions between compulsory and volunteer activities of military personnel: careful record keeping by institutions, with earliest public access consistent with national security: and an inviolable rule of informed consent for subjects. The monumental Final Report concluded with the conviction that public release of the remaining CIA documents about "secret programs" "would be fitting close to an *unhappy chapter in the nation's history.*" 7

Human Rights Issues Remain for the Radiation Victims

Many radiation victims remained dissatisfied. Families of the plutonium victims identified in the Albuquerque Tribune have been awarded $400,000 each.

But a family member objected that "the scientists and hospitals involved" "*got off scot-free.*" 8 The National Association of Radiation Survivors had already attempted to legislate the National Nuclear Ethics Law, which would "criminalize government employees'" "deception of citizens" about radiation exposure. 9 A Task Force for 30 advocacy organizations reproached the Committee for directing compensation to a few small groups, such as subjects of university medical experiments, and leaving the majority of victims – atomic veterans, test site workers, and down winders – to fare poorly under slight modifications of inadequate, existing compensation laws. This Task Force on Radiation and Human Rights introduced an Experiment Victims Rights Bill into Congress 10 and plans to file a human rights complaint in the United Nations. 11

How did the Advisory Committee fall short of international human rights covenants? The Committee states six core principles of obligation, which they claimed, "all morally serious individuals accept." 12 These principles favor duties to the individual over duties to the state, such as, *"One ought not to treat people as mere means to ends,"* and *"One ought not to deceive others."*13

National Association of Radiation Survivors. (1994, November 14). National Association of Radiation Survivors – Summary of Issues. (Brochure.) Live Oak, CA: Author.

H.R. 3946, sponsored by Congressman Robert Torricelli of New Jersey. Rep. Torricelli introduces radiation rights legislation. (1996, Fall). Based on the Universal Declaration of Human Rights and on the International Covenant on Civil and Political Rights, which mandates the right to an effective remedy for <u>unlawful experimentation</u>. Rep. Torricelli (NARS).

At the outset, the "Committee acknowledged a moral dilemma" for physicians in radiation research, between providing health care to subjects and promoting national security projects. "But the Committee never actually arbitrated these competing obligations." Instead, the Final Report tacitly imposed an ethical standard of optimization of the six core principles *after* fulfillment of "quintessential national security activities." 14 The Final Report asked rhetorically:

"Who should have been the subjects of a (plutonium) experiment designed to protect workers vital to bomb production in wartime? What should the subjects have been told about the risks of the "secret" substance with which they were being injected? 15

Here is the sleight of hand: the necessity of the experiment and its "secrecy" were first presumed, and the "ethical" question was how to allocate the damages fairly and most decently.

The Committee criticized "researchers and government officials" for "failure" to minimize risks, to keep records, to provide care and compensation, and to *"tell the truth"* when – in retrospect – national security was *"not"* at stake. The Committee "did not characterize wrongdoers as criminal" but as careless, unaware, short sighted, callous, ambitious, or elitist, and it seemed bewildered by the ethical incompetence it uncovered.

The Story According to Military and Political Intelligence

The mysteries of ethical incompetence may be resolved in another explanation of the radiation experiments, which I (Jean Maria Arrigo) draw from published proceedings of the Consortium for the Study of Intelligence 16 and from intelligence interviewees. From the perspective of military and political intelligence, the proper framework for the story is the history of war, not the history of "radiation experiments." In this account, history demonstrates that every new weapon technology changes strategy and tactics and shifts advantage among nations. 17 The " Office of the Secretary of Defense maintains that U.S. peacetime innovations (in weapons) must be successful at the start of the next war," so as to "exploit change faster than the enemy can adapt to it." (Not deplete in weapons of high technology, but be on guard with your best weapons, authors note). 18 The history of radiation medicine implies that an era of alarming human experimentation ended, whereas the history of war implies it continues as a crucial modern component of weapons development. 19 Indeed, in the midst of the Nuremberg trials, *U.S. military intelligence recruited Nazi scientists to continue their disabling psychochemical experiments on U.S. solders, including "Ernest Garcia," at Edgewood Arsenal, Maryland. 20*

On 7,000 soldiers at Edgewood Arsenal, MD, between 1947 and 1966. Hunt, L. (1991). Secret agenda: The United States government, Nazi scientists, and Project Paperclip, 19451990. New York: St. Martin's.

Similarly, scientists from Japan's biological warfare facility in Manchuria, where American prisoners of war had been killed in field tests, were granted immunity from war crimes prosecution in exchange for their laboratory records and scientific cooperation. – Williams, P. & Wallace, D. (1989). Unit 731: Japan's secret biological warfare in World War II. New York: Free Press.

From the intelligence perspective, the highest good is to defend the nation against internal and external adversaries. Intelligence agrees that ordinary citizens should observe democratic constitutional law among themselves, but the intelligence community itself should protect this morally superior but vulnerable system by using the tactics of the enemy, if necessary, to subdue the enemy. That is, different ethical standards pertain to different social roles. The intelligence community *must* violate the core ethical principles set out by the Advisory Committee: defense requires treating some people, such as expendable covert operators like Ernest Garcia, 21 as mere means to the ends of others; deception is essential to strategy; and so on. In this version of the story, the real problem with the "*human radiation experiments*" has been the recent publicity, which *damages trust in government* far beyond those adversely affected and which impedes the crucial work of intelligence. 22 It was the professional responsibility of the CIA to conceal its records from the Advisory Committee. If the goal is to minimize harm to citizens, then revelations that jeopardize national security, through loss of prestige or otherwise, can only lead to greater harm.

An understanding of the epistemology of intelligence can help to explain the "*extreme secrecy*" and "apparent carelessness in experimentation" that troubled the Advisory Committee. For the intelligence community, the primary epistemological problem is whether the object of observation is *natural deception* perpetrated by the enemy. Has the seismograph recorded a natural earthquake, or has it recorded a deceptive nuclear test in a large underground cavern? 23

To thwart deception and espionage, secrecy is necessary. Secrecy requires compartmentalization of information. Thorough and centralized record keeping and review of proposed experiments by outsiders, as the Advisory Committee demands, would greatly increase vulnerability to deception and espionage. The rule of truly informed consent of voluntary subjects would require truly informed and consenting researchers. But the methodology of intelligence precludes truly informed and consenting personnel throughout the enterprise. "As for the appearance of carelessness in experimentation, the task of intelligence is to leave no possibility uninvestigated, so as to anticipate surprises by the enemy." On the whole, this task is best accomplished through *"diffuse data collection,"* that is, numerous exploratory studies without the scientist's obsession for detail, for maintenance of records, or for consequences to subjects.

Project Sunshine

The difference in "ethical perspective" between science and intelligence may be illustrated with *"Project Sunshine,"* officially dated from 1953. *Project Sunshine* was a *"worldwide program"* to "monitor bone uptake" of "radioactive strontium" from "nuclear explosions," so as to assess the risks of "nuclear testing." *Strontium90* accumulates in bones, "especially the growing bones" of "children," because of its chemical resemblance to calcium. According to the *Final Report*, *"cadavers"* were acquired *surreptitiously* in the *"United States, England, Japan, and South America."*

A project scientist said that good personal contacts in the medical field "did not require you to tell them anything... They could guess, and they probably didn't guess very wrong..." 24 The Advisory Committee condemned Project Sunshine:

"AEC officials and researchers employed deception" in the *"solicitation of bones of deceased babes"* from intermediaries with access to "human remains." It appears that concern for public relations played a key role in keeping the human data gathering, and the very existence of Project Sunshine, "secret." 25

Now for a closer look at the mechanisms of operations available to clandestine research, I (Jean Maria Arrigo) describe *Project Sunshine* 26 in the voice of *"covert actions operator and experimental subject Ernest Garcia, by his permission."* His oral history is one in a series of five I conducted of military and intelligence personnel from the National Association of Radiation Survivors. The materials will be archived at UCLA Special Collections. Garcia also testified to the Advisory Committee at its January 30, 1995, hearing in Santa Fe, New Mexico, on a different matter.

Garcia was born in 1928 in a poor farm community near Los Alamos, a talented boy who picked up several languages from his Indian and immigrant neighbors. His mother died in his childhood, and his severely abusive father demanded extreme obedience. Garcia tells of Einstein and Oppenheimer giving him pennies when they occasionally came to Jemez Springs for meals. 27

I (Jean Maria Arrigo) take poetic license in abbreviating his oral history to focus on *Project Sunshine* and on the mechanisms of covert operation.

At the end of the war I (Ernest Garcia) lied about my age into the service. I was in about a thousand of us army recruits selected to fit the CIA criteria. The training period was very, very aggressive. We would be in very difficult situations, terrains, or in other countries, but never, never telling us where we were going. "Most of the training that we got was how to handle work around scientists, how to work with scientific instructions, scientific chemicals." I was mustered into Panama. They had one of the most sophisticated laboratories, because "all these chemicals have a different behavioral pattern that is consistent with heat and barometric pressure in the tropics." *"Most of the time we was working under the influence of some sort of a mind altering drug – some of those covert operations were pretty horrible that we became extremely strong and fearless, over and above the capacity of humanity."* And "they" changed us around, never kept too many of us too long at a time working together. So if one of us "died," we would just go on.

"The Collection of the Children" (from orphanages and off the streets) – that's a very difficult thing to talk about, the part that I (Ernest Garcia) played in it. "The fact" is that there was some *"children"* that were brought from Sao Paulo into this Latin American country. South America had some very, very sparse areas that lend themselves to these things. But to give you that type of information would immediately..
"They" knew exactly that if we had known what was going to happen, we would have interfered with the operation. I just don't have that in me.

Of course, obedience is mandatory without question – *"we would be exterminated."*

I have paper clippings that have surfaced since then that talked about "fetuses" and "stillborn children" "collected to test radiation." There's no doubt in my mind that some of these *"children"* "we collected" went there because "I was told by a medical physicist here in *"America"* that those "bodies" were "delivered over here" to various laboratories. At the time he became very disturbed. He says, *"This has to be relieved* but I don't know how to do that."

I (Marcel Garcia Jr., author) through the guidance of the Holy Spirit helped Ernest Garcia relieve this horrible experience, and put them behind, by accepting Jesus Christ as his Lord and Savior. Now his sins are forgiven, and now he will have eternal life in the kingdom of heaven, now that is the word of God.

One way to deal with testimony of this sort is to discount it and withhold moral reflection. And this may be valid, but not on the basis of plausibility. "Other fatal experiments" were excluded from the *Final Report*, which only examined records received. For example, "there are several corroborating testimonies of sightings of *men in cages* near Ground Zero at the Nevada Test Site, *'dying horribly'* after the *bomb blasts.*" Recalcitrant witnesses claimed they were "drugged and forced" into psychiatric reprogramming. 28 (One of my other interviewees was a witness, Major Tegtmeyer, an Air Force radiation safety director and counterintelligence agent. 29)

There are recent newspaper reports of Brazilian and Guatemalan *"street children murdered"* by "local police," 30 and dozens of Colombian "garbage pickers have been sold" by "police" to a medical school in Bogota as "cadavers for dissection." 31 Moreover, the *"Nobel Laureate Willard Libby,"* who "advocated" *"Project Sunshine,"* was an extreme elitist: *People are not equal:* you have feed the masses and give them something to do, but don't involve them in decisions (paraphrase must be checked). 32

Garcia continues with description of operational mechanisms.

All operations are normally executed by four different components of the intelligence group. Never, never do they ever let any of the four know what the other ones is doing. If somebody was to question, "Well, how did these "children die?", they just simply have to say it was an accident or something. No one is going to question it.

What the operators do is they tease scientists on their projects sufficient to get them interested to where they can't remove themselves out of it. I can truthfully tell you this from my personal experience that's been involved at both ends of this, (as operator and experiment victim). *They are willing to prostitute themselves, to totally disregard their oaths in the name of secrecy or the name of the betterment of humanity.*

"I have very severe posttraumatic depressions about the children that are very, very devastating."

No, I can't say why it is worse than the people who "died beside me" at Edgewood Arsenal – with everybody screaming and terrified and vomiting. *"Nothing" has bothered me the way these "children" has bothered me.* "We talk right here and my body trembles, just knowing that I was part of it."

Governments that Ordered the Massacre of the Innocent Children and God's Response

- When Moses was born in the year c. 1527 B. C., the Pharaoh the king of Egypt ordered that "every" son who is born you shall cast into the river – the Nile. (Exodus 1:22)
- God's response: And it came to pass "at *midnight*" that the Lord struck all the firstborn in the land of Egypt, from the firstborn of Pharaoh who sat on his throne to the firstborn of the captive who was in the dungeon, and all the firstborn of livestock…there was a great cry in Egypt, for *there was* not a house where *there was* not one dead.
- When Jesus was born in the year 7 or 6 B.C., there was Herod the king, was known as Herod the Great, who reigned over Palestine from 37 B.C. until his death in 4

B.C., he sent forth and put to "death" all the male "children" who were in Bethlehem and in all its districts, from two years old and under. (Matthew 2: 16)
- God's response: Now when Herod was "dead," behold, an angel of the Lord appeared in a dream to Joseph in Egypt, saying, Arise, take the young Child and His mother, and go to the land of Israel, for those who sought the Child's life are dead. (Matthew 2:19)
- *Project Sunshine* was a *"worldwide"* program of the "Atomic Energy Commission" (AEC) of the "United States of America" to monitor bone uptake of radioactive strontium from "nuclear testing." Strontium – 90 accumulates in bones, especially the growing bones of *"children"* because of its chemical resemblance to calcium.
- *"God's response: Yet to come!"*

The Advisory Committee denounced *Project Sunshine*: "AEC officials and researchers employed deception in the solicitation of bones of deceased *"babies"* from intermediaries….It appears that concern for public relations played a key role in keeping the human data gathering, and the very existence of *Project Sunshine, secret.*"

Cynicism cites the character flaws of self-interest, corruption, incompetence, and outright aggression. *Regressive Science* cites the inadequate scientific ethics of earlier eras or scientists' hasty responses to political exigencies. And the *Protection Industry* cites the market evolution of a "mafia like" racket for "protection" in "international transactions." The *Epistemological Explanation,* in contrast, cites flawed moral understanding where there are "genuine moral failures" in "clandestine research."

The *Final Report* (p.794) dates *Project Sunshine* from 1953. Ernest Garcia gave a discreet account of his late 1940s collection of the South American "children," during oral history interviews on October 21 and 22, 1995. In telephone conversation on October 21, 1996, when fully released from the Secrecy Act, he associated the episode with *Project Sunshine.*

Public relations play a key role and reveals the existence of *Project Sunshine,* in this article titled "Dead Infants Secretly Tested for Fallout." The article briefly declares: The U.S. government undertook a "*worldwide campaign*" of deception in the early 1950s "to hide" that is was "gathering human remains," the CIA had a wider involvement in human radiation tests than it has acknowledged, the searches, which followed as many as "*50 bomb test*" in the late 1940s and early '50s "*were made in the United States and more than 20 countries,*" the AEC researchers wanted to test levels of highly radioactive strontium90a fallout product, the "<u>collection of infant skeletons</u>" involved a dozen or more countries including Japan, South Africa, India, Brazil, Colombia, Peru, Chili and Bolivia as well as the United States. The documents show that at least 55 skeletons of stillborn infants – including several from Utah – were tested at the University of Chicago, one of three laboratories involved in the program

. Other Universities involved in experiments with the U.S. Atomic Energy Commission (AEC) as declared by the Wikipedia, the free encyclopedia, and previously revealed under the "Human Radiation Experiments," are; the University of Iowa, The University of Nebraska College of Medicine, plus hospitals and schools, (Pages 193198).

An Inside Look During a Meeting with the AEC and the CIA

Covert Operator Ernest Garcia will provide the richness of detail of his involvement with *Project Sunshine* through his interview with Marcel L. Garcia Jr. (author).
Ernest Garcia is seen sitting in a conference room lessoning to what will be a *"worldwide covert operation" Project Sunshine.*

Ernest Garcia: As I sat at a classified AEC Biophysics Conference and lessoned to the chief of the AEC Division of Biology and Medicine proposed to AEC board member *Willard Libby,* drew some ill feelings into me immediately that just got me sick.

Chief of the AEC: Willard, *how many bombs can we detonate without producing a race of monsters?*

Ernest Garcia, then looked at *Willard Libby* as Willard then got a smirk look on his face and thought that the question was funny, he then said;

Willard Libby: I don't know, let's find out (laughs).

Chief of the AEC: We are establishing a "high priority" of "body snatching" "worldwide", *"especially children,"* and the collection of *"baby bones,"* some will be through personal contacts with foreign doctors. All for the purpose of "Human Radiation Experiments." This will fall under operation *"Project Sunshine."*

Willard Libby is seen bobbing his head up and down in a form of agreement, and then he said:

Willard Libby: I definitely agree that *"body snatching"* is of the highest priority, and "that is an order"!

Possible Scenes Prior to the Annihilation of Certain Victims

In a Home in the U.S. Involving a Mother and Her Daughter

The mother a 30yr. old female, is washing clothes in the laundry room of her house, while her daughter Sandy a 5yr. old girl is playing with her dolls close by, the daughter says:

Sandy: Mommy, can I go outside and play?

Mother: No honey, I can't leave you outside the front yard by yourself, you know that baby.

Sandy: But mommy, I want to play, will you take me to the park and play with me, there's lots of kids there mommy?

Mother: Ok Sandy, when I'm done washing cloths we will go to the park for just a little while, because I have other things I have to do, ok honey?

Sandy: Ok mommy, thank you, I love you mommy.

Mother: I love you to my baby.
In a Very Wooded Park in Brazil, a Father is Training His Son How to Box.

The father a 47yr. old male, is holding up some coaches mitts for his son Gabriel a 12yr. old boy, who is throwing punches at the coaches mitts.

Father: Bueno my son, you need to keep your elbows up a little higher when you throw those hooks, so you could hit with the big knuckles, so don't slap your punches.

The boy stops punching for a moment.

Gabriel: Bueno daddy, like this?

The boy brings the elbow up a little higher while he throws a better hook punch.

Father: That is much better my mi hito, much, much better. You will be a world champion someday my son.

In a College Classroom in London England

A young college student named Juliet age 20yrs. old is seen listening to her teacher Ms. Richardson a 60yr. old woman, standing in front of the class and pointing at the blackboard while she is commenting on a subject just before the class ends.

Ms. Richardson: Now kids, this weekend I want you to study on the subject of, Biophysical and Psychosocial Concepts Related to Health and Illness, and be good kids this weekend.

Juliet is seen exiting from the classroom, and right behind her are two guys talking to each other, one being Thomas a 23yr. old young man, and the other one is Chuck a 22yr. old young man.

Thomas: Damn, I hate it when she keeps calling us kids.

Chuck: It's frustrating man it really bugs me to.

Juliet heard what they said and then she turns around while she is still walking and then says:

Juliet: That's because you both still act like babies.

Both of the guys put a smirk on their face and commented.

Thomas: Hay, what do you mean by that girl?

Two of Juliet's friends suddenly walking up to her side on a crowded hallway, Juliet just smiles. One of her friends is Chantal a 20yr. old female, and her friend walking next to her is Beatrice a 20yr. old female.

Chantal: Now, what was that all about Juliet?
Juliet is suddenly turning around and recognizes her friends.

Juliet: Oh, hi Chantal, no that was nothing; these guys are just acting like babies.

Beatrice is seen looking back at Thomas and Chuck and then she makes her comment while her eyes roll up at the guys.

Beatrice: Well, they certainly don't look like babies to me.

The other two girls are seen looking at each other and Juliet responds:

Juliet: Now Beatrice, you straighten up, you know better than that.

The girls start laughing and are seen tapping each other on the shoulder.

Return to the AEC Biophysics Conference Room

Willard Libby is continuing his conference with the offers while making his demands.

Willard Libby: *"Human samples" are of "prime importance," do you understand?*

Ernest Garcia is seen getting nervous; he is tapping his fingers from his right hand on the table while he is looking at Willard Libby as he speaks.

Willard Libby: And if anybody knows how to do a good job of "body snatching" they will really be serving their country.

Ernest Garcia is seen running his fingers from his left hand through his hair while he bends his head down as a form of depression, as he quietly says to himself:

Ernest Garcia: "Oh my God, are these people stupid or just insane?"

Inside the Office of an Orphanage in the U.S.

The Institution for the Housing and Care of Orphans

A counselor Mrs. McCarthy age 63yrs. old is seen talking to two small children in her office, Johnny who is 6yrs. old, and his sister Kathy who is 8yrs. old, whom both lost their parents recently.

Mrs. McCarthy: Johnny and Kathy, my name is Mrs. McCarthy.

Mrs. McCarthy is seen shaking the children's hand.

Mrs. McCarthy: First of all children, I want to say that I am deeply sorry that you lost both of your parents at the same time due to a car accident. The report says that a drunk driver ran into your parent's car.

Both of the children are thinking of their parents and are now starting to cry.

Mrs. McCarthy: Oh children, I'm so sorry.

Mrs. McCarthy then opens her arms and then she leans down to embrace the children as they come crying into her arms.

Kathy: We miss our mommy and daddy!

Mrs. McCarthy: I know you both miss them but I promise you my love, and that I will do my best to take care of both of you, I promise.

Inside a School of Ballet Dancing in New York City

Inside the school of ballet the instructor Isabella age 37yrs. old female, is instructing a young teenage girl Jessica a 14yr. old female, is holding her left hand on the hand rail and stretching her right leg up and holding her leg with her right hand, as she says:

Jessica: Like this Isabella?

Isabella is now seen guiding Jessica, then Isabella says:
Isabella: Yes, that is much better, but Jessica you must straighten your back more and give me a better posture and lift your head up with pride.

Jessica: Oh yes, I feel much better, how do I look?

Jessica obtains a beautiful form and then she starts to give a brilliant smile. Now Isabella starts to clap her hands as she comments.

Isabella: You look beautiful Jessica, simply beautiful.

Jessica's mother is now seen walking into the dance room; her mother's name is Margaret a 40yr. old female, her mother makes her presence known by saying:

Margaret: Excuse me girls, but it's time to go now Jessica.

On the background Jessica is seen dropping her leg while the instructor picks her right hand up while her fingers gracefully move, and nods her head as a form of approval.

Jessica: Ok mom, let me change and I'll be right there.

Return to the AEC Biophysics Conference Room.

Willard Libby is making a fist with his right hand and prepares to strike the table, as a form of pride, then boldly proclaims:

Willard Libby: I am proud that the President put me in the Atomic Energy Commission.

Willard Libby now strikes the table with pride with a serious look on his face.

Willard Libby: And that was because of my helping on the hydrogen bomb decision.

Willard Libby now pulls his right arm back and then prepares to point upward forty-five degrees, almost like a form of a Hitler salute, and then with his strength and a loud voice he now stretches his arm out and boldly proclaims:

Willard Libby:"Now let's go serve our country to the fullest."

EXT. Mr. Ernest Garcia is seen on the Passenger Side of a Moving Vehicle – in the U.S.A.

Ernest Garcia is seen on the passenger side of a black vehicle with no license plates, and accompanied by two members of the mafia (*Protection Industry*) one being Bernoulli a 30yr. old male, and the second member is Capello a 25yr. old male, and they were fully armed and "extremely dangerous."

Ernest Garcia is looking out the window in seeking in whom he may "kidnap."

Ernest Garcia declares in the interview with Marcel: This is where it all begins, with two members of the mafia and I or maybe I should say two members of the Protection Industry, which were Bernoulli the driver and Capello in the back seat. These are people you do not want to mess with believe me they don't hesitate one bit they get the job done.

Ernest Garcia is focusing up ahead while he reaches towards the driver (Bernoulli) to tell him something.

Ernest Garcia: Bernoulli look, "there is a park full of kids" let's go there and see what I find.

Bernoulli: <u>Do you want me to take out anyone that interferes</u>?

Bernoulli reaches for his gun that is inside his suit while driving with his left hand. Ernest Garcia while he still has his left arm out towards Bernoulli and then he points his index finger upward while he is signaling his hand "no."

Ernest Garcia: No, no killing if all possible, we must do this as clean of a mission as possible.

Garcia brings his left arm back down.

Capello is seen in the back seat pulling out his gun from his coat.

Capello: With the law on our side, we can't go wrong, we get the job done and we get paid for it, I love it.

Ernest Garcia: Bernoulli pull over right here close to where the "children" are playing. Now the moment I "abduct a child" you guys close in and make sure no one comes close to me, you got it?

Bernoulli: You got it senor!

Bernoulli is now pulling over exactly where Ernest Garcia wanted him to be.

Sandy from the previous scene is on the swing and her mother is pushing her from behind. Sandy is thanking her mother for bringing her to the park.

Sandy: Mommy, I'm glad you got the cloths done.

Mother: Now why are you glad that I got the cloths done Sandy?

Sandy: Because you had promised me to bring me to the park, and I love you for that mommy.

Mother; I love you my baby.

Sandy then opens her eyes wider as she remembers something.

Sandy: Mommy, I just remembered that I left my dolly in the car can I go get it?

The mother starts to shake her head no.

Mother: No baby, you can't go to the car alone, there are too many cars going by honey. I'll run to the car and I'll get your doll for you, now you just stay here.

Sandy looks at her mom as she comments to her:

Sandy: Ok mommy but hurry.

The mother starts to run to the car close by.
Mother: Ok my baby; I'll be right back.

While Sandy is watching her mother run off, "suddenly" an arm reached around her waist and pulled her from behind the swing. The force caused Sandy to release her grip. There was intense fear on Sandy's face while she starts to scream out loud.

Sandy: Scream! Mommy, help me!

Ernest Garcia is seen pulling the child away and caring her off on his right side.

The mother immediately turns her head around as she heard her daughter screaming. With a scream for Sandy, the mother starts to run after her.

Mother: Sandy! My baby! No!

The people around the park start to panic as they hear the screaming echoing through the park.

Ernest Garcia is dashing to the car with Sandy on his right arm and his security behind him covering his back with guns in their hand.

The mother is seen running after her daughter while she is still screaming, while the tears are running down her face.

Mother: Bring, my, baby, back!

Ernest Garcia opens the front passenger door of the car while holding Sandy, as she screams out with fear one finale time, with tears pouring out of her eyes, she yells for her mother:

Sandy: Mommy, I love you, please "help me mommy!"

The car is starting to drive off with Sandy struggling to get out from Garcia's grip while she tries to reach out of the passenger window, screaming.

The mother was unable to rescue her daughter; she is seen raising her arms up with intensity.

The mother then screams out:

Mother: Sandy, my baby, come back! Someone, call the police!
The mother then drops to her knees and places her hands on the sides of her face while she watches the car zoom away, as she cries more intensely:

Mother: Oh my baby! My precious beautiful baby! Oh my God!

Return to a previous seen in the wooded park in Brazil

~ 269 ~

While in the wooded park in Brazil with a few families scattered around the park enjoying their family gatherings, a father is coaching his son Gabriel in boxing, while his son is finishing the last few jabs on the coach's mitts the father continues to instruct his son. The father is seen pulling out of his pocket a timer.

Father: That was powerful mi hito, now I need you to keep your endurance up, so now is the time for you to run your laps and I will time you once again. But remember my son every day is different, some days you feel good and some days you don't, so don't ever worry about your skills just keep trying your best, and always keep your faith, and you will be blessed mi hito.

Gabriel: I will daddy, I will always keep trying my best and I promise you that I will always keep my faith, thank you.

Ernest Garcia is hiding behind a large tree in the same park.

Ernest Garcia is seen looking at the father and son training in boxing in the park. Garcia picks up his radio to communicate to his security in the car not too far away.

Ernest Garcia: Bernoulli, come in.

Bernoulli and Capello are seating in the front seat of the black car. Bernoulli hears Garcia

calling for him, and Bernoulli picks up his radio and responses.
Bernoulli: This is Bernoulli go.

Ernest Garcia: I have my eye on what may be a father and a son practicing boxing in the park, my plan is to get the boy, do you have a visual on them?

Bernoulli: Visual is confirmed Mr. Garcia, should we move in?

While Bernoulli is holding the radio up to his ear awaiting Garcia's response, Garcia then comments over the radio by saying:

Ernest Garcia: No, no do not move yet.

Ernest Garcia pauses for a moment, then he notices:
Ernest Garcia: But it looks now like the father is going to send the boy for a run, it looks like the father has a timer on his hand and not only that but it looks like the boy is going to be coming in my direction. So be ready to drive the car to my location and open the back door and I'll grab the boy and bring him in. Do you copy?

Ernest Garcia is awaiting and listening for Bernoulli's response on the radio.

Bernoulli: Yes Mr. Garcia, I copy, the moment I see the boy starting to run I will then drive up for the pickup.

The father is preparing the son Gabriel for his run; the father leans down with the timer in his hand and starts the run for his son.

Father: Ok mi hito are you ready?

Gabriel: Yes daddy, I'm ready, thank you.

Gabriel squats down to prepare his run.

Father: Ok, go!

Gabriel is seen running as fast as he could down the park, straight towards Ernest Garcia.

Bernoulli and Capello are driving just ahead of the boy.
Meanwhile Ernest Garcia is now preparing to kidnap Gabriel and he now comments on the radio to Bernoulli:

Ernest Garcia: Ok guys, let's do this!

Ernest Garcia is seen running right at Gabriel and grabbing him and caring him into the back seat of the car, as Capello is standing outside of the car holding the back door open. Capello now slams the door closed then he gets into the front seat and Bernoulli drives off with speed.

The father is seeing this kidnapping taking place just before his eyes. The father responds with horror in his eyes of unbelief and starts to run after the kidnappers, the father screams out:

Father: Hay, leave my boy alone! Mi hijo! Gabriel
come, back! My baby! Mi Dios ayudar mi!

EXT. In a busy corner street in London England

The Messenger is seen once again this time he is standing on the corner of a busy street in London England. Meanwhile two black cars with four officers in each car are driving behind one another, while Ernest Garcia is on the passenger seat of the front car with the window rolled down, along with him are his team of CIA officers and security (the *Protection Industry*). They are preparing to turn at the corner right where the Messenger is standing, just as they start to turn. The Messenger catches Garcia's attention when he raises both arms upward and stares at Mr. Garcia's eyes.

The Messenger looks deeply into Mr. Garcia's eyes and loudly says:

Messenger: The devil comes but to steal! Kill! And to Destroy!

Ernest Garcia has a look of concern on his face after hearing what the Messenger just said, while driving by Ernest turns his head back, while feeling guilty. The other officers in the car did not make any comments they simply ignored the Messenger.

The two cars with the CIA officers and security are now driving towards the front of a college campus nearby.

There is now a visual on Juliet, Chantal and Beatrice while they are walking out together of the college building in London England. The girls are talking to one another and Juliet comments:

Juliet: Now Beatrice you know that it is not proper for a girl to be throwing herself at the guys like that.

Beatrice: Well I'm only expressing my feelings towards them; there is no harm in that.

Chantal: There is harm in that, if your feeling is just for lust and the greed for money, how could you say that it is not harmful.

Beatrice: Well isn't that what life is all about? That is all men are worth any way.

Juliet: Beatrice your priorities need to be straightened out girl, you really need to change the way you think.

The girls are seen laughing.

The two government cars are seen parked in front of the university, while the officers await Garcia's orders.

Ernest Garcia raises his radio to talk to the other officers in the car behind him. Garcia is looking at Juliet, Chantal and Beatrice, as they are about to come closer towards their cars, Garcia then tells the officers:

Ernest Garcia: Gentlemen I have my eyes on these three girls that are coming closer towards our cars. All of us will come out at the same time and just show them our badges and tell them that they need to come with us. If there is any resistances then restrain them, well take two of the girls and you guys take the other one, ok let's go.

The eight officers are seen coming out of their cars and surrounding the girls.
Ernest Garcia: Girls we are government officials.

The officers are seen showing their badges to the girls.

Ernest Garcia: And all three of you need to come with us.

Juliet takes the lead and speaks on behalf of the other girls.

Juliet: Why, we did not do anything wrong!

Ernest Garcia pulls out some handcuffs from his back and says:

Ernest Garcia: In order to prevent any resistance, it would be best that all of you go along quietly to headquarters with us.

The girls chose to comply with Garcia's orders and got in the cars.

Return to the Institution for the housing and care of orphans in the U.S.A.

Ernest Garcia is sitting in one car with Bernoulli and Capello just outside the Institution for the Housing and Care of Orphans building; Garcia continues to be obedient to his orders, by pursuing in the governments endeavor. The threats and pressure was on Garcia so intensely that he had to continue in the government's program, the objective had to be met. Garcia takes a deep breath and then says:

Ernest Garcia: There are plenty of kids playing in that courtyard at the orphanage, between us three we should be able to grab two each.

Bernoulli: Let's do it!

Ernest Garcia, Bernoulli and Capello make a dash for the kids.

While Kathy and Johnny noticed these men going after the children they look at each other and Kathy says:

Kathy: Johnny, those men are kidnapping the children we better run inside.

Johnny: Ok Kathy, hurry lets go!

Kathy and Johnny take off running but before they get to the door Garcia suddenly got a hold of both of them and carries them off.

Kathy: Screams! Somebody help us! Help!

Johnny is seen trying to punch Garcia, but was unsuccessful in doing any damage. Garcia was just too strong.

Return to the ballet school in New York City

Just outside the School of Ballet in New York City, Ernest Garcia, Bernoulli and Capello are parked behind Margaret's car, which is Jessica's mother. Garcia is telling Bernoulli and Capello inside the car:

Ernest Garcia: Now guys we need to get at least one teenage girl from this dance studio and more than likely that person might be with a guardian, so prepare for anything.

Bernoulli: Ok Mr. Garcia, we are ready whenever you are.

Just then Margaret and Jessica start walking out of the dance studio.

Capello: What perfect timing, just what the doctor ordered.

Margaret is looking out, but does not really notice Mr. Garcia and his security in the car as being an obstacle or a form of danger.

Ernest Garcia now comments to his security:

Ernest Garcia: Alright guys, I'll take the girl that just came out and you guys keep the woman that she is with away from me.

Capello: You got it, consider her yours.

Ernest Garcia: Let's go and get this over with.

As Ernest Garcia and his security are coming out of their car, the view is from the center of the road, so Margaret and Jessica are visible on the background. Jessica is seen walking on Margaret's left side, which puts her closer towards Ernest Garcia, since they were parked behind Margaret's car.

Ernest Garcia made himself known when he approached them and said:
Ernest Garcia: Excuse me.

Ernest Garcia puts his arms around Jessica and lifted her right up off the ground.

The mother Margaret approached Garcia immediately and said:

Margaret: Let go of my daughter, you bastard!

Margaret immediately slapped Garcia across the face with her right hand.

Bernoulli suddenly strikes Margaret very fast and hard across the head with a short club on his right hand.

Immediately Margaret's eyes roll up and she collapses to the ground. Bernoulli watches Margaret fall to the ground and then sys:

Bernoulli: Good night sweetheart.

"There were continuous scenes of government officials abducting children right off the streets all across the world."

- Ernest Garcia, Bernoulli and Capello are seen grabbing kids in central park in New York City.

A report came out in (1993) indicated that poor, abandoned, "molested" and there were "tortures" of "thousands" of Brazilian street "children," and also the street children in Guatemala.

- "Groups of officers" scrambling the streets of Brazil, "filling their arms with abducted children" while they "scream for help."

- "CIA" officers are "seen caring 'sacks' of fetuses and stillborn children out of many abortion clinics."

In a remote camp:

There were numerous CIA officers standing close by while Ernest Garcia gave the orders to be prepared to escort the "subjects" into a large tent nearby.

The CIA officers were dressed in radiation protection outfits and caring weapons. Garcia then gives an order to the CIA officers:
Ernest Garcia: Officers when the "subjects" get here, be prepared to escort them into that large tent and then be sure to follow my orders from there, is that understood gentlemen?

The second in command officer Bradley, responded to Ernest Garcia's order by saying:

Bradley: Yes sir, that is understood sir!

The entire officers there saluted to Ernest Garcia.

Just then three buses were seen coming down the dirt road while Ernest Garcia notices the buses coming, he then comments:

Ernest Garcia: Now that is perfect timing, the buses are now here.

The buses are now parking one behind the other, while the CIA officers are standing by the bus doors, Ernest Garcia waves and announces at the drivers to go ahead and open the doors. The doors from the three buses open almost exactly at the same time, Garcia makes a verbal announcement:

Ernest Garcia: Ok drivers open the doors and release the "subjects."

The so called "subjects" are seen coming out of the buses, which happen to be "<u>CHILDREN</u>" <u>chained together</u>, some were babies being held in the arms of teenagers.

"The children are seen crying out for help and for their family members."

Children: Help! Somebody, help us please!

Garcia declared hearing a child scream and seeing the tears pouring down their faces and fear on their faces like never before seen. The screams and the picture of their faces haunted him for the rest of his life. The child screamed:

Children: Mommy! I want my mommy now! Let me have my mommy!

There were some of the children from the previous scenes there; teenagers caring babies, plus *"retarded children"* were in the same group.

Officer Bradley "commanded the children and teenagers to go to the tent" while he points in the direction of the tent, which happens to be fenced in.

Bradley: "I want all you children and teenagers into that tent right now!"

The children are seen walking into the tent with continuous crying.
Ernest Garcia is now calling for officer Bradley after the children were in the tent.

Ernest Garcia: Bradley, I need you to go ahead and "lock the gates" there.

Bradley: Yes sir, we will get that done immediately, sir.

Officer Bradley and another officer are seen "closing the gates and locking them."

Ernest Garcia is now picking up his dispatch radio and is preparing to communicate with a pilot that is flying overhead, he announces:

Ernest Garcia: "Ok air one, we are ready," do you copy?

While the children are screaming in the background, Ernest Garcia is holding the radio next to his ear and looking straight upward. There was no response from the pilot at first, Garcia makes his statement again while looking upward, and he sees a plane at 5,000 feet, just overhead.

Ernest Garcia: Air one do you copy?

The Air force pilot from air one responds to Ernest Garcia's call.

Pilot: This is air one I copy.

Ernest Garcia: "Give us thirty seconds to clear out and then follow your orders."

Pilot: All is confirmed and the order is on schedule sir.

Ernest Garcia is now looking at his officers and ordering them to clear out.

Ernest Garcia: "All right officers get the hell out and clear out of here quick!"

Just then Garcia could hear the loud cry of the children getting louder and louder while they are screaming to the top of their voices for help. He takes *"a finale glance at the children"* with tears in his eyes and says out loud to himself.

Ernest Garcia: Oh God, forgive me for being a part of this, please forgive me!

"The plane now releases *"the bomb"* the hearts now throb."

Different views are observed at the tent as the "NUCLEAR EXPLOSION" takes place and "ends the lives" of all those "INNOCENT CHILDREN" and "body parts flying around." The "CIA" officers are seen "COLLECTING BODY PARTS" and placing the "subjects" body parts into plastic bags.

As the CIA officers are seen collecting body parts and placing them in plastic bags, Ernest Garcia places another order.

Ernest Garcia: Officers be sure and collect all of the "body parts" and have them hand "delivered to the laboratories in the U.S." for "radiation testing." Meanwhile "this mission just begun," we've got the same work to do with "thousands, worldwide," now see *"whose next"* on the agenda, here are the new orders.

There has been resent killings by government officials of innocent adults in a certain nation due to protesting of what the public called a fraudulent presidential election that was seen on T.V. News in the month of June 2009. But when a government of a nation leads or involves and/or pays other nations to join them in annihilating innocent babies and children worldwide, the question arises; are these people insane, or does Satan possess them? What is the difference?

The Holy Scriptures says:

"You are of God, little children, and have overcome them, because He who is in you is greater than he who is in the world. They are of the world. Therefore they speak as of the world, and the world hears them. We are of God......

he who knows God hears us; he who is not of God does not hear us. By this we know the spirit of truth and the spirit of error (1 John 4: 46)." He who is in the world is the "devil" (5:19). "We know that we are of God, and the whole world lies *under the sway* of the wicked one." Satan does not touch the one born of God (v. 18), but he does have the whole world in his grip and under his dominion. (The Nelson Study Bible, New King James Version).

In The Amazon Mountains

Ernest Garcia and dozens of other officers are armed and seen loading into a plane numerous Amazon Indians. Garcia is heard giving his orders:

Ernest Garcia: Handale hombre, entren, apurense! (Ok men, get in, and hurry)!

In the Streets of Columbia

In the streets of Columbia the police officers are seen abducting garbage pickers, one officers takes hold of a garbage picker and orders him into the police car:

Police Officer: Yo soy la policia, suvase al carro! (I am the police, get in the car)!

A 70yr. old man is complying with the police as he raises his hands up and says:

Garbage Picker: Bueno, bueno, ya vengo, ya vengo. (Ok , ok, I'm coming, I'm coming).

A statement made by Ernest Garcia during his interview with Marcel Garcia.

Ernest Garcia: It is documented that there were newspaper reports of Brazilian and Guatemalan "street children murdered by local police" and dozens of Colombian "garbage pickers have been sold by police" to a medical school in Bogota "as cadavers for dissection." The fact is that there was some children that were brought from Sao Paulo into Latin America country. South America had some very, very sparse areas that lend themselves to these things. But to give you that type of information would "immediately have me exterminated." The economic question would be how "the market demand for cadavers," so clearly stated by *Willard Libby,* "could remain unsatisfied with supplies so evidently available."

EXT. Ground Zero at the Nevada Test Site

Twenty armed officers are seen next to two military buses while civilian men are seen exiting these buses. A commanding officer named Commander Baker (name has been changed) is standing by and will be giving the orders.

The two hundred civilian men that exited the buses are now seen standing in two lines chained together while waiting for their orders from Commander Baker.

Commander Baker: Gentlemen, you are ordered to comply with everything that you are told or you will be exterminated. Now I want all of you to go into that airplane hangar and I'll tell you what to do from there, now get going!

INT. The civilians are seen standing in a line next to four flatbed trucks that have cages on them; the Commander continues to give his orders to the civilians:

Commander Baker: Now gentlemen, I want you to get inside those cages, you need not to worry, we are just going to transport all of you to another location. Now Officer Downing (name changed) here will be kind enough to help you get into those cages.

Officer Downing salutes to Commander Baker while he responds to the order from Commander Baker:

Officer Downing: Yes sir, I will help these civilians into the cages, sir.

There are steps leading from the ground to the top of the truck bed. Each cage allowed room for five men per cage; the cages were sitting on palettes, which made it easier to unload. Some of the chains were unlocked to allow five per group. Officer Downing is seen opening a gate for the civilians to enter. The Commander orders the civilians into the cages with his form of integrity:

Commander Baker: Gentlemen the cages were made to hold five of you at a time, so you could keep each other company. So five of you get in each cage right now and introduce yourselves.

The first five men are seen getting into the cages, there are ten cages per truck. The men are seen introducing themselves as ordered, but with a look of unsure-ness on their face, possibly wondering why they were abducted.

EXT. The four trucks with the caged men are seen driving down a dusty road. As the dust fills the air the men in cages are trying to wipe the dust from their eyes. A forklift is seen attached to the back of the last truck.

A soldier is now seen caring a cage of men on the forklift, the Commander points to a certain direction and informs the soldier driving the forklift:

Commander Baker: Now soldier be sure and separate those cages at fifty yards apart, now there will be markers out there for you, now look for them, you hear me soldier?

The soldier responds:

Soldier: Yes sir, Commander Baker, I'll get the job done right, sir (salutes).

The ten cages equally spaced at fifty yards apart and in a straight row. The men in the cages are seen waving their arms around wondering what's going on. The Commander now gives another order to the forklift driver:

Commander Baker: Now you did a good job on that side soldier, but now I want you to do the same thing on the other three side of that large wooden box on the center there. Now the day is almost gone now, so hurry it up.

The large wooden box in the center was the size of a car.
The soldier caring another cage of civilians responds to the Commanders orders:

Soldier: Yes sir, thank you sir, and I'll hurry it up sir.

It is the end of the day and the setting of the cages is complete and the Commander makes a comment commending the twenty officers on the ground:

Commander Baker: Now I want to commend all of you officers for a job well done. Now this arrangement came out perfect, it looks mighty sharp.

The arrangement from a view from the sky looks like a shape of a plus sign with a wooden rectangular box in the center. The Commander gives another order:

Commander Baker: All right officers let's get the hell out of here and get underground!

The caged men had a look of fear on their faces when they heard that finale comment from the Commander.

INT. Inside an underground shelter Commander Baker is giving an order to Officer Downing, while the other officers are gathered together on the background of the same room.

Commander Baker: All right Officer Downing I'll give you the privilege to press the button that will detonate that "nuclear bomb" underneath that wooden box out there.

Officer Downing: Yes sir, a ten second count down is now commencing, sir.

At the end of the ten seconds Officer Downing finger presses the button and a huge explosion occurs from this *"nuclear bomb"* that shook the earth for miles.

During the explosion photos show the civilians that were closer to the explosion evaporating into dust in their cages and the changes that took place the further the civilians were.

Inside the underground shelter Commander Baker gives another order at the end of the day:

Commander Baker: "Ok officers get your suits on and go gather the remains and take them to the labs and if anyone is still alive take them to psychiatric programming for revisions of their observations."

INT. Inside a Ballroom During a Black Tie Awards Banquet

While inside a very decorative ballroom during a black tie awards banquet, *Willard Libby* is about to be awarded with the Nobel Peace Prize.

Ernest Garcia makes statement in relevance to this subject:

Ernest Garcia: Believe it or not, chemist *Willard Libby* is about to be awarded with the Nobel Peace Prize for the human radiation experiments that were just conducted through *"Project Sunshine"* "for *murder.*"

The host was the chief of the AEC Division of Biology and Medicine; he is standing at the podium preparing to announce the Nobel Peace Prize to *Willard Libby.* While *Willard Libby* is standing on the side, waiting to be presented the Nobel Peace Prize, he stands there straitening his suit with a smile of laughter on his face.

Chief of the AEC: Ladies and gentlemen I am honored to present the Nobel Peace Prize for outstanding achievement in Human Radiation Research, and the public advocate for *Project Sunshine,* ladies and gentlemen Mr. Willard Libby.

The crowd is seen giving Willard Libby a standing ovation as he receives his award and prepares to make his speech at the podium:

Willard Libby: Thank you so much for all of your love and support, I'm sure many of you are proud of the results. You know when I went to high school, my English teacher told the class, "This is a Nobel laureate" turns out she was right. Actually, radiocarbon dating wasn't even my best work, but it caught the imagination didn't it (laughs)?

The crowd is smiling and laughing to Willard's comment, so highly admiring the person. Willard follows up with:

Willard Libby: I'm an ultraconservative, I believe in invention and in great new discoveries; I don't believe in mediocrity and democracy is pretty mediocre, usually. Now, people should be allowed to live and eat and that sort of thing. I'm not for oppressing those who are less fortunate – in fact; I'd give them something useful to do. But people are not equal, in any way at all.

Willard Libby raises his right index finger up for just a moment when he says:

Willard Libby: One of my jobs on the AEC was to allot funds for research. Ninety percent of the support for physical science in this country went through the AEC….

A good part of the time I was on the "commission," I was the "only" scientist on it. Our principle was to give the money to the best people and "let them do what they wanted."

The crowd nodding their head in agreement, with light clapping. Willard Libby prepares for his closing statement with vigor:

Willard Libby: *Project Sunshine* is "the most colossal piece of radiation research ever done," and "instead of banging us," they "*ought to thank us.*" "*It's fantastic!*" And "*it's international!*"

The crowd raised their fist "with joy in their hearts" and cheering. *Willard Libby* has a smile on his face while he laughs; "was his laugh with the people or was his laugh at the people? The same thing goes with the current to be the world dictator or should I say the coming antichrist. Who is proclaiming to save the economy worldwide and bring world peace and confirm a covenant of peace with Israel? So proclaimed in the Holy Scriptures."

Willard Libby: "We used the agency" to get other countries. England did a heck of a lot of work, and "we ran all kinds of tests on people," as well as "food" and "spent millions on it." "So we could not be accused of neglecting our duty!"

~ 294 ~

The crowd was giving *Willard Libby* another standing ovation. * "Whom are they doing their duty for?" *

The statements that *Willard Libby* just made is documented on record.

15

TORTURE – SEC/RET

The Coercive Counterintelligence Interrogation Of Resistant Sources

Restrictions

The purpose of this part of the handbook is to present basic information about coercive techniques available for use in the interrogation situation. It is vital that this discussion not be misconstrued as constituting authorization for the use of coercion at field discretion.

Wikipedia, the free encyclopedia. Research and commentaries by Marcel L. Garcia Jr. (Author).

For both ethical and pragmatic reasons no interrogator may take upon himself the unilateral responsibility for using coercive methods. Concealing from the interrogator's superiors an intent to resort to coercion, or its unapproved employment, does not protect them. It places them, and KUBARK, in unconsidered jeopardy.

The Theory of Coercion

Coercive procedures are designed not only to exploit the resistant source's internal conflicts and induce him to wrestle with himself but also to bring a superior <u>outside</u> force to bear upon the subject's resistance. Non-coercive methods are not likely to succeed if their selection and use is not predicated upon an accurate psychological assessment of the source. In contrast, the same coercive method <u>may</u> succeed against persons who are very unlike each other. The changes of success rise steeply, nevertheless, if the coercive technique is matched to the source's personality. Individuals react differently even to such seemingly nondiscriminatory stimuli as drugs. Moreover, it is a waste of time and energy to apply strong pressures on a hit or miss basis if a tap on the psychological jugular will produce compliance.

All coercive techniques are designed to induce regression. "The Physiological State of the Interrogation Subject as it Affects Brain Function." As a result, "most people who are exposed to coercive procedures will talk and usually reveal some information that they might not have revealed otherwise." "Guilt makes compliance more likely." The response to coercion typically contains at least three important elements: debility, dependency, and dread.

Psychologist and others who write about physical or psychological duress frequently object that under sufficient pressure subjects usually yield but that their ability to recall and communicate information accurately is as impaired as the will to resist. And the use of coercive techniques will rarely or never confuse an interrogate so completely that he does not know whether his own confession is true or false. He does not need full mastery of all his powers of resistance and discrimination to know whether he is a spy or not. Only subjects who have reached a point where they are under delusions are likely to make false confessions that they believe. He is told that the changed treatment is a reward for truthfulness and evidence that friendly handling will continue as long as he cooperates.

The following are the principal coercive techniques of interrogation: arrest, detention, deprivation of sensory stimuli through solitary confinement or similar methods, threats and fear, debility, pain, heightened suggestibility and hypnosis, narcosis, and induced regression. This section also discusses the detection of malingering by interrogates and the provision of appropriate rationalizations for capitulating and cooperating.

Arrest

The manner and timing of arrest can contribute substantially to the interrogator's purposes. "What we aim to do is to ensure that the manner of arrest achieves, if possible, surprise, and the maximum amount of mental discomfort in order to catch the suspect off balance and to deprive him of the initiative.

One should therefore arrest him at a moment when he least expects it and when his mental and physical resistance is at its lowest.

Detention

If, through the cooperation of a liaison service or by unilateral means, arrangements have been made for the confinement of a resistant source, the circumstances of detention are arranged to enhance within the subject his feelings of being cut off from the known and the reassuring, and of being plunged into the strange. Control of the source's environment permits the interrogator to determine his diet, sleep pattern, and other fundamentals. Manipulating these into irregularities, so that the subject becomes disorientated, is very likely to create feelings of fear and helplessness. At any event, it is advisable to keep the subject upset by constant disruptions of patterns.

Deprivation of Sensory Stimuli

The chief effect of arrest and detention, and particularly of solitary confinement, is to "deprive" the subject of many or most of the sights, sounds, tastes, smells, and tactile sensations to which he has grown accustomed. Isolation per se acts on most persons as a powerful stress.

At the National Institute of Mental Health two subjects were suspended with the body and all but the top of the head immersed in a tank containing slowly flowing water at 34.5'C (94.5' F). Both subjects wore blackout masks, which enclosed the whole head but allowed breathing and nothing else. The sound level was extremely low;

The subject heard only his own breathing and some faint sounds of water from the piping. Neither subject stayed in the tank longer than three hours. These findings suggest but by no means prove the following theories about solitary confinement and isolation:

1) The more completely the place of confinement eliminates sensory stimuli, the more rapidly and deeply will the interrogate be affected.
2) An early effect of such an environment is anxiety. How soon it appears and how strong it is depends upon the psychological characteristics of the individual.
3) The interrogator can benefit from the subject's anxiety. As the interrogator becomes linked in the subject's mind with the reward of lessened anxiety, human contact, and meaningful activity, and thus with providing relief for growing discomfort, the questioner assumes a benevolent role.

4) The deprivation of stimuli induces regression by depriving the subject's mind of contact with an outer world and thus forcing it in upon itself. At the same time, the calculated provision of stimuli during interrogation tends to make the regressed subject view the interrogator as a father figure. The result, normally, is a strengthening of the subject's tendencies toward compliance.

Threats and Fear

The threat of coercion usually weakens or destroys resistance more effectively than coercion itself.

The threat to inflict pain, for example, can trigger fears more damaging than the immediate sensation of pain. In fact, most people underestimate their capacity to withstand pain. The same principle holds for other fears.

The effectiveness of a threat depends not only on what sort of person the interrogatee is and whether he believes that his questioner can and will carry the threat out but also on the interrogator's reasons for threatening. If the interrogator threatens because he is angry, the subject frequently senses the fear of failure underlying the anger and is strengthened in his own resolve to resist. Threats delivered coldly are more effective than those shouted in rage. It is especially important that a threat not be uttered in response to the interrogatee's own expressions of hostility.

The threat of death has often been found to be worse than useless. It "has the highest position in law as a defense, but in many interrogation situations it is a highly ineffective threat." If the threat is recognized as a bluff, it will not only fail but also pave the way to failure for later coercive ruses used by the interrogator.

Debility

No report of scientific investigation of the effect of debility upon the interrogatee's powers of resistance has been discovered. The available evidence suggests that resistance is sapped principally by psychological rather than physical pressures. The interrogator should use his power over the resistant subject's physical environment to disrupt patterns of response, not to create them.

Meals and sleep granted irregularly, in more than abundance or less than adequacy, the shifts occurring on no discernible time pattern, will normally disorient an interrogatee and sap his will to resist more effectively than a sustained deprivation leading to debility.

Pain

Everyone is aware that people react very differently to pain. "The sensation of pain seems to be roughly equal in all men, that is to say, all people have approximately the same threshold at which they begin to feel pain, and when carefully graded stimuli are applied to them, their estimates of severity are approximately the same. Yet, when men are very highly motivated they have been known to carry out rather complex tasks while enduring the most intense pain."

Intense pain is quite likely to produce false confessions, concocted as a means of escaping from distress. A time-consuming delay result, while investigation is conducted and the admissions are proven untrue. During this respite the interrogatee can pull himself together. He may even use the time to think up new, more complex "admissions" that take still longer to disprove. KUBARK is especially vulnerable to such tactics because the interrogation is conducted for the sake of information and not for police purposes.

Heightened Suggestibility and Hypnosis

In recent years a number of hypotheses about hypnosis have been advanced by psychologists and others in the guise of proven principles. Among these are the flat assertions that a person cannot be hypnotized against his will?

That while hypnotized he cannot be induced to divulge information that he wants urgently to conceal; and that he will not undertake, in trance or through posthypnotic suggestion, actions to which he would normally have serious moral or ethical objections. If these and related contentions were proven valid, hypnosis would have scant value for the interrogator. In accordance to research, "None of these theories has yet been tested adequately."

Hypnotism used as an operational tool by a practitioner who is not a psychologist, psychiatrist, or M.D. can produce irreversible psychological damage. "There is little or no evidence to indicate that trance can be induced against a person's wishes." The actual occurrence of the trance state is related to the wish of the subject to enter hypnosis." "Whether a subject will or will not enter trance depends upon his relationship with the hypnotist rather than upon the technical procedure of trance induction."

Techniques of inducing trance in resistant subjects through preliminary administration of so-called silent drugs (drugs which the subject does not know he has taken) or through other non-routine methods of induction are still under investigation. "Until more facts are known, the question of whether a resister can be hypnotized involuntarily must go unanswered."

"Material elicited during trance is not reliable." It has been shown that the accuracy of such information would "not be guaranteed" since subject in hypnosis are fully capable of "lying."

Hypnosis is distinctly not a do it yourself project.

Narcosis

Just as the threat of pain may more effectively induce compliance than its infliction, so an interrogatee's mistaken belief that he has been drugged may make him a more useful interrogation subject than he would be under narcosis.

Studies and reports, "dealing with the validity of material extracted from reluctant informants, indicate that there is 'no drug' which can force every informant to report all the information he has." "The more normal, well integrated individuals could lie better than the guilt ridden, neurotic subjects."

Nevertheless, drugs can be effective in overcoming resistance not dissolved by other techniques. Particularly important is the reference to matching the drug to the personality of the interrogatee. The effect of most drugs depends more upon the personality of the subject than upon the physical characteristics of the drugs themselves. Persons burdened with feelings of shame or guilt is likely to unburden them when drugged, especially if the interrogator has reinforced these feelings.

Like other coercive media, drugs may affect the content of what an interrogatee divulges.

Certain drugs "may give rise to psychotic manifestation such as hallucinations, illusions, delusions, or disorientation," so that "verbal material obtained cannot always be considered valid." Their function is to cause capitulation, to aid in the shift from resistance to cooperation. *"Once this shift has been accomplished, coercive techniques should be abandoned both for moral reasons and because they are unnecessary."*

"This discussion does not include a list of drugs that have been employed for interrogation purposes or a discussion of their properties because these are medical considerations within the province of a doctor rather than an interrogator."

The Detection of Malingering

The detection of malingering is obviously not an interrogation technique, coercive or otherwise. But the history of interrogation is studded with the stories of persons who have attempted, often successfully, to evade the mounting pressures of interrogation by feigning physical or mental illness. KUBARK interrogators may encounter seemingly sick or irrational interrogatees at times and places, which make it difficult or next to impossible to summon medical or other professional assistance. Both illness and malingering are sometimes produced by coercive interrogation; a brief discussion of the topic has been included here.

Most persons who feign a mental or physical illness do not know enough about it to deceive the well informed. One such symptom is the delusion of misidentification, characterized by the belief that he is some powerful or historic personage. The malingerer tends to go to extremes in his portrayal of his symptoms; he exaggerates, over dramatizes, grimaces, shouts, is over bizarre, and calls attention to himself in other ways.

Another characteristic of the malingerer is that he will usually seek to evade or postpone examination. The guilty persons were reluctant to take the test, and they tried in various ways to postpone or delay it.

Thus the procedure of subjecting a suspected malingerer to a lie detector test might evoke behavior, which would reinforce the suspicion of fraud.

Under the influence of appropriate drugs the malingerer will persist in not speaking or in not remembering, whereas the symptoms of the genuinely afflicted will temporarily disappear. Another technique is to pretend to take the deception seriously, express grave concern, and tell the "patient" that the only remedy for his illness is a series of electric shock treatments or a frontal lobotomy.

Conclusion

A brief summary of the foregoing may help to pull the major concepts of coercive interrogation together:

1) The principal coercive techniques are arrest, detention, the deprivation of sensory stimuli, threats and fear, debility, pain, heightened suggestibility and hypnosis, and drugs.
2) If a coercive technique is to be used, or if two or more are to be employed jointly, they should be chosen for their effect upon the individual and carefully selected to match his personality.
3) The usual effect of coercion is regression. The interrogatee's mature defenses crumble as he becomes more childlike. During the process of regression the subject may experience feelings of guilt, and it is usually useful to intensify these.
4) When regression has proceeded far enough so that the subject's desire to yield begins to overbalance his resistance, the interrogator should supply a face-saving rationalization. Like the coercive technique, the rationalization must

be carefully chosen to fit the subject's personality.
5) The pressures of duress should be slackened or lifted after compliance has been obtained, so that the interrogatee's voluntary cooperation will not be impeded.

No mention has been made of what is frequently the last step in an interrogation conducted by a Communist service: the attempted conversion. In the Western view the goal of the questioning is information; once a sufficient degree of cooperation has been obtained to permit the interrogator access to the information he seeks, he is not ordinarily concerned with the attitudes of the source. Under some circumstances, however, this pragmatic indifference can be shortsighted. If the interrogatee remains semi hostile or remorseful after a successful interrogation has ended, less time may be required to complete his conversion (and conceivably to create an enduring asset) than might be needed to deal with his antagonism if he is merely squeezed and forgotten.

This reduced version of "The Coercive Counterintelligence Interrogation of Resistant Sources" will now be presented in its original form as a confirmed document, the details are as follows:

The reduced version was systematized by Marcel L. Garcia Jr. (Author)

~ 310 ~

IX. THE COERCIVE COUNTERINTELLIGENCE INTERROGATION OF RESISTANT SOURCES

A. Restrictions

The purpose of this part of the handbook is to present basic information about coercive techniques available for use in the interrogation situation. It is vital that this discussion not be misconstrued as constituting authorization for the use of coercion at field discretion. As was noted earlier, there is no such blanket authorization.

For both ethical and pragmatic reasons no interrogator may take upon himself the unilateral responsibility for using coercive methods. Concealing from the interrogator's superiors an intent to resort to coercion, or its unapproved employment, does not protect them. It places them, and KUBARK, in unconsidered jeopardy.

B. The Theory of Coercion

Coercive procedures are designed not only to exploit the resistant source's internal conflicts and induce him to wrestle with himself but also to bring a superior outside force to bear upon the subject's resistance. Non-coercive methods are not

~ 311 ~

likely to succeed if their selection and use is not predicated upon an accurate psychological assessment of the source. In contrast, the same coercive method may succeed against persons who are very unlike each other. The changes of success rise steeply, nevertheless, if the coercive technique is matched to the source's personality. Individuals react differently even to such seemingly non-discriminatory stimuli as drugs. Moreover, it is a waste of time and energy to apply strong pressures on a hit-or-miss basis if a tap on the psychological jugular will produce compliance.

All coercive techniques are designed to induce regression. As Hinkle notes in "The Physiological State of the Interrogation Subject as it Affects Brain Function"(7), the result of external pressures of sufficient intensity is the loss of those defenses most recently acquired by civilized man: ". . . the capacity to carry out the highest creative activities, to meet new, challenging, and complex situations, to deal with trying interpersonal relations, and to cope with repeated frustrations. Relatively small degrees of homeostatic derangement, fatigue, pain, sleep loss, or anxiety may impair these functions." As a result, "most people who are exposed to coercive procedures will talk and usually reveal some information that they might not have revealed otherwise."

One subjective reaction often evoked by coercion is a feeling of guilt. Meltzer observes, "In some lengthy interrogations, the interrogator may, by virtue of his role as the sole supplier of satisfaction and punishment, assume the stature and importance of a parental figure in the prisoner's feeling and thinking. Although there may be intense hatred for the interrogator, it is not unusual for warm feelings also to develop. This ambivalence is the basis for guilt reactions, and if the interrogator nourishes these feelings, the guilt may be strong enough to influence the prisoner's behavior . . . . Guilt makes compliance more likely. . . ." (7).

Farber says that the response to coercion typically contains ". . . at least three important elements: debility, dependency, and dread." Prisoners ". . . have reduced viability, are helplessly dependent on their captors for the

When an interrogator senses that the subject's resistance is wavering, that his desire to yield is growing stronger than his wish to continue his resistance, the time has come to provide him with the acceptable rationalization: a face-saving reason or excuse for compliance. Novice interrogators may be tempted to seize upon the initial yielding triumphantly and to personalize the victory. Such a temptation must be rejected immediately. An interrogation is not a game played by two people, one to become the winner and the other the loser. It is simply a method of obtaining correct and useful information. Therefore the interrogator should intensify the subject's desire to cease struggling by showing him how he can do so without seeming to abandon principle, self-protection, or other initial causes of resistance. If, instead of providing the right rationalization at the right time, the interrogator seizes gloatingly upon the subject's wavering, opposition will stiffen again.

The following are the principal coercive techniques of interrogation: arrest, detention, deprivation of sensory stimuli through solitary confinement or similar methods, threats and fear, debility, pain, heightened suggestibility and hypnosis, narcosis, and induced regression. This section also discusses the detection of malingering by interrogatees and the provision of appropriate rationalizations for capitulating and cooperating.

C. <u>Arrest</u>

The manner and timing of arrest can contribute substantially to the interrogator's purposes. "What we aim to do is to ensure that the manner of arrest achieves, if possible, surprise, and <u>the maximum amount of mental discomfort</u> in order to catch the suspect off balance and to deprive him of the initiative. One should therefore arrest him at a moment when he least expects it and when his mental and physical resistance is at its lowest. The ideal time at which to arrest a person is in the early hours of the morning because surprise is achieved then, and because a person's resistance physiologically as well as psychologically is at its lowest.... If a person cannot be arrested in the early hours..., then the next best time is in the evening....

" (1)

D. Detention

If, through the cooperation of a liaison service or by unilateral means, arrangements have been made for the confinement of a resistant source, the circumstances of detention are arranged to enhance within the subject his feelings of being cut off from the known and the reassuring, and of being plunged into the strange. Usually his own clothes are immediately taken away, because familiar clothing reinforces identity and thus the capacity for resistance. (Prisons give close hair cuts and issue prison garb for the same reason.) If the interrogatee is especially proud or neat, it may be useful to give him an outfit that is one or two sizes too large and to fail to provide a belt, so that he must hold his pants up.

The point is that man's sense of identity depends upon a continuity in his surroundings, habits, appearance, actions, relations with others, etc. Detention permits the interrogator to cut through these links and throw the interrogatee back upon his own unaided internal resources.

Little is gained if confinement merely replaces one routine with another. Prisoners who lead monotonously unvaried lives ". . . cease to care about their utterances, dress, and cleanliness. They become dulled, apathetic, and depressed." (7) And apathy can be a very effective defense against interrogation. Control of the source's environment permits the interrogator to

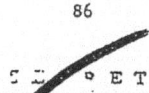

~ 314 ~

determine his diet, sleep pattern, and other fundamentals. Manipulating these into irregularities, so that the subject becomes disorientated, is very likely to create feelings of fear and helplessness. Hinkle points out, "People who enter prison with attitudes of foreboding, apprehension, and helplessness generally do less well than those who enter with assurance and a conviction that they can deal with anything that they may encounter . . . . Some people who are afraid of losing sleep, or who do not wish to lose sleep, soon succumb to sleep loss . . . ." (7)

In short, the prisoner should not be provided a routine to which he can adapt and from which he can draw some comfort -- or at least a sense of his own identity. Everyone has read of prisoners who were reluctant to leave their cells after prolonged incarceration. Little is known about the duration of confinement calculated to make a subject shift from anxiety, coupled with a desire for sensory stimuli and human companionship, to a passive, apathetic acceptance of isolation and an ultimate pleasure in this negative state. Undoubtedly the rate of change is determined almost entirely by the psychological characteristics of the individual. In any event, it is advisable to keep the subject upset by constant disruptions of patterns.

For this reason, it is useful to determine whether the interrogattee has been jailed before, how often, under what circumstances, for how long, and whether he was subjected to earlier interrogation. Familiarity with confinement and even with isolation reduces the effect.

E. Deprivation of Sensory Stimuli

The chief effect of arrest and detention, and particularly of solitary confinement, is to deprive the subject of many or most of the sights, sounds, tastes, smells, and tactile sensations to which he has grown accustomed. John C. Lilly examined eighteen autobiographical accounts written by polar explorers and solitary seafarers. He found ". . . that isolation per se acts on most persons as a powerful stress . . . . In all cases of survivors of isolation at sea or in the polar night, it was the first exposure which caused

"In our experiments, we notice that after immersion the day apparently is started over, i.e., the subject feels as if he has risen from bed afresh; this effect persists, and the subject finds he is out of step with the clock for the rest of the day."

Drs. Wexler, Mendelson, Leiderman, and Solomon conducted a somewhat similar experiment on seventeen paid volunteers. These subjects were "...placed in a tank-type respirator with a specially built mattress.... The vents of the respirator were left open, so that the subject breathed for himself. His arms and legs were enclosed in comfortable but rigid cylinders to inhibit movement and tactile contact. The subject lay on his back and was unable to see any part of his body. The motor of the respirator was run constantly, producing a dull, repetitive auditory stimulus. The room admitted no natural light, and artificial light was minimal and constant." (42) Although the established time limit was 36 hours and though all physical needs were taken care of, only 6 of the 17 completed the stint. The other eleven soon asked for release. Four of these terminated the experiment because of anxiety and panic; seven did so because of physical discomfort. The results confirmed earlier findings that (1) the deprivation of sensory stimuli induces stress; (2) the stress becomes unbearable for most subjects; (3) the subject has a growing need for physical and social stimuli; and (4) some subjects progressively lose touch with reality, focus inwardly, and produce delusions, hallucinations, and other pathological effects.

In summarizing some scientific reporting on sensory and perceptual deprivation, Kubzansky offers the following observations:

"Three studies suggest that the more well-adjusted or 'normal' the subject is, the more he is affected by deprivation of sensory stimuli. Neurotic and psychotic subjects are either comparatively unaffected or show decreases in anxiety, hallucinations, etc." (7)

These findings suggest - but by no means prove - the following theories about solitary confinement and isolation:

1. The more completely the place of confinement eliminates sensory stimuli, the more rapidly and deeply will the interrogatee be affected. Results produced only after weeks or months of imprisonment in an ordinary cell can be duplicated in hours or days in a cell which has no light (or weak artificial light which never varies), which is sound-proofed, in which odors are eliminated, etc. An environment still more subject to control, such as water-tank or iron lung, is even more effective.

2. An early effect of such an environment is anxiety. How soon it appears and how strong it is depends upon the psychological characteristics of the individual.

3. The interrogator can benefit from the subject's anxiety. As the interrogator becomes linked in the subject's mind with the reward of lessened anxiety, human contact, and meaningful activity, and thus with providing relief for growing discomfort, the questioner assumes a benevolent role. (7)

4. The deprivation of stimuli induces regression by depriving the subject's mind of contact with an outer world and thus forcing it in upon itself. At the same time, the calculated provision of stimuli during interrogation tends to make the regressed subject view the interrogator as a father-figure. The result, normally, is a strengthening of the subject's tendencies toward compliance.

F. Threats and Fear

The threat of coercion usually weakens or destroys resistance more effectively than coercion itself. The threat to inflict pain, for example, can trigger fears more damaging than the immediate sensation of pain. In fact, most people underestimate their capacity to withstand pain. The same principle holds for other fears: sustained long enough, a strong fear of anything vague or unknown induces regression,

~ 317 ~

would be given to cause a short period of unconsciousness. When the subject wakens, the interrogator could then read from his 'notes' of the hypnotic interview the information presumably told him." (Orne had previously pointed out that this technique requires that the interrogator possess significant information about the subject without the subject's knowledge.) "It can readily be seen how this... maneuver... would facilitate the elicitation of information in subsequent interviews." (7) Techniques of inducing trance in resistant subjects through preliminary administration of so-called silent drugs (drugs which the subject does not know he has taken) or through other non-routine methods of induction are still under investigation. Until more facts are known, the question of whether a resister can be hypnotized involuntarily must go unanswered.

Orne also holds that even if a resister can be hypnotized, his resistance does not cease. He postulates "... that only in rare interrogation subjects would a sufficiently deep trance be obtainable to even attempt to induce the subject to discuss material which he is unwilling to discuss in the waking state. The kind of information which can be obtained in these rare instances is still an unanswered question." He adds that it is doubtful that a subject in trance could be made to reveal information which he wished to safeguard. But here too Orne seems somewhat too cautious or pessimistic. Once an interrogatee is in a hypnotic trance, his understanding of reality becomes subject to manipulation. For example, a KUBARK interrogator could tell a suspect double agent in trance that the KGB is conducting the questioning, and thus invert the whole frame of reference. In other words, Orne is probably right in holding that most recalcitrant subjects will continue effective resistance as long as the frame of reference is undisturbed. But once the subject is tricked into believing that he is talking to friend rather than foe, or that divulging the truth is the best way to serve his own purposes, his resistance will be replaced by cooperation. The value of hypnotic trance is not that it permits the interrogator to impose his will but rather that it can be used to convince the interrogatee that there is no valid reason not to be forthcoming.

A third objection raised by Orne and others is that material elicited during trance is not reliable. Orne says, "...it has been shown that the accuracy of such information... would not be guaranteed since subjects in hypnosis are fully capable of lying." Again, the observation is correct; no known manipulative method guarantees veracity. But if hypnosis is employed not as an immediate instrument for digging out the truth but rather as a way of making the subject want to align himself with his interrogators, the objection evaporates.

Hypnosis offers one advantage not inherent in other interrogation techniques or aids: the post-hypnotic suggestion. Under favorable circumstances it should be possible to administer a silent drug to a resistant source, persuade him as the drug takes effect that he is slipping into a hypnotic trance, place him under actual hypnosis as consciousness is returning, shift his frame of reference so that his reasons for resistance become reasons for cooperating, interrogate him, and conclude the session by implanting the suggestion that when he emerges from trance he will not remember anything about what has happened.

This sketchy outline of possible uses of hypnosis in the interrogation of resistant sources has no higher goal than to remind operational personnel that the technique may provide the answer to a problem not otherwise soluble. To repeat: hypnosis is distinctly not a do-it-yourself project. Therefore the interrogator, base, or center that is considering its use must anticipate the timing sufficiently not only to secure the obligatory headquarters permission but also to allow for an expert's travel time and briefing.

J. Narcosis

Just as the threat of pain may more effectively induce compliance than its infliction, so an interrogatee's mistaken belief that he has been drugged may make him a more useful interrogation subject than he would be under narcosis. Louis A. Gottschalk cites a group of studies as indicating "that 30 to 50 per cent of individuals are placebo reactors, that is, respond

with symptomatic relief to taking an inert substance.". (7)
In the interrogation situation, moreover, the effectiveness
of a placebo may be enhanced because of its ability to placate
the conscience. The subject's primary source of resistance
to confession or divulgence may be pride, patriotism,
personal loyalty to superiors, or fear of retribution if he is
returned to their hands. Under such circumstances his
natural desire to escape from stress by complying with the
interrogator's wishes may become decisive if he is provided
an acceptable rationalization for compliance. "I was drugged"
is one of the best excuses.

Drugs are no more the answer to the interrogator's
prayer than the polygraph, hypnosis, or other aids. Studies
and reports "dealing with the validity of material extracted
from reluctant informants...indicate that there is no drug
which can force every informant to report all the information
he has. Not only may the inveterate criminal psychopath lie
under the influence of drugs which have been tested, but the
relatively normal and well-adjusted individual may also
successfully disguise factual data." (3) Gottschalk reinforces
the latter observation in mentioning an experiment involving
drugs which indicated that "the more normal, well-integrated
individuals could lie better than the guilt-ridden, neurotic
subjects." (7)

Nevertheless, drugs can be effective in overcoming
resistance not dissolved by other techniques. As has already
been noted, the so-called silent drug (a pharmacologically
potent substance given to a person unaware of its administration)
can make possible the induction of hypnotic trance in a
previously unwilling subject. Gottschalk says, "The judicious
choice of a drug with minimal side effects, its matching to
the subject's personality, careful gauging of dosage, and a
sense of timing...[make] silent administration a hard-to-equal
ally for the hypnotist intent on producing self-fulfilling and
inescapable suggestions...the drug effects should prove...
compelling to the subject since the perceived sensations originate
entirely within himself." (7)

Particularly important is the reference to matching the drug to the personality of the interrogatee. The effect of most drugs depends more upon the personality of the subject than upon the physical characteristics of the drugs themselves. If the approval of Headquarters has been obtained and if a doctor is at hand for administration, one of the most important of the interrogator's functions is providing the doctor with a full and accurate description of the psychological make-up of the interrogatee, to facilitate the best possible choice of a drug.

Persons burdened with feelings of shame or guilt are likely to unburden themselves when drugged, especially if these feelings have been reinforced by the interrogator. And like the placebo, the drug provides an excellent rationalization of helplessness for the interrogatee who wants to yield but has hitherto been unable to violate his own values or loyalties.

Like other coercive media, drugs may affect the content of what an interrogatee divulges. Gottschalk notes that certain drugs "may give rise to psychotic manifestations such as hallucinations, illusions, delusions, or disorientation", so that "the verbal material obtained cannot always be considered valid." (7) For this reason drugs (and the other aids discussed in this section) should not be used persistently to facilitate the interrogative debriefing that follows capitulation. Their function is to cause capitulation, to aid in the shift from resistance to cooperation. Once this shift has been accomplished, coercive techniques should be abandoned both for moral reasons and because they are unnecessary and even counter-productive.

This discussion does not include a list of drugs that have been employed for interrogation purposes or a discussion of their properties because these are medical considerations within the province of a doctor rather than an interrogator.

~ 321 ~

K. The Detection of Malingering

The detection of malingering is obviously not an interrogation technique, coercive or otherwise. But the history of interrogation is studded with the stories of persons who have attempted, often successfully, to evade the mounting pressures of interrogation by feigning physical or mental illness. KUBARK interrogators may encounter seemingly sick or irrational interrogatees at times and places which make it difficult or next-to-impossible to summon medical or other professional assistance. Because a few tips may make it possible for the interrogator to distinguish between the malingerer and the person who is genuinely ill, and because both illness and malingering are sometimes produced by coercive interrogation, a brief discussion of the topic has been included here.

Most persons who feign a mental or physical illness do not know enough about it to deceive the well-informed. Malcolm L. Meltzer says, "The detection of malingering depends to a great extent on the simulator's failure to understand adequately the characteristics of the role he is feigning.... Often he presents symptoms which are exceedingly rare, existing mainly in the fancy of the layman. One such symptom is the delusion of misidentification, characterized by the...belief that he is some powerful or historic personage. This symptom is very unusual in true psychosis, but is used by a number of simulators. In schizophrenia, the onset tends to be gradual, delusions do not spring up full-blown over night; in simulated disorders, the onset is usually fast and delusions may be readily available. The feigned psychosis often contains many contradictory and inconsistent symptoms, rarely existing together. The malingerer tends to go to extremes in his protrayal of his symptoms; he exaggerates, overdramatizes, grimaces, shouts, is overly bizarre, and calls attention to himself in other ways...."

"Another characteristic of the malingerer is that he will usually seek to evade or postpone examination. A study

of the behavior of lie-detector subjects, for example, showed
that persons later 'proven guilty' showed certain similarities
of behavior. The guilty persons were reluctant to take the
test, and they tried in various ways to postpone or delay it.
They often appeared highly anxious and sometimes took a
hostile attitude toward the test and the examiner. Evasive
tactics sometimes appeared, such as sighing, yawning,
moving about, all of which foil the examiner by obscuring
the recording. Before the examination, they felt it necessary
to explain why their responses might mislead the examiner
into thinking they were lying. Thus the procedure of subjecting
a suspected malingerer to a lie-detector test might evoke
behavior which would reinforce the suspicion of fraud." (7)

Meltzer also notes that malingerers who are not
professional psychologists can usually be exposed through
Rorschach tests.

An important element in malingering is the frame of
mind of the examiner. A person pretending madness
awakens in a professional examiner not only suspicion but
also a desire to expose the fraud, whereas a well person
who pretends to be <u>concealing</u> mental illness and who
permits only a minor symptom or two to peep through is
much likelier to create in the expert a desire to expose
the hidden sickness.

Meltzer observes that simulated mutism and amnesia
can usually be distinguished from the true states by
narcoanalysis. The reason, however, is the reverse of
the popular misconception. Under the influence of appropriate
drugs the malingerer will persist in not speaking or in not
remembering, whereas the symptoms of the genuinely
afflicted will temporarily disappear. Another technique
is to pretend to take the deception seriously, express
grave concern, and tell the "patient" that the only remedy
for his illness is a series of electric shock treatments
or a frontal lobotomy.

~ 323 ~

L. Conclusion

A brief summary of the foregoing may help to pull the major concepts of coercive interrogation together:

   1. The principal coercive techniques are arrest, detention, the deprivation of sensory stimuli, threats and fear, debility, pain, heightened suggestibility and hypnosis, and drugs.

   2. If a coercive technique is to be used, or if two or more are to be employed jointly, they should be chosen for their effect upon the individual and carefully selected to match his personality.

   3. The usual effect of coercion is regression. The interrogatee's mature defenses crumbles as he becomes more childlike. During the process of regression the subject may experience feelings of guilt, and it is usually useful to intensify these.

   4. When regression has proceeded far enough so that the subject's desire to yield begins to overbalance his resistance, the interrogator should supply a face-saving rationalization. Like the coercive technique, the rationalization must be carefully chosen to fit the subject's personality.

   5. The pressures of duress should be slackened or lifted after compliance has been obtained, so that the interrogatee's voluntary cooperation will not be impeded.

No mention has been made of what is frequently the last step in an interrogation conducted by a Communist service: the attempted conversion. In the Western view the goal of the questioning is information; once a sufficient degree of cooperation has been obtained to permit the interrogator access to the information he seeks, he is not ordinarily concerned with the attitudes of the source. Under some circumstances, however, this pragmatic indifference can be short-sighted. If the interrogatee remains semi-hostile or remorseful after a successful interrogation has ended, less time may be required to complete his conversion (and conceivably to create an enduring asset) than might be needed to deal with his antagonism if he is merely squeezed and forgotten.

Definition of Torture
According to the Webster's Dictionary

Torture: the act of inflicting excruciating pain, as punishment or revenge, as means of getting a confession or information, or for sheer cruelty. To afflict with severe pain of body or mind.

Definition of Interrogate

Interrogate: to ask questions of (a person), sometimes to seek answers or information that the person questioned considers personal or secret.

Definition of Coerce (coercive)

Coerce: to compel by force, intimidation, or authority, esp. without regard for individual desire or volition. To dominate or control, esp. by exploiting fear, anxiety. To hold in, restrain.

State-Sponsored Torture Interrogation

Neurologist Lawrence Hinkle explained the physiological difficulties:

"The human brain, the repository of the information that the interrogator seeks, functions optimally within the same narrow range of physical and chemical conditions that limit the functions of human organs in general... Any circumstance that impairs the function of the brain potentially affects the ability to give information as well as the ability to withhold it."

Torture interrogation creates a sort of mix-min problem, in which pain and injury play off against cognitive function.

Routine participation of medical personnel in state sponsored torture interrogation has been documented worldwide. Health professionals have administered non-therapeutic drugs, monitored the victim for endurance under torture, resuscitated the victim, treated the victim to prepare for further abuse, issued false health certificates on release, falsified autopsy reports, and issued false death certificates. In a study by the Danish Medical Group, 41 of 200 torture victims from 18 countries reported that "doctors assisted in their torture."

If the prisoner gives the information requested, the examination is quickly terminated; if not, "specialists" must "force his secret from him"...Science can easily place at the army's disposition the means for obtaining what is sought.

The success of interrogation research in the United States may possibly be estimated by successes in a related specialty, "psychiatric reprogramming," that is, revision of memory or belief through psychiatric procedures. Outspoken witnesses of "caged men" near ground zero at the

"Nevada Test Site," both before and after bomb blasts, reported that they were forced to undergo, through psychiatric programming, revisions of their observations. The U.S. Supreme Court ruled to keep secret the names of the 185 MKULTRA researchers. This ruling set strong precedent for legal cover for future clandestine research: Courts do not have sufficient background or expertise to formulate a knowledgeable decision as to what may be harmful to the intelligence gathering procedures used by this country or other countries.

16

TERRIFYING EVENTS YET TO COME

Weapons of Mass Destruction

A **weapon of mass destruction (WMD)** is a weapon that can "kill large numbers of humans" and/or cause great damage to manmade structures (e.g. buildings), natural structures (e.g. mountains), or the biosphere in general.

The term is often used to cover several weapon types, including nuclear, biological, chemical (NBC), and radiological weapons.
Additional terms used in a military context include atomic, biological, and chemical (ABC) warfare and chemical, biological, radiological, and nuclear (CBRN) warfare.

The phrase was predominantly used in reference to nuclear weapons during the Cold War; following the collapse of the Soviet Union and increasing tensions between the Middle East and the Western powers, the term broadened to its modern, more inclusive definition. It entered widespread usage in relation to the U.S. led 2003 invasion of Iraq.

Early Uses of the Term

The first use of the term "weapons of mass destruction" on record is from *The Times* (London) in 1937 in reference to the aerial bombardment of Guernica, Spain:

"Who can think at this present time without a sickening of the heart of the appalling slaughter, the suffering, the manifold misery brought by war to Spain and to China? Who can think without horror of what another widespread war would mean, waged as it would be with all the new weapons of mass destruction?"

At that time, there were no nuclear weapons; biological weapons were already being researched by Japan,(2) and chemical weapons had seen wide use, most notably in World War I.

Following the atomic bombings of Hiroshima and Nagasaki, and progressing through the Cold War, the term came to refer more to nonconventional weapons.

The application of the term to specifically nuclear and radiological weapons is traced by William Safire to the Russian phrase *oruziye massovovo porazheniya.*

He credits James Goodby (of the Brookings Institution) with tracing what he considers the earliest known English language use soon after the nuclear bombing of Hiroshima and Nagasaki (although it is not quite verbatim): a communiqué from a November 15, 1945 meeting of Harry Truman, Clement Attlee and Mackenzie King (probably drafted by Vannevar Bush – or so Bush claimed in 1970) referred to "weapons adaptable to mass destruction."

That exact phrase, says Safire, was also used by Bernard Baruch in 1946 (in a speech at the United Nations probably written by Herbert Bayard Swope).(3) The same phrase found its way into the UN resolution to create the Atomic Energy Commission (predecessor of the International Atomic Energy Agency (IAEA), which used the wording "atomic weapons and of all other weapons adaptable to mass destruction."

An exact use of this term was given in a lecture "Atomic Energy as an Atomic Problem" by J. Robert Oppenheimer. The lecture was delivered to the Foreign Service and the State Department, on September 17th, 1947. The lecture is reprinted in *The Open Mind* (New York: Simon and Schuster, 1955).

"It is a very far reaching control which would eliminate the rivalry between nations in this field, which would prevent the surreptitious arming of one nation against another,...

which would provide some cushion of time before atomic attack, and presumably therefore before any attack with weapons of mass destruction, and which would go a long way toward removing atomic energy at least as a source of conflict between the powers."

An early use of the exact phrase in an international treaty was in the Outer Space Treaty of 1967, however no definition was provided.

Evolution of its use

During the Cold War, the term "weapons of mass destruction" was primarily a reference to nuclear weapons. At the time, the U.S. arsenal of thermonuclear weapons were regarded as a necessary deterrent against nuclear or conventional attack from the Soviet Union, and the euphemism "strategic weapons" was used to refer to the American nuclear arsenal.

The term "weapons of mass destruction" continued to see periodic use throughout this time, usually in the context of nuclear arms control; Ronald Reagan used it during the 1986 Reykjavik Summit, when referring to the 1967 Outer Space Treaty.(4) Reagan's successor, George H.W. Bush, used the term in an 1989 speech to the United Nations, using it primarily in reference to chemical arms.(5)

The end of the Cold War "reduced U.S. reliance on nuclear weapons as a deterrent, causing it to shift its focus to disarmament." "This period coincided with an increasing threat to U.S.

interest from Islamic nations and independent Islamic groups."

With the 1990 invasion of Kuwait and 1991 Gulf War, Iraq's nuclear, biological, and chemical weapons programs became a particular concern of the first Bush Administration.(6) Following the war, the Clinton Administration and other western politicians and media continued to use the term, usually in reference to ongoing attempts to dismantle Iraq's weapons program.

After the September 11, 2001 attacks and the 2001 anthrax attacks, an increased fear of nonconventional weapons and asymmetrical warfare took hold of the United States and other Western powers. This fear reached a crescendo with the 2002 Iraq disarmament crisis and the alleged existence of weapons of mass destruction in Iraq that became the primary justification for the 2003 invasion of Iraq. However, no WMD were found in Iraq.

Because of its prolific use during this period, the American Dialect Society voted "weapons of mass destruction" (and its abbreviation, "WMD") the word of the year 2002, (7) and in 2003 Lake Superior State University added WMD to its list of terms banished for *"Misuse, Overuse and General Uselessness."*(8)

Definitions of the term

The most widely used definition of "weapons of mass destruction" is that of nuclear, biological or chemical weapons (NBC), although there is no treaty or customary international law that contains an authoritative definition. Instead, international law has been used with respect to the specific categories of weapons within WMD, and not to WMD as a whole.

The acronym NBC (for nuclear, biological and chemical) is used with regards to battlefield protection systems for armored vehicles, because all three involve insidious toxins that can be carried through the air and can be protected against with vehicle air filtration systems.

However, there is an argument that nuclear and biological weapons do not belong in the same category as chemical and "dirty bomb" radiological weapons, which have limited destructive potential (and close to none, as far as property is concerned), whereas nuclear and biological weapons have the unique *"ability to kill large numbers of people with very small amounts of material,"* and thus could be said to belong in a class by themselves.

The NBC definition has also been used in official U.S. documents, by the U.S. President,(9)(10) the U.S. Central Intelligence Agency, (11) the U.S. Department of Defense,(12) (13) and the U.S. Government Accountability Office. (14)

Other documents expand the definition of WMD to *"also include radiological or conventional weapons."* The U.S. military refers to WMD as:

"Weapons that is capable of a high order of destruction and/or of being used in such a manner as to destroy large numbers of people. Weapons of mass destruction can be high explosives or nuclear, biological, chemical, and radiological weapons, but exclude the means of transporting or propelling the weapon where such means is a separable and divisible part of the weapon. (15)

The significance of the words *separable and divisible part of the weapon* is that missiles such as the Pershing II and the SCUD are considered weapons of mass destruction, while aircraft capable of carrying bomb loads are not.

Within U.S. civil defense organizations, the category is now **Chemical, Biological, Radiological, Nuclear, and Explosive (CBRNE)**, which defines WMD as:

> *(1) Any explosive, incendiary, poison gas, bomb, grenade, or rocket has a propelling charge of more than four ounces (113 g), missile having an explosive or incendiary charge of more than one quarter ounce (7 g), or mine or device similar to the above. (2) Poison gas. (3) Any*

weapon involving a disease organism. (4) Any weapon that is designed to release radiation at a level dangerous to human life. This definition derives from US law, 18 U.S.C. Section 2332a(16) and the referenced 18 USC 921.(17) Indictments and convictions for possession and use of WMD such as truck bombs,(18) pipe bombs,(19) shoe bombs,(20) cactus needles coated with botulin toxin,(21) etc. have been obtained under 18 USC 2332a.

WMD Use, Possession and Access

Nuclear weapons

The only country to have used a nuclear weapon in war is the United States.

There are eight countries that have declared they possess nuclear weapons and are known to have tested a nuclear weapon, as of the date of July 10, 2009, only five of which are members of the NPT. The eight include: People's Republic of China; France; India; Pakistan; Russia; The United Kingdom; the United States of America; and North Korea.

Israel is considered by most analysts to have nuclear weapons numbering in the low hundreds as well, but maintains an official policy of nuclear ambiguity, neither denying nor confirming its nuclear status.

Iran is suspected by western countries of seeking nuclear weapons, a clam that it denies. While the truth is unknown, the Nov. 2007 NIE on Iran stated that Iran halted its nuclear weapons program in the fall of 2003. (25)

South Africa developed a small nuclear arsenal in the 1980s but disassembled them in the early 1990s, making it the only country to have fully given up an independently developed nuclear weapons arsenal. Belarus, Kazakhstan, and Ukraine inherited stockpiles of nuclear arms following the breakup of the Soviet Union, but relinquished them to the Russian Federation.

Countries with access to nuclear weapons through nuclear sharing agreements include: Belgium, Germany, Italy, the Netherlands, and Turkey. North Korea has claimed to have developed and tested nuclear devices. Although outside sources have been unable to unequivocally support the state's claims, "North Korea has officially been identified to have nuclear weapons."

Nuclear Terrorism

Nuclear terrorism denotes the use, or threat of the use, of nuclear weapons or radiological weapons in acts of terrorism, including attacks against facilities where radioactive materials are present.(1) In legal terms, nuclear terrorism is an offense committed if a person unlawfully and intentionally "uses in any way radioactive material...with the intent to cause death or serious bodily injury," according to International conventions.(2)

The notion of terrorist organizations using nuclear weapons (especially very small ones, such as suitcase nukes) has been a threat in America rhetoric and culture. It is plausible that terrorists could acquire a nuclear weapon.(3)

Two of the main dangers associated with nuclear reactors are nuclear proliferation and nuclear terrorism. Terrorism involving nuclear weapons or radioactive materials could take a variety of forms. Terrorists could:

- Attack a nuclear reactor.
- Disrupt critical inputs (eg., water supply) for the safe running of a nuclear reactor.
- Steal nuclear fuel or waste.
- Acquire fissile material and fabricate a crude nuclear bomb.
- Acquire a readymade nuclear weapon or take over a nuclear-armed submarine, plane or base.(4)

Graham Allison, a well-known defense analyst, has said that the danger of terrorists acquiring a nuclear weapon is greater than 50 percent. (5)

Radiological Weapons

It is possible for a terrorist group to detonate a radiological or "dirty bomb." A "dirty bomb" is composed of any radioactive source and a conventional explosive. The radioactive material is dispersed by the detonation of the explosive. Detonation of such a weapon is not as powerful as a nuclear blast, but can produce considerable radioactive fallout. There are other radiological weapons called radiological dispersal devices where an explosive is not necessary. A radiological weapon may be very appealing to terrorist groups as it is highly successful in instilling fear and panic amongst a population (particularly because of the threat of radiation poisoning), and would contaminate the immediate area for some period of time, disrupting attempts to repair the damage. The economic losses could be enormous, easily reaching into the tens of billions of dollars.

Radiological Assassinations

It is also possible that a terrorist group could utilize radiological agents (such as thallium or polonium) in order to poison officials or members of government. These agents could be injected into or ingested by the target, resulting in radiological poisoning and death, either immediately or over an extended period of time. Although no such act has yet been committed by "terrorist," "some covert intelligence agencies have been accused of using this tactic in the past." Examples include:

- Poisoning of Nikolai Khokhlov by radioactive thallium poisoning in Frankfurt in 1957 by KGB (6)
- Assassination of Alexander Litvinenko with radionuclide polonium210 on November 1, 2006.(7) (8) (9)
- Death of Yuri Shchekochikhin on July 3, 2003 in Moscow. (10) (11) (suspected)

Allegations of Preparations to Nuclear Sabotage

The highest ranking GRU defector Stanislav Lunev described alleged *"Soviet plans for using tactical nuclear weapons for sabotage against the United States in the event of war."* He described Soviet made "suitcase nukes" identified as RA115s (or RA11501s for submersible weapons) "which weigh from fifty to sixty pounds." These *portable bombs* "can last for many years" if wired to an electric source. "In case there is a loss of power, there is a battery backup. If the battery runs low, the weapon has a transmitter that sends a coded message either by satellite or directly to a GRU post at a Russian embassy or consulate." (12)

Lunev was personally looking for hiding places for weapons caches in the Shenandoah

Valley area.(12) He said that *"it is surprisingly easy to smuggle nuclear weapons into the US,"* *"either across the Mexican border or using a small transport missile that can slip through undetected when launched from a Russian airplane."*(12) US Congressman Curt Weldon supported claims by Lunev. Searches of the areas identified by Lunev who admits he never planted any weapons in the US have been conducted, "but law enforcement officials have never found such weapons caches, with or without portable nuclear weapons." (14)

Allegations of Privately Owned Nuclear Weapons

According to high ranking Russian SVR defector Tretyakov, he had a meeting with two Russian businessmen representing a state created *Chetek* corporation in 1991. They came up with a fantastic project of destroying large quantities of chemical wastes collected from Western countries at the island of Novaya Zemlya (a test place for Soviet nuclear weapons) using an underground nuclear blast. The project was rejected by Canadian representatives, but one of the businessmen told Tretyakov that he keeps his own nuclear bomb at his dacha outside Moscow. Tretyakov thought that man was insane, but the "businessmen" (Vladimir K. Dmitriev) replied: "Do not be naive. With economic conditions the way they are in Russia today, anyone with enough money can buy a nuclear bomb. It's no big deal really."(15)

Planned and Attempted Attacks

In June 2002, U.S. citizen Jose Padilla was arrested for allegedly planning a radiological attack on the city of Chicago; however, he was never charged with such conduct. He was instead convicted of charges that he conspired to "murder, kidnap and maim" people overseas.

In November 2006, M15 warned that Islamic terrorists, specifically the al-Qaida were planning on using nuclear weapons against cities in the United Kingdom by obtaining the bombs via clandestine means.

"In June 2007 Fox News claimed that the FBI released to the press the name of the operations leader for developing tactical <u>plans for detonating 'nuclear bombs' in several American cities 'simultaneously'</u> as Adnan Gulshair el Shukrijumah."

This report only makes common sense that one of the ways to "destroy our nation would be from the inside out" and as previously said that terrorists may possibly even use "dirty bombs" along with the 'nuclear weapons," with the possible intention to "<u>destroy the U.S. in one day</u>." This may coincide with events in the Holy Scriptures when certain nations were attacked at "midnight" and destroyed by the morning of the same day. Other upcoming reports from different sources also seem to support the same concept; the terrorists *"intense intentions seem to be of their highest priority in meeting this horrifying objective."*

Former OSS/CIA agent and covert operator Ernest Garcia doubted that the bomb location could be extracted from the nuclear terrorist.

Ernest Garcia and H.W. Rood, who taught, in military intelligence schools, Rood responds:
If they're going to put a bomb in New York City, they're going to use it to *exploit* something. If they just want to say, "Shit, why don't we blow up New York City?" then they blow up New York City. *"They don't fool around"* so that some terrorist can be captured before it happens. On the other hand, if they're using this to extort something from the United States, then, of course, their terrorist will be captured. But he probably won't be the one who knows where anything is.

"The utilitarian argument would be that *you don't get anything out of the terrorist by torturing him,*" and that you use a lot of your people up in torturing other human beings, and you don't get any return. I mean, you could pick out this *one* incident where this guy really is ticklish on the bottom of his feet, so you can get him to tell you where the bomb is. "But one of the things is that the folks who want to put bombs in places like that really don't pick out people who are ticklish – that it's such a rare instance." "And so why would you build an institution to torture people?"

In a counter terrorist operation, many agencies must coordinate. A military newspaper (29) complained of "an unwieldy array of more than 40 different federal agencies, bureaus, and offices" to manage the threat of a terrorist strike with weapons of mass destruction: "A major bioterrorism simulation exercise conducted in March 1998 revealed glaring "coordination problems" within the response structure." Reliability and accountability are crucial. Outlaws and madmen could not be hired as torturers by an otherwise well-ordered agency. The torturers would have to be well trained and professional, according to Rood.

Garcia agreed with Rood on the logic of operations and the institutional paths of cause and effect. But in his portrayal, state sponsored torture interrogation has already borne the predictable consequences.

---

28. Rood, Harold William. (1997, February 14). Commentary on the transcript of the oral history of Hal Brody and on Levin's defense of torture interrogation. Interview conducted by Jean Maria Arrigo at Claremont McKenna College.

Garcia described gross mistreatment by the OSSCIA of their field agents in South America after World War II. Agencies of unknown legitimacy, too, were able to command obedience because of the dangers of assessing putative authorities. "It was very; very difficult to know who you were dealing with at the time. You just had to be respectful and not insubordinate only to survive." He found widespread disillusionment and alienation among covert operators, "which led to corruption and large scale political problems." Garcia comments:

"They (covert operators in South America) had become so frustrated with the system and everything else that *they themselves became the worst enemies of the country.*" And "they sold out a lot of information," "sold out a lot of weapons." "As a matter of fact, that can truthfully be accounted for how the "Middle East" has saturated, proliferated themselves with those chemical warfare and nuclear weapons." That just goes to show how well these "people operated even inside of the military," that they were able to unload out of the ship "literally cases of ammunition and small arms."

In Garcia's view, state sponsored torture interrogation continued into the Korean and Vietnam wars, and the institutional effects of torture and other abuses are already out of hand.

A Palestinian in an Israeli prison confirmed this point: "We learned about all the types of ill-treatment and the techniques that the secret police use, and we learned to observe the behavior of enemy officers during our interrogation." –Qouta, Samir, Punamaki, RaijaLeena, & Sarraj, Eyad El. (1997). Prison experiences and coping styles among Palestinian men. Peace and Conflict: Journal of Peace Psychology, 3 (1), 1936. P. 26

Like H. W. Rood, Ernest Garcia *"doubted that the bomb location could be extracted"* from the hypothetical nuclear terrorist.

Various people have been trained from birth to be extremely resistant and they're just as stout as a frozen turnip. *"These people are actually taught to be tortured."* They will acclimate themselves to excruciating types of torture in anticipation of what they might be facing in the future. *"And they're so terribly brainwashed by their government that these people don't have any other option but to just to go ahead and do exactly what they've been trained to do."*

Arrigo: Suppose you are assigned the job of getting the bomb location out of this fellow. Do you think you can do it?

Garcia: I'll be real, real candid with you in this respect. *"They've already blew it."* The thing is that (by incarcerating the terrorist) they already made him understand that there was an extraordinary amount of pressure that was going to be applied on him, "that he was going to wish that he was dead." This person knows what is coming and he's going to try to destroy himself.

He's caught between a stone and a hard place here. There is zero tolerance where these people are coming from (that is, the terrorist group that sent them). And this man, woman, or whatever have absolutely nothing to look forward to but try to resist and survive, and the other option that there is for them is to *"just take their secrets with them to their death."*

Arrigo: The philosopher says if we can't get the story out of that terrorist, then we'll torture his innocent wife and children. What complications or possibilities does this add to the case?

Garcia: It's been my experience that this kind of people has very, very little sentiment. "I think they're already conditioned to sacrifice even their own family." "It would be an extraordinary achievement if anybody could break these people."

Arrigo: Let's suppose Levin said: "Well, Ernest Garcia, what we need is the cleanest, most honorable, most effective operation. Will you set this up for us? What could you do?

Garcia: First of all, what you'd have to do is find a way to somehow penetrate what their method of operation was. And just get in there and circulate with them. You yourself become a terrorist, participating in planning or even in the dry run.

Arrigo: So you might do some pretty horrible things along the way?

Garcia: Absolutely. You have to be ready to do that. "You've got to find them in best faith. You can't do it while they're either angry or they're working in the field where they have expectations of the possibility of being caught. You have to do it in a very different type of setting. Once you've gained confidence and you become one of them, then they start spitting information and you start gathering the weakest places. You start commercializing on that. I've done it with some of the worst that there is."

And I reversed the process very, very adequately.

Unfortunately, we're dealing here with a situation where the accused is already incarcerated so we have to use that kind of environment. "We've lost the best moves." From that point on it turns hard. Very, very hard. (32)

The former FBI historian mentioned before agreed that infiltration is effective. Before civil liberties reforms in 1976, she said, "Government spies agreed that it was better to infiltrate groups that used inflammatory rhetoric than to wait for those groups to omit violence…*Many people in law enforcement believe that they now are unable to protect Americans from terrorism and subversion." (33)*

Garcia's plan would trade the moral problems of torture interrogation for the problems of infiltration. (34) The supporting clandestine research would shift from biomedical and psychiatric techniques to social process.

By the analyses of Rood and Garcia, "state sponsored torture interrogation "is not" an efficient practice in a democracy."

This was the conclusion "Ken Kendall" reached in his analysis of Levin's reasoning from the battlefield model of an unprepared interrogatee: (41)

"Now (the terrorist) might go ahead and talk right away, but if he's not willing to talk quick enough and you do have access to his wife and child then you would bring them in and 'start at the smallest.' I'll cut off a finger or toe or whatever."

Arrigo: And you think that would work?

Kendall: "Well, it would work with me." I may have wanted to hold out myself, and held out with all kinds of beating or torture or whatever it needed to be, because I believe in something. But as far as I go I wouldn't want anything happening to my wife and child, and I would be more inclined to talk… "Then morally I would say once you've got what information you need then – it's hard to do but go ahead and *"finish killing them"* and "*erase them from existence,*" and then that would cover you from the dilemma of having to admit that you did something like this."

If there's only a small number of people involved that could ever get out and say anything, then you can insist that they didn't know what they were talking about. – "This guy sung his head off. We didn't have to do nothing with his wife and child. We don't know where they're at." This is probably what I would advise, how this went and all. "Primarily based on my past experience."

Arrigo: "*So in "our list of people" who were "sacrificed" here we might have to "include the people who were involved" in this torture and the "liquidation" of the wife and child.*" But that would run by the same utilitarian argument?

Kendall: Pretty close, yeah. "Then as time goes by, passions die, people forget. – Live and let live. – And that's why there's not so much fuss about us atomic veterans, because time has gone by, and the great hue and cry is not there to do anything." "*So much for this being a hypothetical issue*"

The morality of the practice in favorable instances by rogue outfits with expendable agents may still be argued though. In Garcia's view, highly principled Intelligence theorists like Rood do the important work of upholding standards within their reach, but their reluctance to consider programmatic atrocities inadvertently covers abuses by Intelligence units that are kept unintegrated and unaccountable.

Arrigo: If we could imagine Professor Rood saying directly to you that there are always excesses or slippage on the edges of operations but certainly "none of this is a part of high level policy decision," how would you respond to that?

Garcia: How could he convince me of that? How *could* he? "How could anybody convince me of that?" "*This is a high level of policy.*" I can only say one thing that, after seeing not one but several of this type of behaviors, that "it is a common norm and *it is executed as well orchestrated operations that are formulated by intelligent people in high positions*" – way before they happened.

Garcia would bring Ethics to bear on compartmentalization of operations for moral disguise; on the mistreatment of field agents assigned to commit hands on, face-to face abuses of human beings – whatever the higher-level justification of these actions; and on the social procession of terrorism and infiltration.

Rood: It seems to me that torture, for us, is inexcusable. And so, you know, "*you lose New York City. That's life.*" If you're going to torture, do it yourself for Christ's sake. Carry the weight.

Brief Outline of End Time Events Predicted in the Holy Scriptures

The research, documents, and interviews were established for the purpose of education and awareness of things to come, which are relevant to Biblical Eschatology, which necessarily embrace both fulfilled and unfulfilled prophecy, the former providing an important guide to the character of prediction embraced in the latter. *The signs of the "End Times" are currently under way.* Presented by Marcel L. Garcia Jr.

I. Events are presented as Before, During, and After the Seven Year End Time Period (This seven year period is the 70th "seven" of Daniel, Dan. 9: 27.) Although some of the current *"signs"* seem to signify that we may be <u>very close</u> to the beginning of the Tribulation. The outline is as follows:

A) Events immediately before the seven year period
1. *Church ruptured (John 14: 13; 1 Cor. 15: 5152;*
   1 Thes. 4: 1618; Rev. 3: 10)
2. Restrainer removed (2 Thes. 2: 7)
3. Judgment seat of Christ (in heaven, 1 Cor. 3: 1215;
   2 Cor. 5: 10)
4. Antichrist rises to power over the Roman confederacy
   (Dan. 7: 20, 24)

B) Event at the beginning of the seven year period
   1. *Antichrist (the coming "ruler") makes a covenant with Israel (Dan. 9: 2627)*
C) Events in the first half of the seven year period
   1. Israel living in peace in the land (Ezek. 38:8)
   2. Temple sacrifices instituted (Rev. 11: 12)
   3. World church dominates religion and the Antichrist (Rev. 17)
D. Events perhaps just before the middle of the seven year period
   1. *Gog and his allies invade Palestine from the north (Ezek. 38: 2, 56, 22)*
   2. Gog and his allies destroyed by God Himself (Ezek. 38: 1723)
E. Events at the middle of the seven year period
   1. Satan cast down from heaven and energizes the Antichrist with enragement (Rev. 12: 1217)
   2. Antichrist breaks his covenant with Israel, causing her sacrifices to cease (Dan. 9: 27)
   3. The 10 kings under the Antichrist destroy the world church (Rev. 17: 1618)
   4. The 144,000 Israelites saved and sealed (Rev. 7: 18)
F. Events of the second half of the seven year period, These
   last three and one-half years, of the seven year period are called "the Great Tribulation" (Rev. 7: 14; cf. "great distress,"

Matt. 24: 21; "times of distress,"
Dan. 12: 1; and "a time of trouble for Jacob," Jer. 30: 7)
1. Rebellion (apostasy) against the truth in the professing church (Matt. 24: 12; 2 Thes. 2: 3)
2. Antichrist becomes a world ruler (1st seal, Rev. 6: 12)
with support of the Western confederacy (Rev. 13: 5,
7; 17: 1213)
3. Antichrist revealed as "the man of lawlessness," "the
lawless one" (2 Thes. 2: 3, 89)
4. War, famine, and death (2nd, 3rd, and 4th seals, Rev. 6:
38)
5. Converted multitudes from every nation martyred (5th
seal, Rev. 6: 911; 7: 914; Matt. 24: 9)
6. Natural disturbances and worldwide fear of divine
wrath (6th seal, Rev. 6: 1217)
7. *Antichrist's image (an "abomination") set up for*
worship (Dan. 9: 27; Matt. 24: 15; 2 Thes. 2: 4; Rev.
13: 1415)
8. Two witnesses begin their ministry (Rev. 11: 3)
9. The "false prophet" promotes the Antichrist, who is

worshiped by nations and unbelieving Israel (Matt.
24: 11‑12; 2 Thes. 2: 11; Rev. 13: 4, 11‑15)
10. Mark of the beast used to promote worship of the
Antichrist (Rev. 13: 16‑18)
11. Israel scattered because of the anger of Satan (Rev.
12: 6, 13‑17) and because of the "abomination"
12. Jerusalem overrun by Gentiles (Luke 21: 24; Rev. 11:
2)
13. Antichrist and false prophets *"deceive many people"*
(Matt. 24: 11; 2 Thes. 2: 9‑11)
14. The gospel of the kingdom proclaimed (Matt. 24: 14)
15. Israel persecuted by the Antichrist) Jer. 30: 5‑7; Dan.
12: 1; Zech. 13: 8; Matt. 24: 21‑22)
16. Trumpet judgments (Rev. 8‑9) and bowl judgments
(Rev. 16) poured out by God on Antichrist's empire
17. Blasphemy increases as the judgments intensify (Rev.
16: 8‑11)

G. Events concluding the seven year period
   1. Two witnesses slain by the Antichrist (Rev.
      11: 7)
   2. Two witnesses resurrected (Rev. 11: 11‑12)

3. The king of the South (Egypt) and the king of the North fight against the Antichrist (Dan. 11: 40)
4. Antichrist enters Palestine and defeats Egypt, Libya, and Ethiopia (Dan. 11: 4043)
5. Armies from the East and the North move toward Palestine (Dan. 11: 44; Rev. 16: 12)
6. Jerusalem is ravaged (Zech. 14: 14)
7. Commercial Babylon is destroyed (Rev. 16: 19; 18: 13, 2124)
8. *Signs appear in the earth and sky* (Isa. 13: 10; Joel 2: 10, 3031; 3: 15; Matt. 24: 29)
9. *Christ returns with the armies of heaven (Matt. 24: 2731; Rev. 19: 1116)*
10. Jews flee Jerusalem facilitated by topographical changes (Zech. 14: 5)
11. Armies unite at Armageddon against Christ and the armies of heaven (Joel 3: 911; Rev. 16: 16; 19: 1719)
12. *Armies are destroyed by Christ (Rev. 19: 19, 21)*
13. *The "beast" (Antichrist) and the false prophet are thrown into the lake of fire (Rev. 19: 20)*

H. Events following the seven year period of the tribulation
   1. Final re-gathering of Israel (Isa. 11: 1112; Jer. 30: 3;
   Ezek. 36: 24; 37: 114; Amos 9: 1415; Micah 4: 67;
   Matt. 24: 31)
   2. A remnant of Israelites turn to the Lord and are

forgiven and cleansed (Hosea 14: 15; Zech. 12: 10;
   13: 1)
3. National deliverance of Israel from the Antichrist
   (Dan. 12: 1; Zech. 12: 10; 13: 1; Rom. 11: 2627)
4. Judgment of living Israel (Ezek. 20: 3338; Matt. 25:
   130)
5. Judgment of living Gentiles (Matt. 25: 3146)
6. *Satan cast into the abyss (Rev. 20: 13)*
7. Old Testament saints resurrected (Isa. 26: 19; Dan. 12: 13)
8. Tribulation saints resurrected (Rev. 20: 46)
9. Daniel 9: 24 fulfilled
10. Marriage supper of the Lamb (Rev. 19: 79)
11. Christ begins His reign on earth (Ps. 72: 8; Isa. 9: 67;
    Dan. 2: 1435, 44; 7: 1314; Zech. 9: 10; Rev. 20: 4)

II. Characteristics and Events of the Millennium
 A. Physical characteristics
   1. Topography and geography of the earth changed (Isa.
      2: 2; Ezek. 47: 112; 48: 820; Zech. 14: 4, 8, 10)
   2. Wild animals tamed (Isa. 11: 69; 35: 9; Ezek. 34: 25)
   3. Crops abundant (Isa. 27: 6; 35: 12, 67; Amos 9: 13; Zech. 14: 8)
   4. Human longevity increased (Isa. 65: 2023)

B. Spiritual and religious characteristics and events
  1. Satan confined in the abyss (Rev. 20: 13)
  2. Millennial temple built (Ezek. 40: 543: 27)
  3. Animal sacrifices offered as memorials to Christ's death (Isa. 56: 7; 66: 2023; Jer. 33: 1718; Ezek. 43: 1827; 45: 1346: 24; Mal. 3: 34)
  4. Feast of the New Year, Passover, and Tabernacles reinstituted (Ezek. 45: 1825; Zech. 14: 1621)
  5. Nations worship in Jerusalem (Isa. 2: 24; Micah 4: 2; 7: 12; Zech. 8: 2023; 14: 1621)
  6. Worldwide knowledge of God (Isa. 11: 9; Jer. 31: 34; Micah 4: 5; Hab. 2: 14)
  7. Unparalleled filling of and empowerment by the Holy Spirit on Israel (Isa. 32: 15; 44: 3; Ezek. 36: 2429; 39: 29; Joel 2: 2829)
  8. New Covenant with Israel fulfilled (Jer. 31: 3134; Ezek. 11: 1920; 36: 2532)
  9. Righteousness and justice prevails (Isa. 9: 7; 11: 4; 42: 14; Jer. 23: 5)
C. Political characteristics and events
  1. Israel reunited as a nation (Jer. 3: 18; Ezek. 37: 1523)
  2. Israel at peace in the land (Deut. 30: 110; Isa. 32: 18; Hosea 14: 5, 7; Amos 9: 15; Micah 4: 4; Zech. 3: 10
  3. Abrahamic Covenant land-grant boundaries
    established (Gen. 15: 1821; Ezek. 47: 1348:8, 23
  27)

4. Christ in Jerusalem rules over Israel (Isa. 40: 11;
Micah 4: 7; 5: 2)
5. Davidic Covenant fulfilled (Christ on the throne of
David, 2 Sam. 7: 1116; Isa. 9: 67; Jer. 33: 1726;
Amos 9: 1112; Luke 1: 3233)
6. Christ rules over and judges the nations (Isa. 11: 35;
Micah 4: 23; Zech. 14: 9; Rev. 19: 15)
7. Resurrected saints reign with Christ (Matt. 19: 28;
2 Tim. 2: 12; Rev. 5: 10; 20: 6)
8. Universal peace prevails (Isa. 2: 4; 32: 1718; 60: 18;
Hosea 2: 18; Micah 4: 24; 5: 4; Zech. 9: 10)
9. Jerusalem made the world's capital (Jer. 3: 17; Ezek.
48: 3035; Joel 3: 1617; Micah 4: 1, 68; Zech. 8: 2
3)
10. Israel exalted above the Gentiles (Isa. 14: 12; 49: 22
23; 60: 1417; 61: 59)
11. The world blessed through Israel (Micah 5: 7)
D. Events following the Millennium
1. Satan released from the abyss (Rev. 20: 7)
2. Satan deceives the nations (Rev. 20: 8)
3. Global armies besiege Jerusalem (Rev. 20: 9)

4. Global armies destroyed by fire (Rev. 20: 9)
5. Satan cast into the lake of fire (Rev. 20: 10)
6. Evil angels judged (1 Cor. 6: 3)
7. The wicked dead resurrected (Dan. 12: 2; John 5: 29)
8. The wicked judged at the Great White Throne (Rev. 20: 11-14)
9. The wicked cast into the lake of fire (Rev. 20: 14-15; 21: 8)

III. Eternity

A. Christ delivers the mediatorial (millennial) kingdom to
    God the Father (1 Cor. 15: 24)
B. *Present heavens and earth demolished (Rev. 21: 1)*
C. *New heavens and new earth created (2 Peter 3: 10;*
    Rev. 21: 1)
D. New Jerusalem descends to the new earth (Rev. 21: 2,
    10-27)
E. Christ rules forever in the eternal kingdom (Isa. 9: 6-7;
    Ezek. 37: 24-28; Dan. 7: 13-14; Luke 1: 32-33; Rev.
    11: 15)

Notes
1. Some identify Antichrist's initial rise to power with
   the first seal judgment (Rev. 6: 1-2)

2. Some place the battle of Gog and his allies at the very middle of the seven year period; others place it later.
3. Some say the 144,000 will be saved and sealed in the first half of the seven year period.
4. According to some, this apostasy will begin in the first half of the seven year period.
5. Many pre-millenarians place the seal judgments in the first half of the seven year period.
6. Some Bible scholars say the work of the two witnesses will be in the first half of the seven year period.
7. Some suggest that the two witnesses will be slain and resurrected in the first half of the seven year period.
8. Some equate these events with the battle of Gog and his allies.
9. Some say that the Christians have to suffer for their sins and go through a portion of the tribulation.
10. Some Bible scholars say that the false prophet is a

Jew, there is no support for this. "*The false prophet is a religious character who supports the political ruler.*"

The "Covenant with Death" and the "Agreement with Hell"

Therefore thus says the Lord God: Isaiah 28: 18, speaks of the "covenant with death" and the "agreement with hell" for which "*God will punish Israel.*" This must refer to the covenant of Daniel 9: 27, when Israel "*seeks peace*" from the hands of men rather than from the hand of the Lord. For this covenant, Isaiah says, they will be punished "when the overflowing scourge shall pass through, then ye shall be trodden down by it." This scourge could hardly be the occupation by "the *Beast*, for he was a party to the covenant," but must refer to the invasion by the "Assyrian" who will be used by the Lord to chasten Israel. The destruction of the Assyrian in the passages referred to seem to parallel the destruction of the armies of Gog in Ezekiel 38 – 39, and thus, is considered parallel references. *"God could not punish Israel for this false covenant until after the covenant had been made."*

What is this covenant with death and Sheol? Daniel tells us about a "future" covenant which Israel will make with the "Antichrist," the prince who is coming, the "Man of Sin," the godless man, the willing king, "the beast" out of the sea and the "beast" out of the land, the one is *"controlled by Satan"* (see Dan. 9: 27).

The city, which contains the sanctuary, that is, Jerusalem, would be "destroyed by the people of the ruler who will come." The ruler who will come is that final head of the Roman Empire, *"the little horn"* of Daniel 7:8.

It is significant that the *people* of the ruler, not the ruler himself, "will destroy Jerusalem." Since he will be the "final" Roman ruler, the people of that ruler must be the Romans themselves. This, then, is a prophecy of the *"destruction of Jerusalem"* about which Christ spoke in His ministry. Christ warned them, He also warned the nation that Jerusalem would be destroyed by Gentiles (Luke 21: 24), that it would be desolate (Matt. 23: 38), and that the destruction would be so complete that not one stone would be left on another (Matt. 24: 2).

Daniel 9: 27a. This verse unveils what will occur in the 70th seven years. This seven year period will begin after the Rapture of the church (which will consummate God's program in this present Age). The 70th "seven" will continue till the return of Jesus Christ to the earth. Because Jesus said this will be a time of "great distress" (Matt. 24: 21), this period is often called "the Tribulation."

"*A significant event that will mark the beginning of this seven year period is the confirming of a covenant.*" This covenant will be made "with many" that is, with Daniel's people, the nation Israel. "The ruler" who will come, (Daniel 9: 26) will be this covenant maker, for that person is the "antichrist" of the word he in verse 27. As a "yet future" ruler he will be the "final head of the fourth "empire" (the little horn of the fourth beast, 7: 8).

The "covenant" he will make will evidently be a *"peace covenant,"* in which he will "guarantee Israel's safety in the land."

This suggest that Israel will be in her *"land"* but will be "unable to defend herself" "for she will have lost any support she may have had previously." Therefore she will *"need"* and "welcome" the *"peacemaking"* role of this head of the "confederation" of 10 European (Roman) nations. In offering this covenant, this ruler will pose as a *"prince of peace,"* and Israel will accept his "authority." But then in the middle of that "seven," after three and one-half years, he will break the covenant. According to Daniel 11: 45, he will then move from Europe *"into"* the *"land of Israel."*

This ruler will end ... sacrifice and offering. This expression refers to the entire Levitical system, which suggests that Israel will have restored that system in the first half of the 70th

"seven." "After *this ruler gains worldwide 'political' power*, he will assume power in the 'religious' realm as well and *will cause the world to worship him*" (2 Thes. 2: 4; Rev. 13: 8). To receive such worship, "he will terminate all organized religions. Posing as the world's rightful king and god and as Israel's "prince of peace," he will then turn against Israel and become her "destroyer and defiler."

Revived Roman Empire

The Roman Empire died and disappeared from human history between three and four hundred A.D. just simply rotted away or (was wounded). Now as we approach the end times, there has to be a Roman Empire back on the scene, but it won't be the old empire of the Caesar, but a revived Roman Empire. When World War II ended and the original ten nations of Western Europe got together and decided late in the 40s or early 50s they were going to set up a ….

United States of Europe. They may not of known that they were fulfilling Bible prophecy, but I assure you that it was God's will. They put together a system that involved these major 10 nations of Western Europe, which we still call the Western European Union and everything that they are doing is reestablishing "politically" "economically" and "spiritually" a revival of that old Roman Empire. They have established a NATO like organization that will include all the nations along both sides of the Mediterranean and out across the Middle East and even including India and part of China. Those are the exact borders of the old Roman Empire. Everything that these men have done was to bring about the *"New Revived Roman Empire."* Out of this "Revived Roman Empire" will rise the "Antichrist" the "world dictator." That *will "deceive" human kind with flattery, and take away their sovereignty (freedom) and take "control" of "everyone and everything," and no one will be able to buy or sell unless you except the mark of the "beast" and if you refuse you will be killed, just when the people had cried out for a "change"* (Dan. 7: 8, 20; 8: 23) (Ezek. 28: 6), so that his (antichrist or world political authority) position over the nations is by their own consent (Rev. 17: 13). He rules over the nations in his federation with absolute "authority" (Dan. 11: 36, where he is depicted as doing his own will. *This "authority" is manifested through the "change" in laws and customs* (Dan. 7: 25). *His chief interest is in "might and power" and to bring his followers to Hell with him (Dan. 11: 38). He is the head of Satan's lawless system (2 Thes. 2: 3).*

<u>"People are destroyed for lack of knowledge</u>."
(Hosea 4: 6)
The minute you get away from the Word of God you're doomed to failure.

"Those Who Are Anti EU Are Terrorists"

Crusade Media reports on the 16th June 2008, comments made by the members of the European Union:

- Italian President Giorgio Napolitano said: *"Those who are anti EU are terrorist."* It is psychological terrorism to suggest the specter of a *European super state.*
- European Commission President Jose Manuel Barroso said: "Sometimes I like to compare the EU as a creation to *the organization of empires.* We have the dimension of Empire but there is a great difference. Empires were usually made with force with a center imposing diktat, a will on the others." *"Now what we have is the first non-imperial empire."*

Irish voters on June 12 said "No" to the *"superpower"* ambitions of European political elites, who want all 27 member-states of the European Union to ratify the 269page (about 3000 pages with annexes) Lisbon Treaty that would turn the EU into a bureaucratic *"super state."* "European politicians will almost certainly find a way to keep it alive."

One of the main objectives of the virtually unreadable treaty is to turn the EU into a *"global geopolitical actor"* that can counterbalance the "United States" on the world stage. European elites say the EU needs to speak with "one voice" in international affairs.

In this context, the new treaty is designed to create the job position of (an unelected) European president as well as a "powerful European foreign minister." It would also establish a European diplomatic corps with European embassies and a *"European army."*

As many observers of European politics know, democracy does not come easy on a continent where "European elites" view themselves as an "aristocracy" entitled to *"rule over the ignorant masses."* Indeed, the entire European social welfare state has been built upon the unspoken quid pro quo of "bread and circuses" for the general populace, in exchange for their *"loyal submission to the political and intellectual classes."*

"Thus it should come as no big surprise that the word 'No' does not exist in the European political lexicon."

THE "PEACE COVENANT"

2 Thessalonians 2: 3; *"The man of sin is revealed,"* the son of perdition, who opposes and exalts himself above all that is called God or that is worshiped, so that he sits as God in the temple of God, showing himself that he is God. (1 Tim. 4: 1; Dan. 7: 25; 8: 25; 11: 36; John 17: 12).

It seems probable that the man of sin will be identified by some people living then when he makes a "covenant with Israel" at the beginning of the 70th week of Daniel (Dan. 9: 27); but when he breaks the "covenant" three and a half years later (Dan. 9: 27), he will be widely recognized for who he really is, "the antichrist" (Isaiah 28: 18; 2 John 8).

The Jerusalem Post, May 20, 2009

Amid much speculation over US President Barack Obama's upcoming address to the Muslim world, report published on Wednesday outlined the details of his *"Middle East peace plan,"* which are said to include a demilitarized Palestinian state.

The US president's initiative, which was formulated in consultation with Jordan's King Abdullah II during the two leaders' recent meetings at the White House, reportedly does not significantly stray from the pan Arab peace initiative proposed in 2002. Rather, it bolsters certain details within the Saudi proposed plan.

"The Obama Abdullah plan" was put together in response to concerns from both Israel and the US that the Arab plan was too general and intransigent, and according to a report in Wednesday's *Yediot Ahronot,* will call on Arab countries to take *"trust building measures"* in order to clear the air with Israel.

Obama is expected to present the initiative in an address to the Arab and Muslim world from

Cairo in three weeks, and set out conditions for a demilitarized Palestinian state, with *"east Jerusalem as its capital,"* within the next four years. *Yediot* reported that *"Obama's vision"* for an 'independent,' 'democratic' and 'contiguous' Palestinian state "would not" have its own army and would be "forbidden from making military agreements with other states," in order to provide for *"Israel's security."*............
* (I Thessalonians 5: 3) – For when they say, *"Peace and safety!" then sudden destruction comes upon them.*

Jerusalem Post (continued)

The matter of *"borders"* would be solved with territorial exchanges between Israel and the Palestinians, and the
"Old City of Jerusalem would be established as an international zone."

(Daniel 11: 45) – *"And he shall plant the tents of his palace between the seas and the glorious holy mountain; yet he shall come to his end, and no one will help him."*
(The antichrist will make his headquarters in Jerusalem).

The initiative would require the Palestinians to give up their claim of a *"right of return,"* according to *Yediot,* and Europe and the US would arrange compensation for refugees, including foreign passports for those residing abroad.

"Obama's plan" would also promote holding simultaneous talks between Israel and the Palestinians, and Syria and Lebanon. *Yediot* said that when such talks come to an agreement on Palestinian statehood, "diplomatic and economic relations" would be established between Israel and Arab states.

The Jerusalem Post, May 19, 2009

Netanyahu faces US pressure on settlements

Prime Minister Binyamin Netanyahu refused to make any commitments concerning settlements during his first official trip to Washington, even though a construction freeze is a *"top US demand."*

Jerusalem Post (continued)

US President Barack Obama treaded more lightly on the settlements issue, but still stressed that such construction "must end."

"Settlements have to be stopped in order for us to move forward," he said alongside Netanyahu in the Oval Office. "That's a difficult issue. I recognize that, but it's an important one, and it has to be addressed."

During the talks in Washington, "Netanyahu also repeated" a number of times that "Israel was willing to begin negotiations with the Palestinians" "immediately," and that what was holding up a renewal of the talks was not Israel, but the Palestinian Authority.

The Palestinians have stated that they will only resume negotiations after Israel commits itself to a two state solution and ends settlement construction.

Netanyahu said that the key issue related to the Israeli-Palestinian *"peace process"* to emerge during his talks in Washington was the importance American officials were placing on "Arab states playing a role."

"The new thing here is that President Obama says that not only Israel must give, but also the Palestinians and the Arab states, and not at the end of the process, "but now." They must take concrete steps to improve relations with Israel and begin to move forward with reconciliation," he said.

(Rev. 12: 12) – *"he knows he has a short time."*

Jerusalem Post (continued)

Netanyahu emphasized, at the Kerry meeting, *"the threat of Iran"* and again rejected the idea of linking the issue to the Israeli-Palestinian conflict, "while noting that he would like to see progress on both fronts."

"We intend to pursue the peace track independently of what happens in Iran, but in point of fact...it should be done in parallel," he said.

Israel and America have been disagreeing over how to prioritize the issues, with *"Israel urging action on Iran first"* and the US stressing how progress with the Palestinians could aid the struggle to keep Iran from going nuclear.

"Israel has also wanted to see the US impose a tight timeline on negotiations with Iran" over its nuclear program, "worrying" that "talks would allow Teheran to run out the clock." Israeli officials have suggested that "three months would be a sufficient time frame for engagement efforts," but Obama rejected "artificial deadlines" at the joint press conference Monday.

He did, however, offer a time frame of his own, suggesting that the emerging US policy of diplomatic engagement – which he indicated would begin in earnest after Iran's June elections – would be reassessed at the "end of the year."

"The important thing is to make sure that there is a clear timetable, at which point 'we say' these talks don't seem to be making any serious progress," Obama said. "By the end of the year, I think we should have some sense as to whether or not these discussions are starting to yield significant benefits, whether we're starting to see serious movement on the part of the Iranians."

Channel 2 reported Tuesday night that Netanyahu made clear after meeting with the president that *"Israel retained the right to defend itself."*

Speaker of the US House of Representatives Nancy Pelosi, who met with Netanyahu after Kerry did, also stressed the importance America put on the Iranian issue. "It is important for all of us to work together to be sure that Iran 'does not' develop a weapon of mass destruction."
Netanyahu said, "Israel and many of our Arab neighbors understand the threat posted by Iran's quest to develop nuclear weapons capability," he said. "I was assured yesterday by President Obama that the 'United States' is continuing to prevent that from happening, and I think that is important "not only" for "security, but for peace."

(Daniel 9: 27) – *"When Israel 'seeks peace' from the hands of men rather than from the hand of the Lord."* "The ruler who will come" (Dan. 9: 26) will be this covenant maker, for that person is the antecedent of the word he in verse 27. "Understand, son of man, that the vision *refers* to the *time of the end.*" (Daniel 8: 17), (Isaiah 28:

22) – "A *destruction determined even upon the whole earth.*"

Jerusalem Post (continued)

Secretary of State Hillary Clinton also addressed the settlement issue at a press conference on Tuesday. She said "the US was committed to a two-state solution, and "obviously, underlying that commitment is the conviction that the Palestinians deserve a viable state. And therefore, nothing should be done to undermine the potential resolution of the "peace effort" that could prevent such a two-state solution from taking hold."

Clinton reiterated that "we are, as always, committed to the "*safety and security of Israel*," but our goal is to see the people living together."

"The covenant he will make will evidently be a "*peace* covenant," in which he will "*guarantee Israel's safety* in the land." This suggests that Israel will be in her land but will be unable to defend herself "for she will have lost any support she may have had <u>*previously*</u>." Therefore she will need and welcome the "peacemaking" role of this head of the confederation. (*Isaiah 29: 57*) – "Yes, it shall be in an instant, suddenly." "You will be punished by the Lord of hosts with thunder and earthquake and great noise. *With storm and tempest and the flame of devouring fire.* The multitude of "all the nations" who fight against Jerusalem." In I Thessalonians 5: 3, the people are quoted as saying, "Peace and safety," before the "Great Tribulation" overtakes them. The peace will tragically turn out to be a "false peace" and the prelude to her unprecedented time of trouble when *"two out of three Israelites will perish in the land" (Zech. 13: 8).* "For I will gather "all the nations" to battle against Jerusalem" (Zech. 14: 2).

Jerusalem Post, May 20, 2009

PM returns from US, aide calls focus on 2state idea "childish"

As Binyamin Netanyahu returned to Israel from Washington late Wednesday afternoon, an aide to the prime minister said that media focus on the idea of a two-state solution to the Israel-Palestinian conflict was *"childish and stupid."*

"On the Iranian issue, there was a consensus that there is a joint understanding between Israel and the US that its *"nuclear program must be stopped."* President Obama made it clear that the process of dialogue is not without a time limit."

"The prime minister said there was also an understanding that *Israel preserves the right to defend itself,"* Netanyahu said.

On the Palestinian issue, he stressed that "there was an agreement that we need to *immediately begin the peace process.*"

"I said I am willing to open peace talks with the Palestinians, by the way with Syrians as well, of course without preconditions, but I made it clear that in any peace agreement there must be a solution to *Israel's special security needs*," said the "prime minister."

"Netanyahu also said" both agreed on the need to extend the *"Middle East Peace" process to "Arab countries."*

Jerusalem Post, July 10, 2009 – 4:13 AM
Top adviser to Netanyahu: Israel will not leave entire Golan even in peace deal
Jerusalem – Israel will not withdraw from the entire Golan Heights in return for a peace deal with Syria, Prime Minister Benjamin Netanyahu's top policy adviser said in an interview published Friday, rejecting Syria's key demand for an agreement with Israel.

The two countries could split the territory, suggested Uzi Arad, Netanyahu's national security adviser and the aide widely seen as closest to Netanyahu. But in the comments in the daily Haaretz newspaper, he said *"Israel must remain on the Golan Heights to a depth of several miles and cannot withdraw in full even in return for a peace agreement."*

Israel captured the Golan Heights in the 1967 Mideast War and annexed the territory in 1981, a move that was never internationally recognized. Syria has always maintained that peace will be possible only if Israel withdraws entirely from the Heights.

Jerusalem Post, June 14, 2009

Prime Minister Binyamin Netanyahu's speech at the BeginSadat Center at BarIlan University:

"Peace has always been our people's most ardent desire." "Our prophets gave the world the vision of peace, we greet one another with wishes of peace, and our prayers conclude with the word "peace."

Jerusalem Post (continued)

Two and a half months ago, I took the oath of office as the prime minister of Israel. I pledged to establish a national unity government – and I did. I believe, and I still believe, that "unity was essential" for us "now more than ever" as we face three immense challenges – *"the Iranian threat," "the economic crisis"* and *"the advancement of peace."*

In relevance to *the economy at the end times* Revelations 13: 16, declares; He causes "all," both small and great, rich and poor, free and slave, to receive *a mark on their right hand or their foreheads,* and that "no one may buy or sell except one who has the mark or the name of the beast, or the number of his name. (Revelations 14: 9) – If "anyone" worships the beast and his image, and receives his mark on his forehead or on his hand, he himself shall also drink of the wine of the wrath of God, which is "poured out full strength" into the cup of His indignation. He shall be tormented with fire and brimstone in the presence of the holy angels and in the presence of the Lamb. And *the smoke of their torment ascends "forever and ever."* (Revelation 13: 12) – "Authority is given to the beast." (Revelation 13: 14) – "And he "deceives" those who dwell on the earth."

"Satan will deceive the world by giving full authority to the beast, *the beast will then have full control of the "economy" worldwide,* where no one will be able to buy or sell without the mark of the beast, and with full *control* of every human being. (Revelation 13: 15) – "As many as would not worship the image of the beast to be killed."

Jerusalem Post (continued)

"The Iranian threat looms large before us," as was further demonstrated yesterday. "The greatest danger confronting Israel, the Middle East, the entire world and human race, is the nexus between radical Islam and nuclear weapons." For years, I have been working tirelessly to forge an

international alliance to prevent Iran from acquiring nuclear weapons.

I share the president's desire to bring about *"a new era"* of reconciliation in our region. To this end, I met with President (Hosni) Mubarak in Egypt and King Abdullah in Jordan to elicit the support of these leaders in expanding the *"circle of peace"* in our region.

"I turn to all Arab leaders" tonight and I say: Let us meet. *"Let us speak of peace"* and *"let us make peace."* I am ready to meet with you at any time. I am willing to go to Damascus, to Riyadh, to Beirut, to any place – *including Jerusalem.*

I turn to you, our Palestinian neighbors, led by the Palestinian Authority, and I say: "Let's begin negotiations *"immediately"* without preconditions."

"We want to live with you in peace," as good neighbors. We want our children and your children to never again experience war: that parents, brothers and sisters will never again know the agony of losing loved ones in battle; that our children will be able to dream of a better future and realize that dream; and that "together we will invest our energies in plowshares and pruning hooks, not swords and spears."

Jerusalem Post (continued)

"If we join hands and work together for *peace*," there is no limit to the development and prosperity we can achieve for our two peoples – in the *"economy*," agriculture, trade, tourism and education – most importantly, in providing our youth a better world in which to live, a life full of tranquility, creativity, opportunity and hope.

We evacuated every last inch of the Gaza strip, we uprooted dozens of settlements and evicted thousands of Israelis from their homes, and in response, we received a hail of missiles on our cities, towns and children.
I believe that with goodwill and international investment, this humanitarian problem can be permanently resolved.

"In my vision of *peace*," in this small land of ours, two peoples live freely, side by side, in amity and mutual respect. Each will have its own flag, its own national anthem, its own government. Neither will threaten the *"security"* or survival of the other.

"I have come tonight to give expression to that unity, and to the principles of *'peace'* and *'security'* on which there is broad agreement within Israeli society. These are the principles that guide our policy."

I have already stressed the first principle – recognition. Palestinians must clearly and unambiguously recognize Israel as the state of the

Jewish people. The second principle is demilitarization. The territory under Palestinian control must be demilitarized with ironclad security provisions.

Jerusalem Post (continued)

We don't want Kassam rockets on Petah Tikva, Grad rockets on Tel Aviv, or missiles on BenGurion Airport. *"We want peace."*

In order to achieve *peace,* we must ensure that Palestinians will not be able to import missiles into their territory, to field an army, to close their airspace to us, or to make pacts with the likes of Hizbullah and Iran.

"On a matter so *critical* to the existence of Israel, we must first have our *security* needs addressed."

And here is the substance that I now state clearly: If we receive this *"guarantee"* regarding demilitarization and Israel's *"security"* needs, and if the Palestinians recognize Israel as the state of the Jewish people, then we will be ready in a future *"peace agreement"* to reach a solution where a demilitarized Palestinian state exists alongside the Jewish state.

"The covenant that the "antichrist" will make evidently will be a "peace covenant," in which he

(the antichrist) will "guarantee" Israel's "safety" in the land." (Daniel 9: 27).

Israel needs defensible borders, and Jerusalem must remain the united capital of Israel with continued "religious freedom" for all faiths.

"Our microchips" are powering the "world's computers."
"(Revelation 13: 1518) – The mark of the beast."

Published: Sunday, July 19, 2009

Jerusalem – Israel on Sunday rejected a U.S. demand to suspend a planned housing project in east Jerusalem, threatening to further complicate an unusually tense standoff with its strongest ally over settlement construction.

Settlements built on captured *"lands"* claimed by the Palestinians have emerged as a major sticking point in relations between Israel and the Obama administration because of their potential to disrupt *"Mideast peacemaking."*

On Sunday, Netanyahu told his Cabinet there would be no limits on Jewish construction anywhere in "unified Jerusalem."

"We cannot accept the fact that Jews wouldn't be entitled to live and buy anywhere in

Jerusalem," Netanyahu declared, calling Israeli sovereignty over the entire city "indisputable."

"I can only imagine what would happen if someone suggested Jews could not live in certain neighborhoods in New York, London, Paris or Rome. There would certainly be a major international outcry," Netanyahu said.

East Jerusalem is an especially volatile issue because it is the site of key Jewish, Christian and Muslim holy sites. The Palestinians want the traditionally Arab sector of the city to be the capital of their future state.

Although Barack Obama said: <u>"The Old City of Jerusalem would be established as an international zone."</u>

The Prophecy of Possession of the Land of Israel

Genesis 12: 7. The narrative of the *"promise of the land"* This was part of the original revelation that God gave to Abram when he was still in Ur (v.1). Now it became an *"important proof"* of God's continuing purpose for Abram and his people. "
"The land became one of the central features of God's prophetic program for Israel."

The point is that Abram had a future temporal hope – the land – as well as the eternal hope the New Jerusalem.

Deuteronomy 3: 21-22. The promise of the land being inherited by Israel was repeated once again. This prophecy will be fulfilled (Ezek. 45-48); Amos 9: 14-15).

Joshua 21: 43-45. The Lord had not failed to keep His promise even though Israel had failed by faith to conquer all the land.

Judges 1: 1-8. The familiar picture of Israel's failure in the time of Judges was described in God's statement to Israel, "Yet you have disobeyed Me. Why have you done this? Now therefore I tell you that I will not drive them out before you; they will be thorns in your sides and their gods will be a snare to you" (vv.2-3).

Judges 2: 20-23. Further revelation was given concerning the Lord's anger with Israel: "Therefore the Lord was very angry with Israel and said, 'Because this nation has violated the covenant that I laid down for their forefathers and has not listened to Me, I will no longer drive out before them any of the nation's Joshua left when he died. I will use them to test Israel and see whether they will keep the way of the Lord and walk in it as their forefathers did.' The Lord had allowed those nations to remain; He did not drive them out at once by giving them into the hands of Jashua" (vv. 20-23).

Psalm 25: 12-2. The godly man was promised "days in prosperity" and that "his descendants will inherit the land" (v.13). No one who trusts the Lord will "be put to shame" (v. 2). This is fulfilled in history and will be fulfilled in the Millennium.

Isaiah 28: 1419. Because you said, *"We have made a covenant with death, and with Sheol (Hell) we have an agreement."* Then your covenant with death will be annulled, and your agreement with Sheol (Hell) will not stand; when the overwhelming scourge passes through, you will be beaten down by it.

"Jerusalem's leaders rejoiced over their alliance with other leaders for protection, rather than from the hand of the Lord." The overwhelming whip passes through, (the Assyrian army), as the meaning of their repeated calamities dawns on the people, it intensifies their terror (it will be sheer terror to understand the message), therefore thus says the Lord God (Isaiah 28: 1419).

Barak's name is in the Old Testament in relevance to a "peace offering"

Judges 4: 69; "Barak" summoned the tribes of Israel and "led the army to victory."

Judges 5: 2; That the leaders took the lead in Israel, that "the people offered themselves willingly," bless the Lord!

Judges 5: 8,9; "***When new gods were chosen,***" *"then war was in the gates."* Was shield or spear to be seen among forty thousand in Israel? My heart goes out to the commanders of "Israel who offered themselves 'willingly' among the people." Bless the Lord. The kings came; they fought in "Megiddo" (vs. 19).

"Offered themselves willingly," all the people with praise and song gladly cooperated (cf. v. 9). This verb (Hb. *nadab*) is related to the noun for "freewill offering" (Hb. *nedabah*), which were "one" of the 'three types' of offerings making up the "*peace offerings*"

Judges 7: 11-36; And this is the law of the sacrifice of "peace offerings" that one may offer to the Lord (vs.11). If he offers it for a "thanksgiving" (vs.12). But if the sacrifice of his offering is a "vow" offering or a "freewill offering," (vs. 16).

"The peace offering as seen here is subdivided into three types, according to their associated motivations: thanksgiving, a vow, and freewill."

Judges 10: 6; The people of Israel again did what was evil in the sight of the Lord. "***Go and cry out to the gods whom you have chosen; let them 'save you' in the time of your distress***" *(vs. 14).*

Deuteronomy 32: 38-39; Let them rise up and help you; let them be your protection! *"See now that I, even I, am he, and there is no god beside me; I kill and I make alive; I wound and I heal; and there is 'none' that can deliver out of my hand."*

"On Israel's twenty-first anniversary, of a motto in the auditorium at Tel Aviv, written in Hebrew and English. It said, "Science will bring peace to this land." The Old Testament says that Messiah will bring peace to that land, *so apparently they are chasing a new messiah today."*

Revelation 14: 7; "Fear God and give him glory, because *the hour of his judgment has come*, and worship him who made heaven and earth, the sea and the springs of water."

Revelation 17: 10; they will stand far off, in fear of her torment, and say, "Alas! Alas! You great city, you mighty city, Babylon! *"For in a single hour your judgment has come."*

Revelation 18: 2021; "Rejoice over her, O heaven, and you saints and apostles and prophets, for God has given judgment for you against her!" "So will Babylon the great city be thrown down with violence, and will be found no more" (vs. 21).

Prepare for the Wrath of Destruction

1 Thessalonians 5: 3; while people are saying, *"There is peace and security,"* then *"sudden destruction will come upon them" as labor pains*

come upon a pregnant woman, and *"they will not escape."*

Deuteronomy 32: 4041; *"For I lift up My hand to heaven and "swear," As I live "forever," if I sharpen my flashing sword and my hand takes hold on judgment, "I will take vengeance on my adversaries" and will repay those who hate me."*

Ezekiel 39: 2123; *"all nations" "shall see My judgment"* which I have executed, and My hand which I have laid on them. So the house of Israel shall know that I *am* the Lord their God from that day forward. The Gentiles shall know that the house of Israel went into captivity for their iniquity; *"because they were unfaithful to Me,"* therefore I hid My face from them. I gave them into the hand of their enemies, and "they all fell by the sword."

Ezekiel 38: 16; The word of the Lord came to me: Son of man, set your face toward Gog, of the land of Magog, the chief prince of Meshech and Tubal *(capital of Russia)*, and prophesy against him and say, Thus says the Lord God: Behold, I am against you, O Gog, chief prince of Meshech and Tubal. And I will turn you about and put into your jaws, and I will bring you out, and all your army, horses and horsemen, all of them clothed in full armor, a great host, all of them with buckler and shield, wielding swords. Persia (*Iran*), Cush (Arabia), and Put (Libya – although this is usually identified with the Libya in Africa) are with them,

all of them with shield and helmet; Gomer (Germany) and all his hordes; Bethtogarmah (*Turkey or Armenia*, although it is extended by some to include central **Asia**) from the uttermost parts of the north with all his hordes many people are with you.
Ezekiel 38: 8; "In the latter years" "you will go against" the land that is restored from war, (*the mountains of Israel*).

The prophecy against Gog is one of the most dramatic predictions of Ezekiel. The main thrust of the prediction is not difficult to understand. The passage predicted an invasion of Israel by a great army that will attack Israel from the north.

This passage is a part of the predictions of the great world conflict that will characterize the years just before the Second Coming of Christ. It is plausible that preceding this event the predictions of the *"revived Roman Empire,"* a ten nation confederacy, will be fulfilled. This will be considered in the prophecies of Daniel 2 and Daniel 7.

A political leader will arise who will head up the ten nations and make the Mediterranean Sea a Roman lake as it was in the New Testament times. The political leader was referred to in 9: 26 as "the ruler who will come." "This ruler will be associated with the people who destroyed the city of Jerusalem" in A.D. 70, that is, the Roman people and, accordingly, "he will fulfill the role of a Roman leader" in the "end time" as "heading up this ten nation confederacy."

This may be the forerunner and the major event that leads up to the "world government" predicted for the last three and a half years leading up to the Second Coming of Christ. As the battle described here is a disaster for the invading countries, "it may change the political power structure" to such an extent that it will be possible for the "Roman leader" of the ten nations to become "*a world dictator.*" The Great Tribulation (Dan. 11: 4045; Rev.16: 1216), should be distinguished from the war described in Ezekiel 3839 which is "not" a world conflict but a war between a select group of nations attacking Israel.

In the quarter of a century since World War II Russia has risen to be one of the great military powers of the modern world. To a far greater extent than ever before Russia has become a prominent nation, especially in its influence on the Middle East. With both "*Russia and Red China*" constituting a major political bloc, the question of a future war between Russia and Israel becomes a possibility, *especially since God declared that this is a part of His plan, 'this event will occur,'* maybe right after "Israel makes a military strike on Iran?"

"*God is Israel's only source of help.*" He himself will deal with Russia. "War will break out." The *Great* Tribulation will begin (which is the final three and one-half years of the Tribulation Period) in all of its frenzied fury. *"The whole earth will be a holocaust." "Judgments, one right after the other, will come upon the earth."*

The remarkable aspect of this prophecy is that the Scriptures do "not" reveal "any opposing army attacking the invaders." Rather, it will be a time when "God Himself by supernatural actions destroys the army." What ever happened to the declared support of the government of the United States of America? "Will America be completely annihilated from the inside out, or will the American government just turn their back to Israel?"

The International Jerusalem Post
No. 2301 December 10, 2004 27 KISLEV 5765
WMDs on US?

An al-Qaida attack on the US with nonconventional weapons is virtually "inevitable," and the organization is likely "tying up the knots" for such an attack.

The International Jerusalem Post (continued)

Yosef Bodansky, former director of the US Congressional Task Force on Terrorism and Unconventional Warfare, told *The Jerusalem Post* last Sunday.

"All of the warnings we have today indicate that a major strike – something more horrible than anything we've seen before – is all but inevitable," he said.

Bodansky, in Israel for the second annual Jerusalem Summit, an international gathering of conservative thinkers, added that "the primary option" for the next al-Qaida attack on "US soil" would be one that would use "weapons of mass destruction."

"I do not have a crystal ball, but "this is" what "all the available evidence" tells us, "we will have a bang," Bodansky said.

He said that al-Qaida has not carried out a second major attack on the US until now for internal psychological and ideological reasons, but after the reelection of President George W. Bush, it has gotten *"the green light"* to do so from leading "Islamic religious luminaries," as well as from "the elites of Arab world."

According to Bodansky's reading of Osama bin Laden's mindset, after the elaborate attacks of 9/11 there was no need for the "bin Laden's of the world" to carry out a second major attack in the US, both because the target audience of the attacks – "the Arab and Islamic world" – had gotten the message that *"America could be penetrated,"* …….

and because *"a second attack would necessarily have to be more grandiose."*

Following the attacks and the US led war on terror, a debate started within the operational arm of the organization over *"the potential use of weapons of mass destruction,"* Bodansky said.

If, in pre9/11 days, the theme used by bin Laden was that perpetual confrontation and *"jihad against the US"* was "the only way to protect Islam," the argument now used is "the ability to punish American society," Bodansky said.

"Just as the West was challenging the quintessence of Islam by means of the *"globalization"* era, there was a parallel need by Islamic extremists to strike at – and hurt – the core of American society, this time with 'weapons of mass destruction,"* Bodansky said.

A subsequent theological debate emerged within the organization and its supporters in the Arab world, he said, over whether *"the mass killing of innocent is permissible."*

Bodansky said that while there may still be some vestiges of debate and doubt within Islamic circles, he *"believes"* that *"planning for such an attack is finished."* "They got the kosher stamp from the Islamic world to use nuclear weapons," he said.

Moreover, Bodansky said that "America is losing the war against terrorism."

The International Jerusalem Post (continued)

Noting the number of recruits bin Laden is able to count on as his call to arms gains widespread support throughout the Muslim world.

"In the pre9/11 world, Bodansky said, jihadists could count on 250,000 individuals trained and willing to die, and 2.5 million5 million people willing to help them in one way or another. He cited intelligence estimates from this summer that suggest that as many as *500,750,000 people are willing and training to die,* 10 million are willing to actively support them, short of killing, while another 50 million are willing to support such a movement financially."

"What or who exactly was associated with the controlled "globalization" spoken about by the Islamic religious luminaries, as well as from elites of the Arab world? Does this organization want to rule the world? Or, whom did Satan work through in establishing the "Revived Roman Empire" that the Holy Scriptures talks about?"

One World Economy – Dr. Dwight Pentecost – Defined a reunited Roman Empire, as One World Government. In which the nations of the world will worship the economic dictator in which he will enforce a *"One World Economy."*

"Those associated with this system and the head or world dictator (antichrist), are controlled by Satan himself."

"What other titles does this *Revived Roman Empire* have?"

A New World Order – Webster Tarpley (Author Historian) – At the United Nations, September 1990, President Bush Sr., announced, "Now we can see a new world coming into view, a world in which there is a very real prospect of a *New World Order.*"

Webster Tarpley defines the *New World Order* – The *New World Order* is a more ponder able name to the "*Anglo American New World Empire,*" the planetary domination of London, New York, Washington over the West coast. They had to change the name to a *New World Order* in order to get others to join them. It's really the Old World Order, it's the British Empire working into the American Empire, the U.S., and British World Empire is what you get.

Agents of the Bank of England attempted to assassinate president Andrew Jackson on multiple occasions, because of his resistance against a "*private central bank*" to be set up in the United States.

Before his death, president Woodrow Wilson apologized to the public, regretting that he had been deceived by a group of *"international bankers"* and the country's financial system had fallen into their iron grip, being the Federal Reserve Bank of 1913.

The *"military industrial complex"* is taking over the country.

Only three years after reaching office, president Eisenhower pathetic warning concerning the threat posed to our system of government by the *"military industrial complex came to pass."*

President John F. Kennedy, had enraged the entire elite network. Executive order no. 11110, signed by President Kennedy began the process of abolishing the "private Federal Reserve." Kennedy was also pushing for real civil rights reform and had begun the process of pulling the troops out of Vietnam.

The message to future U.S. presidents and leaders across the world was clear, *"Do as your told or die."*

Suddenly the *"Wall Street Journal"* tells us that the "North American Union" is here. And that is getting rid of the dollar, for a common currency with Canada and Mexico, is good.

The *"Financial Times of London"* published by a member of the "Bilderberg" group wrote; "That a *"dictatorial royal world government"* "had been kept in the shadows for our own good" and that *"it was now time for it to emerge from behind the "curtains" of national security."*

In the 1964 book "With No Apologies" Senator Berry Goldwater said; "The Trilateral Commission" is intended to be "the vehicle for multinational consolidation of the commercial and banking interest," by *"seizing control" "of the political government of the United States."* The Trilateral Commission represents, the skillful coordinated effort to *"seize control and consolidate the four centers of power; political (seeking power in the government), monetary (coinage or currency), intellectual (to a high degree of intellect), and ecclesiastical (the church or the clergy)."*

Objective

"What the *"Trilateral Commission" intends; is to create a "Worldwide Economic Power" "superior to the political governments of the nation's states involved."* As managers and creators of the system, *"they will rule the future."* (infowars.com)

The Holy Scriptures
The Final Form of the Gentile World Power

The final form of the Gentile power is marked by a federation of that which is *"weak"* and that which is strong, autocracy and democracy, the iron and the clay (Dan. 2: 42).

There will be, before the age closes, the most remarkable union of two apparently "contradictory" conditions – a universal head of empire, and separate independent kingdoms besides, each of which will have its own king; but that one man will be the emperor over all these kings. Till that time comes, every effort to unite the different kingdoms under one head will be a *"total failure."* Even then it will be not by fusing them together into one kingdom, but each independent kingdom will have its own king, though all subject to one head. *"God has said they shall be divided."* This then is what is shown us here. *"They shall not cleave one to another, even as iron is not mixed with clay."* And if ever there was a portion of the world that has represented this incoherent system of kingdoms, it is modern Europe. There will be a universal monarchy; while in virtue of the clay there will be separate kingdoms. The federation is not brought about by force; else this condition would not continue. But it is brought about by mutual consent, so that each member in the alliance retains its own identity. This is in harmony with Revelation 17: 13.

This final "authority" over the empire is welded by one who is marked by blasphemy, "hatred of God's people," *disregard for established law and order*, who will continue for three and one-half years (Dan. 7: 26). This final form of world power will have *"worldwide"* influence (Dan. 7: 23).

This whole development is attributed to *"satanic power"* (Rev. 13: 4). As the Roman empire had been the "agency" through which Satan attacked Christ at His first advent, that empire in its final form will be the "agency" through which "Satan works against the Messiah at His second advent."

The final form of Gentile power resides in an individual called an "eighth" king, who comes into authority over that kingdom ruled by the previous seven (Rev. 17: 1011).

The course of this fourth world empire is given in Revelation 17: 8. "The Beast which thou sawest was, and is not; and shall ascend out of the bottomless pit, and go into perdition." "Was," describes the empire in the period of its impotency. "Shall ascend out of the abyss" shows the coming form of the empire. "Goes into perdition" depicts its *"future destruction."* The one particular object of the hatred of the form of Gentile world power is Jesus Christ. "These shall make war with the Lamb" (Rev. 17: 14). "The godlessness of the world powers, which seek world dominion," manifests itself in animosity against the One to whom all dominion has been given (Phil. 2: 910; Rev. 19: 16). As each of the four successive powers had enemies who contested their right to rule, so, at the time of the end of Gentile world power, "there will be kingdoms and federations of nations who contest the authority of the so called Revived Roman Empire" or *"New World Order."*

*The International Jerusalem Post
January 1218, 2007*

"Yazdi is one of the most radical people in Iran today," the official said. "He is also Ahmadinejad's spiritual mentor and has a great deal of influence over him."

He noted that while Khamenei is certainly antiIsrael and a radical, he is more moderate than Ahmadinejad. "The president's antiIsrael and a rhetoric and focus on the Holocaust does not make Khamenei happy," he said.

"A more remarkable aspect of Ahmadinejad's ideology is his devotion to the "hidden imam," a messiah like figure in Shi'ism who will appear at the "end of days." He believes that his government needs to prepare the country for his return."

"One of the first decisions" of Ahmadinejad's government was to invest millions of dollars in renovating the Jamkaran Mosque, where the devout drop notes for the "hidden imam" into a "holy well." As mayor of Tehran, he invested millions in expanding a main thoroughfare "it is believed the imam will use when he returns."

~ 401 ~

In a recent interview on CNN, former prime minister Benjamin Netanyahu compared Ahmadinejad to David Koresh, leader of the Branch Davidians from Waco, Texas.

"It's the cult of the Mahdi, a holy man that disappeared a thousand years ago, and the president of Iran believes that he was put here on Earth to bring this holy man back in a *"great religious war."*

The International Post (continued)

This war would be between the true Muslim believers and the infidels, Netanyahu said. "Ahmadinejad, the president of Iran, is first trying to develop nuclear weapons and then going about his mad fantasy of global conflict."

"There is no way to stop Iran anymore except with military action," says one high-ranking officer. "At this point, sanctions will only leave a dent, but they will not stop the program."

But if the diplomatic track reaches a dead end, "it will still be necessary to stop Iran's atomic plan," "even at a heavy price." Olmert has said numerous times in public that "Iran cannot be allowed to obtain nuclear weapons." He has also said that "Iran has what to be afraid of."

"The government needs to decide what its red line is," he says. "Once that line is crossed then we need to attack."

Israel seems to be preparing for the possibility that it will have to *"go it alone"* against Iran. A recent escalation in rhetoric seems to indicate that the country is getting ready for such an option.

President George W. Bush will not order a military strike.

"The entire movement in the US is toward dialogue, not military action," says one high-ranking intelligence official. *"Countries are beginning to come to terms with the fact that there will be a nuclear Iran."*

The International Jerusalem Post (continued)

In addition to the underground reinforcement at certain nuclear sites, "the Iranians have also beefed up their air defenses in preparation for a possible air strike." But the strong air defenses do not protect fixed Iranian targets against standoff precision guided weapons fired from out of range of the antiaircraft missiles.

The Iranian Air Force is comprised of MiG29 squadrons and other planes, some dating back 30 years. Air defense systems, which are currently heavily deployed near the various nuclear sites, feature Russian SA2, SA5, SA6 and shoulder launched SA7 missiles, according to the Military Balance prepared by the Jaffee Center. The Iranians also have aged US made Hawk missiles and have been seeking to purchase the sophisticated S300P from Russia.

"Israel can do it," the former head of the Air Force says. "All you have to do is pick a number of essential targets and destroy them. This way you postpone the process and wait to see what happens."

Brom warned that Israel would also have to take into account Iranian use of *"chemical weapons."* For that purpose, the Arrow 2 antiballistic missile defense system, which according to senior IAF officers is capable of intercepting all of Iran's missiles, was developed.

"The fallout of a preemptive attack would be painful," admits a high-ranking security official. "But we need to think of the tradeoff: A nuclear bomb could destroy the State of Israel."

The International Jerusalem Post (continued)

Within the Israeli leadership, there is one clear voice – Prime Minister Ehud Olmert – that refuses to come to terms with a nuclear Iran and claims that *"Teheran must be stopped, even at a heavy price,"* from obtaining weapons of mass destruction and "rocking the balance of power in the Middle East."

Once Iran completes the construction of the centrifuges and masters the technology, it will still take another year to reach SQ and then another two years to assemble a nuclear device, putting current assessments for when *"Iran Will Have a Nuclear Weapon at 2010."*

"The way things look now, D-Day might not be too far away."

According to Meridor's report, success for Iran would set off a race to join the nuclear club throughout the Middle East.

"The region," the report states would become uncontrollable.

"That day might not be too far away." With Iran pushing ahead with its program in defiance of the UN and the international community, Egypt, Algeria, Saudi Arabia, Morocco, Tunisia and the United Arab Emirates announced in early November (2006) that they intended to begin upgrading their nuclear energy programs. Of the six, the most advanced by far are Egypt and Algeria. Turkey is also reported to be toying with the idea of starting a nuclear program.
The International Jerusalem Post (continued)

"To remain a player in the region, these Arab countries will have no choice but to "quickly" develop nuclear weapons," says a senior government official responsible for formulating strategic policy.

The countries that would be most affected by Iranian success, Meridor's report claims, are Saudi Arabia and Egypt, both heavily "dependent on American military support and afraid to lose their place of dominance in the region." Saudi Arabia is a leading Sunni power while Iran is a Shi'ite dominated country.

"The Saudis will not be able to stand by and let their archenemies overtake them military," said the official. "Egypt is the same and will want to retain its military superiority in the region."

This was actually pointed out three years ago in a report – "Saudi Arabia – a New Player on the Nuclear Scene?" – published in the Jaffee Center for Strategic Studies' *Notes* by Ephraim Asculi, a veteran of the Israeli Atomic Energy Commission.

Asculi claimed that a Sunni *"fear"* of a Shi'ite nuclear bomb prompted "Saudi Arabia" to "strike a deal with Pakistan" under which it would contribute to the Pakistani nuclear project and in return receive a commitment from Islamabad to provide it with a *"nuclear umbrella."* Saudi Arabia can also launch the weapons; it purchased 36 CSS2_missiles, with a range of 3,000 kilometers, from China in the late 1980s.

1998 United States Congressional Commission

In *"1998"* the United States Congress both Democrats and Republicans put together a commission analyzing the venerability of the United States to ballistic missile attacks from third world countries. "This commission, which would receive material from American intelligence sources, concluded that the Iranians could build an International range missile that could strike the eastern seaboard of the United States within "5 years," within taking the decision of doing so. And it would be clear to American intelligence military leaders that in fact the Iranian leaders had taken that decision. And "that was more 10 years ago," Is Iran ready?

The International Jerusalem Post
December 1521, 2006

Would-be president Senator John McCain has declared *"there's only one thing worse than the United States exercising the military option. That is a nuclear armed Iran."*

But newly confirmed Defense Secretary Robert Gates contends that such military action is almost unthinkable, "except as a last resort and if we felt that our vital interest were threatened" – *"suggesting that the US could tolerate a nuclear Iran."*

"The Russians have been the hamperer sin chief." "China has not been far behind."

The IAEA has also contributed to the fostering of the desired Iranian impression that *it's all too late now anyway; that Iran cannot be stopped.*

The International Jerusalem Post
February 28, 2007

The goal the Nazis put forward was of racial superiority and here the goal is the superiority of a religious creed. The other difference is that "Hitler embarked on a world conflict and then sought to develop nuclear weapons, and Ahmadinejad is doing (it the other way around). And, further, that there weren't a billion Germans in the world to infect with this mad faith."

"There is reason to believe that Iran is now governed by these wide-eyed believers who have no inhibitions and apocalyptic goals… *These are people who are planning to get control of weapons of mass genocide without any hesitation in using them.*"

"Getting the nuclear genie back into the Iranian bottle once it has been released will not be feasible. *"When the "chief of the Mossad" says that within three years (2010) Iran will have a nuclear weapon, that's 1,000 days, and each day that goes by is a 'day lost' to our efforts to stop this."*

The International Jerusalem Post
May 2531, 2007

Iran as an Islamic Republic is a mortal threat to Israel, and it is also a challenger to the United States. There are three ways of dealing with this: You can surrender to Iran – by saying, "We'll give you the Middle East and then we'll go away." (Some Americans want to do this, because they don't have the stomach for anything else).

The Wall Street Journal – World News
Wednesday, July 15, 2009

Obama Puts Arms Control at Core of New Strategy – "I believe we are at a tipping point," says Brent Scowcroft, who was national security adviser to President George H.W. Bush and has long pushed for nonproliferation issues to return to the top of the agenda. "If we fail in Iran, we're going to have a number of countries go the same route Iran has just in self-defense. Egypt will, Saudi Arabia will, Turkey will. In northeast Asia, "if we can't deal with North Korea, the Japanese are going to say: 'We'll have to do it ourselves.'"

The International Jerusalem Post
August 713, 2009

President and prime minister. The Americans believe that pressure was necessary to shift Netanyahu – on Palestinian statehood.

"*An increasing body of Israeli opinion holds that the Obama administration is foolish,*" nonetheless, or worse – that it has gone over the top in its focus on a stringent settlement freeze, alienating the Israeli mainstream, dissipating any pressure on the Palestinians to compromise and thus undermining its own good peacemaking intentions.

Since Taking office, *the Obama administration might be regarded as having acted like the school principal* who walks out into the playground to confront two squabbling students, grabs each by the ear and drags them off toward his office. The Israeli kid, protesting his innocence, has struggled and screamed the whole way, complaining about the unfairness.

The International Jerusalem Post (continued)

"The mullahs of Teheran are deeply unpleasant people who are not susceptible to diplomatic engagement" and cannot be trusted with a nuclear capability.

"In time, the Obama administration will likely ratchet up the sanctions on Teheran, but by too little and far too late." There are not a few influential officials in Washington who are now convinced that, sooner rather than later, and despite the immense complexities and uncertain consequences, *"Israel will come to the conclusion that its survival requires a military strike on an Iran that is both avowedly 'seeking our destruction' and closing in on the means to achieve this."*

What will then become of a painstakingly constructed Middle East peace table is, frankly, anyone's guess?

Crusade Media

The Strategic Threat of Nuclear Terrorism

Featuring Rolf MowattLarssen, Director, Department of Energy Office of Intelligence and Counterintelligence

June 16, 2008

On June 16, 2006, Rolf Mowatt-Larssen, director of the U.S. Department of Energy's Office of Intelligence and Counterintelligence addressed *The Washington Institute's Special Policy Forum.* The following is the prepared text of his remarks.

In 1998, Osama bin Laden said that it was an Islamic duty to acquire weapons of mass destruction, and it is through this prism that most people view the threat of nuclear terrorism.

Al-Qaida obtained a *fatwa* in May 2003 from Saudi cleric Naser alFadh that attempted to justify the use of weapons of mass destruction. Moreover, al-Qaida spokesman Suleyman abu Ghayth said in 2003 that it is al-Qaida's right to "*kill 4 million Americans*" in retaliation for Muslim deaths that al-Qaida blames on the United States. In January 2006, bin Laden threatened that "*operations are being prepared and you will see them in your own backyard,*" and past experience strongly suggest that "*they will strive to conduct an attack more spectacular than 9/11.* Based on such information, most people would agree that alQaeda personifies today's nuclear terrorism threat.

Crusade Media

Iran Has Technology for a Nuclear Warhead to Fit Shehab3 Missile

16th June 2008

Some Western military and intelligence were shocked that "*Iran had the blueprints for making a nuclear warhead that could fit onto its Shehab3 missiles.*" The discovery was released by the former UN weapons inspector, David Albright, Sunday, June 16, ahead of the report on his investigation of the nuclear smuggling ring run by the father of the Pakistan nuclear bomb Abdul Qadeer Khan. He alleged that the nuclear blueprints passed to Libya, Iran and North Korea included ....

Crusade Media (continued)

On May 22, Swiss President Pascal Couchepin, disclosed that, last December, the destruction had been ordered of a batch of 30,000 "documents detailing construction plans for nuclear weapons, gas ultracentrifuges to enrich weapons grade uranium and *guided missile delivery systems,*" "<u>evidence</u>" in a criminal case of a Swiss family of three engineers involved in the Khan ring.

Sources disclosed on May 30 that these nuclear blueprints were sold in underhand deals to those countries – and possibly also to al Qaeda – in the second half of the 1990's. "Tehran has therefore had those designs far between 10 and 13 years."

"This discovery makes nonsense of the supposedly definitive judgment in Western and Israel intelligence that Iran lacks the technology for building a nuclear missile delivery system." Because of these estimates, Western governments have been able to keep *their sanction scum diplomatic track with Iran rolling as though tomorrow would never come.*

"It is now evident that not only North Korea and Iran have known for some time how to build and deliver a nuclear warhead, but unknown recipients of A.Q. Khan's merchandise, including terrorist organizations, may also command hazardous nuclear knowledge."

The three Swiss engineers, members of the Tinner family, are; the father, Friedrich, whose ties with Khan went back decades, and his sons, Urs and Marco.

Crusade Media (continued)

The Khan ring set up marketing headquarters in Dubai and Malaysia. The brothers have awaited trail for four years in a Swiss jail. Their father is out on bail and confined to Switzerland. The evidence against Urs Tinner, the hard disk he stole containing the incriminating nuclear documents, has now been destroyed by the Swiss authorities under the supervision of the UN nuclear watchdog.

Military experts reported on May 30: If Urs Tinner, a small cog in the Khan network, was able to steal a hard drive containing a mass of the network's nuclear secrets, three conclusions are inescapable:

1. That Khan did not retain an efficient security system for the data he was selling. Therefore, his system was full of holes and his confederates and agents, whether employed on the technical or marketing side of the business, were able to help themselves to documents, diagrams and other illicit nuclear materials that were put on sale and, perhaps, go into business on their own.
2. It is an open secret among the American and Western intelligence services involved in uncovering the Khan ring that large sections are still going strong out in Pakistan, the Far East and the Middle East through channels still unexposed. They are

bound to assume that the documents destroyed by the Swiss government may exist in copies still in circulation.
3. Some of their holders may have hung onto them for the last four years and then destroyed them when the Khan ring was exposed ...

Crusade Media (continued)

for fear of being linked to the trafficker. On the other hand, *it is possible that some of A.Q. Khan's agents and accomplices sold his nuclear plans and secrets to terrorists linked to al Qaeda.*

"A similar report comes to surface a year later on August 20, 2009"

It is obviously recognizable that procrastination is playing a major role. As a Grandmaster in the martial arts field, there was always a saying; "that he who hesitates has lost." When a person or government hesitates, this shows that there is lack of skill and/or fear, if not both. *"But yet there is no hesitation when it comes to taking innocent lives, but yet there is hesitation when it comes to saving lives."* But yet there is a judge that sees it all, and will judge all.

In relevance to the similar report as previously indicated, brings to rise a few questions. Has the U.N. been sitting on a report for over a year now, in relevance to Iran's alleged nuclear weapons experiments? Has Iran actively pursued research into developing nuclear warheads and the way to deliver them has been available since September, 2008 or even longer?

The Jerusalem Post
Sep. 4, 2009

"*The U.S. and key allies contend the Islamic republic is covertly trying to build an atomic bomb.*"

The Jerusalem Post (continued)

Teheran has bristled at the agency's latest report, which accuses Iran of defiantly continuing to enrich uranium and refusing to clear up lingering questions about possible military dimensions to its nuclear program.

But it takes sharp aim at Washington for giving the UN nuclear watchdog unspecified intelligence and other evidence allegedly recovered from a laptop computer that reportedly was smuggled out of Iran.

"*US intelligence later assessed the information as indicating that Teheran had been working on 'details of nuclear weapons,' including missile trajectories and ideal altitudes for exploding warheads.*"

The material on the laptop also included videos of what intelligence officials believe were "*secret nuclear laboratories in Iran.*"

The IAEA itself has pressed the US and other governments to share more details on Iran related intelligence. In its latest report on Iran, the UN agency noted that "constraints placed by some member states on the availability of information to Iran are making it more difficult for the agency to conduct detailed discussions with Iran."

But it cautions that there are "a number of outstanding issues which give rise to 'concerns' and which need to be clarified to exclude the existence of possible military dimensions."

Is the Gog and Magog war of Ezekiel 3839 within a twinkle of an eye?

In Ezekiel 39: 11, He says, "And *it shall come to pass* in that day, that I will give unto Gog a place there of *graves in Israel.*" But "*there will be a slaughter the like of which has not been seen in the history of the world.*"

The retaliation from an attack against Iran's nuclear facilities may commence the Gog and Magog war, with Russia, Iran and its allies invading Israel. But every person must take very seriously, that if God says that it shall come to pass, "*it will come to pass!*" Even if there was no attack on Iran's nuclear facilities, this event will "still come to pass." In Ezekiel 38: 4, He says, "And I will turn thee back, and *put hooks into thy jaws, and I will bring thee forth*, and all thine army, horses and horsemen, all of them clothed with all sorts of armour, even a great company with bucklers and shields, all of them handling swords. *"It will come to pass."*

The following articles will declare the closeness of this upcoming event that will come to pass "the window is closing."

The Wall Street Journal
Wednesday, July 8, 2009, Page A9

U.S. Military Chief Warns of Iran Nuclear Weapon

Washington – The top U.S. military officer *warned that the "window is closing"* for preventing Iran from acquiring a nuclear weapon, highlighting the difficult choices facing Obama administration in the wake of last month's elections.

The Wall Street Journal (continued)

He (Adm. Mike Mullen, chairman of the Joint Chiefs of Staff), also cautioned that a possible Israeli military strike on Iran risked destabilizing the broader Middle East and triggering retaliatory Iranian attacks elsewhere in the world.

The U.S. and its allies are *"running out of time"* to persuade Iran to abandon its nuclear program. "Iran is very focused on developing this capability," (nuclear weapon), he said at the Center for Strategic and International Studies. *"The clock is ticking and that's why I'm as concerned as I am."*

Vice President Joe Biden had signaled a "change" in administration policy when he told a television interviewer that "Israel can determine for itself" whether to bomb Iran's nuclear facilities.

Still, Adm. Mullen made clear that an Israeli strike was far more likely than an American one.

"Israel has signaled that it may be preparing for a military strike on Iran. Earlier this week, an Israeli submarine believed to be carrying nuclear tipped missiles returned to the Mediterranean after crossing the Red Sea and moving towards Iran.

Russiatoday.com/Top_ News
22 September, 2008

"For the first time in modern history, a Russian naval squadron is making its way towards Latin America."

Russia Today (continued)

The nuclear powered cruiser 'Peter the Great', an antisubmarine ship and two support vessels will sail from the Arctic to the Caribbean to take part in joint maneuvers with Venezuela.

After covering 15,000 nautical miles, in November the ships will perform several *combat training tasks*, including missile and artillery exercises. The exercises will give the ships an opportunity to showcase their advanced weaponry, and test out the new technology in a realistic setting.

Russiatoday.com/Top News
02 December, 2008

Russia and Venezuela have begun joint naval exercises in the Caribbean. The move has been seen in the West as a response by Moscow to the visit of the U.S. Navy to Georgia earlier this year.

Two Russian warships, the nuclear powered missile cruiser Peter the Great and submarine hunter Admiral Chabanenko, together with two auxiliary vessels and 12 Venezuelan warships, are taking part in the two day war games.

Startribune.com/world
February 25, 2009

Iranians and Russians announce test run has begun at Iran's first nuclear power plant

Star Tribune (continued)

BUSHEHR, Iran – Iranian and Russian engineers carried out *a test run of Iran's first nuclear power plant* Wednesday, a major step toward starting up a facility that the U.S. once hoped to prevent because of fears over Tehran's nuclear ambitions.

"Russia is providing enriched uranium fuel for the plant in the southern port of Bushehr."

State Department spokesman Robert A. Wood said in Washington. "It also demonstrates that Iran does not need to develop any kind of indigenous uranium enrichment capacity."

Yahoo! News
5/20/2009

Iran says it tests missile, Israel within range

TEHRAN, Iran – President Mahmoud Admadinejad said Iran test fired a new "advanced missile" Wednesday with a range of about 1,200 miles, *"far enough to strike Israel,"* southeastern Europe and U.S. bases in the Middle East.

"Defense Minister (Mostafa Mohammad Najjar) has informed me that the Sajjil2 missile, which *"has very_advanced technology,"* was launched from Semnan and it landed *precisely on the target*."

Ahmadinejad has repeatedly called for Israel's elimination, and the Jewish state has not ruled out a military strike.

Jerusalem Post
July 14, 2009

2 IDF warships cross Suez to Red Sea

In a new signal to Iran, two Sa'ar 5class Israeli Navy ships crossed through the Suez Canal from the Mediterranean to the Red Sea on Tuesday to beef up Israel's naval presence near Eilat.

The passage of the ships comes several weeks after a Dolphin class submarine passed through the international waterway *"for the first time."*

One of the ships, the INS *Hanit,* already crossed the canal in June, in what an Egyptian source said *"was the first time"* a large missile ship used the strategic waterway, which is the fastest route to get Israeli Navy vessels from the Mediterranean, where they are based, to the Red Sea and beyond.

The other ship to cross on Tuesday was the INS *Eilat.*

Iran has recently deployed several of its navy ships in the Gulf of Aden and near Eritrea.

In the event of a conflict with Iran, and if Israel decided to involve its three Dolphin class submarines – which according to foreign reports can fire nuclear tipped cruise missiles and serve as a second-strike platform – the quickest route would be to sail them through the Suez Canal. Going through the canal would also be the way to get to the Gulf of Oman without refueling.

TIMES ON LINE
July 16, 2009

Israeli navy in Suez Canal prepares for potential attack on Iran

Israel will soon test an Arrow interceptor missile on a US missile range in the Pacific Ocean. The system is designed to defend Israel from ballistic missile attacks by Iran and Syria. Lieutenant General Patrick O'Reilly, the director of the Pentagon's Missile Defense Agency, said that Israel would test against a target with a range of more than 630 miles (1,000km) – too long for previous Arrow test sites in the eastern Mediterranean.

The Israeli air force, meanwhile, will send F16C fighter jets to participate at Nellis Air Force base in Nevada this month. Israeli C130 Hercules transport aircraft will also compete in the Rodeo 2009 competition at McCord Air Force base in Washington.

"Diplomats said that Israel had offered concessions on settlement policy, Palestinian land claims and issues with neighboring Arab states, to facilitate a possible strike on Iran."

"Israel has chosen to place the Iranian threat over its settlements," said a senior European diplomat.

Jerusalem Post
July 29, 2009

"Russia, Iran to hold naval maneuver"

Jerusalem Post (continued)

"For the first time, Russia and Iran" will hold a joint naval maneuver in the Caspian Sea, The Iranian Mehr News Agency reported Wednesday.

According to the report, the maneuver *will include 30 Russian and Iran ships, as well as helicopters.*

"*Moscow* is building Iran's first nuclear plant in Bushehr, has provided Teheran with weapons and needs Iranian assistance on the Caspian Sea and other regional issues."

Iran is paying Russia more than $1 billion (C630 million) to build the "light water reactor" and has already received several shipments of enriched uranium for its operation.

World News
Wednesday August 26, 2009

Russia wants to buy French warship

ULAN BATOR (Reuters) – Russia wants to buy from France an advanced warship that can launch amphibious assaults, a general said on Wednesday.

The ship can be used to launch amphibious assaults or as a mobile command and control center. It would be Russia's biggest single purchase of weapon abroad.

This amphibious assault ship able to carry helicopters, personnel, armed vehicles and tanks for thousands of miles.

The International Jerusalem Post
August 1420, 2009

"*President Mahmoud Ahmadinejad has announced*" this or that dramatic breakthrough, telling the TV cameras that, as a consequence, "*the threshold has been crossed and the drive to nuclear power is now unstoppable*" – that his country has taken up membership in the select global nuclear club.

Briefing the Knesset's Foreign Affairs and Defence Committee on August 4, Brig.Gen. Yossi Baidatz, the head of research in the IDF's Military

Intelligence division, related bleakly to the two criteria that would determine Iran's capacity to go nuclear. First, he reported, Iran's program was progressing smoothly and *"by the end of the year"* would have cleared all technological hurdles – rendering the acquisition of *"a bomb a matter of choice* rather than scientific and practical challenge." And second, he asserted, the international community was plainly reconciling itself, however reluctantly, to the notion of a nuclear Iran.

Most notably, the United States remained committed in principle to diplomatic engagement even though there was no prospect of serious diplomacy so much as beginning, and *"meanwhile precious weeks and months were slipping by."*

Rhetorically, it should be stressed, "successive Israeli governments have declared flatly that the Jewish state will not tolerate the Iranian regime attaining the capacity" *"to wipe us out."*

The International Jerusalem Post (continued)

"Not this Iranian leadership, so overtly committed to the destruction of Israel. Not this regime, which cannot be relied upon to act rationally and rein itself in according to the deterrent model of mutual assured destruction."

On the summit of Mount Scopus, 'we' will "guarantee peace" for Jerusalem and for the State of Israel

August 23, 2009

Israeli Prime Minister, Benjamin Netanyahu statements made at the Israeli National Defense College Graduation Ceremony on August 3, 2009.
 Our first problem that makes it difficult with regard to our national security is that we have a very small country. Some of whom negate the State of Israel's existence and use all means in order to abrogate our existence – this creates problems of national security which don't exit in any other country or for any other people. Our attempts to achieve peace with the Palestinians, we need to respond to two problems: on the one hand, the problem of the denial of our rights to exist, and on the other hand, the problem of security which stems from Israel's geographic dimensions.

 When *'we'* sign a peace agreement with the Palestinians, which "I believe will happen" – *'we'* want it to be a final <u>agreement</u>" – "<u>an end</u> to conflict," an "<u>end</u> to the conflict's claims."

Israeli Prime Minister, Benjamin Netanyahu statements (continued)

 "<u>We</u>" are talking about an *"international guarantee,"* "headed by the United States," for the demilitarization arrangements that *"we"* will establish.

"We" can even go further: we are actually ready to consider the "military" "protection" by NATO" (*instead of from God*) of an 'agreement' reached by Israelis and Palestinians on the bases of equality within a Federal State that is also a nation state for the Jewish people.
The "freedom of movement" and establishment, as developed in the careful case law and legislation of the European Union. Again, we propose that such a right to free movement be "*a central element of the 'agreement,*" to be refined further in the way successfully charted by the "Europeans since the Treaty of Rome in 1957."

"This is why advancing "*economic peace*" and development is integral for helping to promote "*peace.*"

"The only thing that can postpone and disrupt the rate of the extinguishing of radical Islam is the possibility that it will be armed with a nuclear weapon." "*Today, this is so dangerous*" that I would go so far as to say that understanding of this danger is permeating governments, leaders, public opinion shapers, and even armies.

"On the summit of Mount Scopus, *"we"* will '*guarantee peace*' for Jerusalem and for the State of Israel."

We have made a covenant with death, and with Hell we have an agreement

ISAIAH 28: 21

"*Therefore hear the word of the Lord,*" "you scoffers, who rule this people in Jerusalem!" Because '*you*' have said, "*We'* have made a '*covenant'* with death, and with Hell '*we*' have an '*agreement,*' when the overwhelming whip passes through it will not come to us, for '*we*' have made *lies* our refuge, and in falsehood '*we*' have taken *shelter*" (vs. 1415).

Then your '*covenant*' with death will be "annulled," and your *agreement* with Hell will "not stand"; when the overwhelming scourge passes through, "*you will be beaten down by it*" (vs. 18).

"God rebukes the scoffing stupidity of Judah's leaders. Jerusalem's leaders rejoiced over their alliance, for *protection and peace.*" "*The judgment of God will now come upon them* as like an overwhelming scourge passing through, they will be "beaten down" by it, says the Lord thy God."

"**What happened to their faith in God.**"

It is amazing, and how precisely God's prophecy is and so accurate. Not only His prophesy, but also even *"every word that was said, was prophesied."* This prophecy was foretold thousands of years ago, and now just recently those exact words were just mentioned. The Lord said this would occur at the end times, which is more than obvious "today" (found by Marcel L. Garcia Jr. – author).

Jerusalem Post
Aug. 5, 2009

A recipe for even more delay on Iran

US President Barak Obama will not prevent Iran from acquiring nuclear weapons.

Defense Secretary Robert Gates stating on July 16 that an Iranian bomb is *"the greatest current threat to global security."* But the same administration has no plan to ensure that the threat does not materialize – and is attempting to ensure that Israel doesn't either.

The Iranians have already called Obama's bluff. An "Iranian newspaper" referred to the "American agenda" on July 26 this day :"(T)he Obama administration is prepared to *"accept the prospect of a nuclear armed Iran"*…They have no long-term plan for dealing with Iran…Their strategy consists of "begging us" to talk with them."

This is an administration more worried about ensuring a *Judenrein* future Palestinian state (settlements being only the tip of the iceberg) than ensuring the safety of the Jewish state or preventing the dramatic shift in the balance of power that will come with an Iranian nuclear weapon.

As Assistant Secretary of State Philip Crowley put it a day later: "We'll have to wait and see where Iran is…Obviously, right now, the government has its hands full."

In effect, the administration is giving Iran a timeout for brutality.

Jerusalem Post (continued)

In the meantime, there is no American push for tough immediate sanctions in response to Iran's massive violations of the Nuclear Non-Proliferation Treaty (NPT) and human rights. On the contrary, Obama declared in July: "This notion that we were trying to get sanctions…is not accurate."

If and when the administration reverses course on sanctions, its first stop will be the UN. It will start by "begging" the Security Council for another resolution with "significant" sanctions. Except that nobody believes the Security Council will deliver. "More than six years ago the UN's International Atomic Energy Agency found Iran was violating the NPT." *"And here we are on the brink of disaster five trivial resolutions later."*

In short, Obama's Iran policy has two prongs. "Set a snail's pace on engagement and sanctions. And send waves of brass knuckled emissaries to Jerusalem in an effort to take military action off the table."

The "only" question now is whether Obama's fundamental disrespect for Jewish self-determination will convince Israel not to take the military steps necessary to forestall an Iranian nuclear bomb. If it does, "Ahmadinejad's reign of *terror will have only just begun.*"

Netanyahu seeks economic pressure on Iran
8/30/2009 11:39AM

After talks with German Chancellor Angela Merkel, Netanyahu *"warned of a mortal threat to Israel's survival posed by Iran."*

Netanyahu seeks economic pressure on Iran (continued)

Netanyahu said; *"There is not much time"* to halt Tehran's nuclear ambitions, he told reporters.

Netanyahu and Merkel said they were convinced the time was right to jumpstart *"peace talks"* between Israel and the Palestinians.

"I hope that in a time frame of a month or two we can re-launch negotiations," Netanyahu said.

"Let's just get on with it. We have a job to fend off the radicals and move forward."

"We cannot allow those who call for the destruction of the Jewish state to go unchallenged," he said in reference to Ahmadinejad as he took "possession of the plans."

"We cannot allow evil to prepare the mass deaths of innocents."

The Rapture of the Church

1 Thessalonians 4: 17
"Then we (believers) who are *alive*, who are left, will be *"caught up"* together with them in the clouds to meet the Lord in the air, and so *we will always be with the Lord* (vs. 17)." "While people are saying, "There is peace and security," then sudden destruction will come upon them as labor pains come upon a pregnant woman, and they will not escape (5: 3)." *"For God has not destined us (believers) for wrath, "but to obtain salvation" through our Lord Yahshua, (5: 9)."*

The Rapture of the Church (continued)

Hebrews 10: 39

"But we (believers) 'are not' of those who shrink back and are destroyed, but of those who have faith and preserve their souls."

"In a moment, in the twinkling of an eye, the living and the dead are "caught up" from the earth into the air to meet Yahshua "our" Lord and Savior." The Greek for "caught up" (harpazo, "to grab or seize suddenly, to snatch, take away") gives a sense of being forcibly and "suddenly lifted upward," to meet the Lord in the air (see also John 6: 15; Acts 8: 39)."

Jerusalem Post
Sep. 7, 2009

ElBaradei: Nuclear 'stalemate' with Iran

ElBaradei told the IAEA board; "Iran 'has not' suspended its enrichment related activities or its work on heavy water related projects as required by the Security Council, nor has Iran implemented the Additional Protocol," which would open its nuclear facilities to unannounced and more intrusive inspections.
(This was a statement made at the 35nation board of the International Atomic Energy Agency (IAEA) – which is taking a hard look at Iran and Syria – Mohamed ElBaradei urged the Islamic Republic to "substantively reengage" with the international community).

Jerusalem Post (continued)

ElBaradei also criticized Syria for failing to disclose details about a desert site bombed by Israel in 2007.

"Syria has not cooperated with the agency to confirm Syria's statements regarding the nonnuclear nature of the destroyed building on the Deir aZour site, nor has it provided the required access to information, locations, equipment or materials," he said.

ElBaradei had a terse assessment of North Korea, which conducted its second nuclear test explosion in May. The IAEA pulled out its inspectors after North Korea suspended all cooperation with the IAEA in April, and since has been unable to monitor or verify Pyongyang's nuclear activities.

Before the meeting, Iranian President Mahmoud Ahmadinejad said, *"his country will neither halt uranium enrichment nor negotiate over its nuclear rights,* but is ready to sit and talk with world powers over "global challenges."

"From our point of view, Iran's nuclear issue is over. We continue our work within the framework of global regulations and in close interaction with the International Atomic Energy Agency," he said. "We will never negotiate over obvious rights of the Iranian nation."

Jerusalem Post
Sep. 7, 2009

IDF preparing for US missile systems

Jerusalem Post (continued)

The Defense Ministry is preparing for the possibility that the United States will decide to leave missile defense systems in Israel following a joint missile defense exercise the two countries will hold next month, senior officials said Sunday.

The Israeli Air Force's Air Defense Division will hold a joint drill, called Juniper Cobra, with the US Military's European Command (EUCOM) and the US Missile Defense Agency (MDA) next month in what is being described as the *"largest joint exercise ever held by the two countries,"* during which they will jointly test three different ballistic missile defense systems.

Juniper Cobra, which will be held in October in Israel, will include the newly developed Arrow 2 as well as America's THAAD (Terminal High Altitude Area Defense) and the ship based Aegis Ballistic Missile Defense System. While Israel and the US have held Juniper Cobra exercises for the past five years, the upcoming drill is planned to be *"the most complex and extensive to date."*

Meanwhile Sunday, Iranian television claimed that the Iranian military had developed an "anti-cruise missile system. Announcing the latest milestone in domestic military industrial achievements, Air Force Brig.Gen. Ahmad Miqani said, "(Despite) 30 years of military sanctions by the enemy, the armed forces have taken appropriate steps toward self-sufficiency and have been able not only to update their equipment, but also to achieve wide-ranging progress in the military and aerospace sector."

Jerusalem Post (continued)

"Today we are able not only to identify stealth cruise missiles, but also to destroy them," he elaborated on Press TV.

Jerusalem Post
Sep. 3, 2009

'Russia confirms MiG jet sale to Syria'

The Russian daily newspaper *Kommersant* has reported that Russia is expected to provide Syria with powerful MiG fighter jets but has not yet begun delivering the planes.

Israeli defense officials said they were not surprised by Russia's intention to sell Syria the advanced jets but expressed concern that if the deal went through "it would alter the balance of power in the region."

Jerusalem Post

Sep. 12, 2009

Meridor urges "immediate action on Iran": "The clock is ticking"

Intelligence Minister Dan Meridor on Saturday urged "immediate action on the Iranian nuclear threat," during an interview with Reuters. "The clock is ticking," he "warned."

His comments came less than 24 hours after the six world powers the US, Russia, China, France, Britain and Germany.

Jerusalem Post (continued)

The Islamic republic attaining nuclear ability was "not very far away."

"I don't want to go into details but they are going in that direction…It's not in the distant future," he said.

Khaleej Times
September 12, 2009

Iran defiant as "Putin warns against attack"

TEHRAN – Iran on Friday stood firm against intense new international pressure over its disputed nuclear program, and "Russian Prime

Minister Vladimir Putin" "warned the West against staging an attack."

Supreme leader Ayatollah Ali Khamenei insisted that Iran must defend its right to nuclear power.

"We must stand firm for our rights. If we give up our rights, whether nuclear or other rights, this will lead to decline of society," said Khamenei, who has the final say in all national issues.

"We will walk the path of decline if instead of using 'freedom' for scientific and ethical progress, "we use it to_spread sin," instead of standing against arrogance, aggressors and international looters, we feel weak in front of them and retreat, and instead of frowning at them we smile at them."

Khaleej Times (continued)

While warning that any attack on Iran over its nuclear project would be unacceptable, "Russia's Putin" also urged Tehran to show restraint.

"This would be very dangerous, unacceptable, this would lead to an 'explosion of terrorism,' increase the influence of extremists," he said when asked about the possibility of an attack.

"I doubt very much that such strikes would achieve their stated goal."

"Iranian President Mahmoud Ahmadinejad said the 'Jewish state is doomed' to be "wiped off the map."

The Leaders of the Only Nation that Supports Israel will 'Betray them' and Have Chosen to be "Fainthearted"

Lamentations 4: 17; Still our eyes failed us, *Watching* vainly for our help; In our watching we watched for a nation *that* could not save *us*.

Jeremiah 37: 7; "Thus says the Lord, the God of Israel: Behold, the army which has come up to help you will return to their own land."

Job 30: 15; "<u>Terrors are turned upon me</u>." Lamentations 2: 22; "<u>The terrors that surround me</u>."

Jeremiah 15: 8; "I will cause anguish and terror to fall on them" "suddenly."

Zechariah 12: 3; "And it shall happen in that day that I will make Jerusalem a very heavy stone for all peoples; all who would "heave it away" "will surely be cut in pieces," though "all nations" of the earth "are gathered against it." In that day, says the Lord, I will strike every horse with confusion, and its rider with madness.

"Two metaphors describe how God will use Jerusalem as a foil to destroy the nations:

1) Jerusalem will be a cup of reeling (vs. 2). This common prophetic phrase describes divine judgment (cf. Isa. 51: 17, 2122; Jer. 25: 1528).
2) Jerusalem will be an immovable rock (Zech. 12: 3). The defeat of the Armageddon armies is thus likened to a man who drinks more than he can hold, or tries to move a weight heavier than he can lift. Those who attack Jerusalem will do so to their own ruin. "He who is not with Me is against Me," (Matthew 12: 30). The Lord says that "all nations" are gathered against Jerusalem. If you personally are not saved, "prepare for your judgment that is against you." Although I pray for your salvation.

The Holy Scriptures continues to prevail in the Truth and that in God's prophecies they are currently becoming a reality before your eyes, no matter what news comes out, your guidance is in the truth of God's word and His Holy Spirit, and not man's words. Every manner of peace and salvation comes "only" through Yahshua.

Everyone will deceive his neighbor, and will not speak the truth

Jeremiah 9: 36; "And like their bow they have bent their tongues for lies." "For they proceed from evil to evil, and they do not know Me," says the Lord (vs. 3). "Everyone take heed to his neighbor, and do not trust any brother," (vs. 4). "Everyone will deceive his neighbor," and "will not speak the truth"; they have taught their tongues to speak lies, (vs. 5). "Through deceit they refuse to know Me," says the Lord, (vs. 6).

The Leaders of Nations are Deceptive with One Another
Daniel 11: 27; "Both these kings' hearts *shall* be bent on evil, and they shall speak lies at the same table; but it shall not prosper, for 'the end' *will* still *be* at the appointed time."

The Mayan Prophecy
The End Time Date
December 21, 2012

According to the Maya calendar (13.0.0.0.0 in the Long Count) on the date *December 21st, 2012*, this date is supposed to mark the "end of the world," or the "ending" of a Maya calendar cycle. Some would even go as far as saying that it is an "end time date." Another one of the devils lies! You may notice that God's word is always deceived by Satan. The devil will turn even the "eagle" in Isaiah 40:31, and use it as the "*eagle god*," of Satan, and look at how many nations use the eagle as a symbol (Satan working through the nations). Plus notice how some nations use Grecian symbols at the capitol of that nation.

According to the Holy Scriptures

"No One Knows the Day or Hour!"

Supporting verses and statements (continued)

Matthew 24: 36; "But of that day and hour 'no one knows,' not even the angels of heaven, but My Father only."
It is calculated that the "Great Tribulation" will last three and one-half years.

Revelation 11: 3; "And I will give *power* to my two witnesses, and they will prophesy one thousand two hundred and sixty days, clothed in sackcloth." Rev. 12: 6; "one thousand two hundred and sixty days." Daniel 7: 25; "Then the *saints* shall be given into his hand for 'a time and times and half a times." Daniel 12: 7; "Then I heard the man clothed in linen, who *was* above the waters of the river, when he held up his right hand and his left hand to heaven, and swore by Him who lives forever, that it *shall be* for 'a time, times, and half *a time;* and when the power of the holy people has been completely shattered, all these *things* shall be finished."

"If" the Mayan prophecy was correct, that the 'end of the world' is to come on December 21st, 2012. And if you subtract the three and one-half years that the word of God says the great tribulation will last. Then you would land in the summer of 2009, it is now the month of September 2009, and we 'are not' in the "Great Tribulation."

"But the word of God does say that 'a period of time that the Lord would shorten' because of His mercy." Which means that God will place a limit on the tribulation; Christ will intervene and prevent complete genocide.

Supporting verses and statements (continued)

The Signs of the Times and the End of the Age
The Great Tribulation
The Words that came from Jesus Christ

Matthew 24: 2122; "For then there will be "*great tribulation*," such as has 'not been' 'since the beginning of the world' until "this time", no, nor "ever shall be." "And unless those days were shortened, no flesh would be *saved*; but for the elect's sake 'those days will be shortened" (vs.22).

"Then this may tell us that the "rapture of the church" and the "judgment against the evil of this world," from all mighty God, will soon commence."

"Today's factual news confirms that we are currently experiencing what the Lord has planned for the end times." The earth will move out of her place (Isaiah 13:13)

THE WALL STREET JOURNAL
Friday September 18, 2009

U.S. Missile UTurn Roils Allies

President Barack Obama's decision to drop plans to deploy a ballistic missile defense shield in Central Europe drawing immediate cheers in "Moscow" and criticism elsewhere is a "gamble" by the U.S. that scaling back its "defense" ambitions will improve security in the long run.

The scripture says the Russians and Allies will now attack.

The People of the World Have Been Warned by the Word of God

Ezekiel 38: 1012; "Thus says the Lord God: "On that day it shall come to pass *that* 'thoughts' will arise in your mind, and you 'will' make an 'evil plan': You will say, "I will go up against a land of 'un-walled villages': I will go to a peaceful people, who dwell safely, all of them 'without walls' and having neither bars nor gates" – to take plunder and to take booty, to stretch out your hand against the waste places *that are again* inhabited, and 'against a people gathered from the nations.'

While the Missile Defense system (the walls) is being brought down the Russians continue to prepare for the invasion, just as God said.

Russian News
Kommepcahtb
News of 14:22 13 September 2009

Venezuela may buy Russia's anti-ship missiles Club
Venezuelan President Hugo Chavez, who said on the prompt delivery of Russia's missiles with a range of up to 300 km, is likely to mean a system of anti-Club.

"Apparently, it is a coastal missile system Club, designed to attack ground and sea targets, and allows to build a universal system of defense," – said on Sept. 13, RIA Novosti source in the military industrial complex. According to him, a set of Club can hit targets at a distance of 300 km altitude missiles – from 10 to 50 am…..

Kommepcahtb News (continued)

Please remember that Hugo Chavez, who visited this week, Russia, September 12, announced plans to supply Russia's tanks T90, as well as high precision missiles.

Khaleej Times
12 September 2009

Chavez announces Russian missile purchase

CARACAS – Amid rising tensions with neighboring Colombia, Venezuelan President Hugo Chavez announced late Friday that his country would soon take delivery of Russian made missiles with a range of 300 kilometers (185 miles).

"We have signed some agreement with Russia. Soon we will begin receiving some missiles," Chavez said during a meeting with supporters in front of the presidential palace.

But the announcement came amid rising tension between Caracas and Bogota over Colombia's decision to allow the United States access to several military bases on its territory.

But Russian President Dmitry Mededev said Russia would sell weapons to its "friend" Venezuela.

Separately, a consortium of Russian oil companies and Venezuelan state oil company PDVSA signed an agreement establishing a joint venture to develop the Junin 6 oil field along Venezuela's Orinoco River.

Khaleej Times (continued)

Recent Russian arms sales to Venezuela also include 24 fighter jets Sukhoi30, 50 combat helicopters and 100,000 Kalshnikov assault rifles. Moscow has also granted Venezuela a one billion dollar credit to finance the acquisition of its weapons.

THE WALL STREET JOURNAL
Wednesday, July 8, 2009

Pope Calls for a Group to Oversee World Markets
United Nations and Other International Bodies Need 'Real Teeth' to Prevent Future Crises, Encyclical Says

ROME – Pope Benedict XVI issued a rare papal critique of the global economic crisis Tuesday, calling for a "true world political authority" charged with exercising greater oversight of financial markets.

In a letter titled "Caritas in Veritate," or "Charity in Truth," Pope Benedict said the United Nations and other international bodies 'need' to "acquire real teeth" to properly monitor markets, stem the current crises and prevent future ones. "There is urgent need of a true world political authority," the pope wrote in the 44page encyclical.

The pope is expected to give a copy of the encyclical to President Barack Obama when the two meet at the Vatican on Friday, said Cardinal Renato Martino, a top Vatican official.

The Washington Journal (continued)

Also on the agenda is a document – drawn up by Italy and approved last month by G8 finance ministers – that seeks to establish a new set of internationally accepted rules for transparent and ethical behavior in finance, business, trade and fiscal policy. Italy, the G8 host nation, has made this so-called Legal Standard a major tenet of its agenda.

Yet critics said that many of the rules and guidelines already exist; and difficulty lies in having them enforced.

The Scriptures Describes "The Second Beast" as a False Prophet – a Religious Character

Revelation 13: 1112; "And I beheld another beast coming up out of the earth; and he had two horns like a lamb, and he spoke as a dragon. And he exercises all the power of the first beast before him, and causes the earth and them which dwell therein to worship the first beast, whose deadly wound was healed."

If the sea, mentioned as the source of the first beast (Rev. 13: 1), represents the mass of humanity indicating the racial background of the first beast as a Gentile, the reference to the second beast as coming out of the earth instead of the sea indicates that this character, who is later described as a false prophet (Rev. 16: 13; 19: 20), is a creature of earth rather than heaven. He is pictured, however, as having two horns like a lamb and as speaking like a dragon. The description of him as a lamb seems to indicate that he has a religious character, a conclusion supported by his being named a prophet.

His speaking as a dragon indicates that he is motivated by the power of 'Satan' who is "the dragon."

As a supporting character to the first beast, he is active on behalf of the first beast and "exercises his authority," and he has authority in the "economic" realm to control all commerce (Rev. 13: 1617); (11) he has the mark that will establish his identity for those who live in that day (13: 15). "The mark or brand (as used at the times of slavery) of the beast symbolizes that the person that accepts this mark no longer belongs to God but to man or 'Satan,' the mark is 666, is the number of man (whom runs the one world order) a lawless system. Apparently the mark of the beast is some sort of identifiable proof of ownership."

There is some evidence pointing to the conclusion that the second beast is the "head of the apostate church." With the rise of the first beast to a place of worldwide dominion, the 'apostate church" is destroyed in accordance to Revelation 17: 16, and then the worship of the entire world is directed to the beast out of the sea (the antichrist). The second beast, however, survives the destruction of the church, which had been under his control, and he assists the beast in making the transition. It is clear that he shares prominence and leadership with the first beast until they are both cast alive into the lake of fire at the close (19: 20).

"We are presented, then, with a 'Satanic trinity,' the unholy trinity, or the trinity of hell: the Dragon (Satan), the Beast (antichrist), and the False Prophet (Rev. 16: 13). The places currently occupied by God, by Jesus Christ, and by the Holy Spirit which is discharged by the False Prophet."

MYSTERY, BABYLON THE GREAT, THE MOTHER OF HARLOTS AND OF THE ABOMINATIONS OF THE EARTH (Revelation 17: 5)

Revelation 17 outlines the judgment on the great harlot or the evil woman, the apostate religious system. The evil woman symbolizes the religious system of Babylon, and the waters symbolize 'peoples, multitudes, nations, and languages" (vs. 15). The angel informed John that the kings of the earth had committed adultery with the woman; in other words, they had become a part of the religious system, which she symbolized (cf. 14: 8). The system is a leader in ecclesiastical affairs (Rev. 17: 2, 5). The system is a leader in political affairs (Rev. 17: 3). It is seen to be controlling the Beast upon which it sits. The system has become very rich and influential (Rev. 17: 4).

The woman was dressed in purple and scarlet, and was glittering with gold, precious stones, and pears. Her adornment is similar to that of religious trappings of ritualistic churches today. It was Satan's effort to delude mankind with an imitation so like the truth of God that they would not know the true Seed of the woman when He came in the fullness of time.

From Babylon this mystery religion spread to all the surrounding nations. Everywhere the symbols were the same, and everywhere "the cult of the mother and the child" became the popular system; the image of the queen of heaven with the babe in her arms was seen everywhere. Within 1000 years Babylonianism had become the religion of the world, which had rejected the Divine revelation.

The Bible is full of information about Babylon as the source of false religion, the record beginning with the building of the tower of Babel (Gen. 1011). The name "Babel" suggests "confusion" (Gen. 11: 9). Later the name was applied to the city of Babylon which itself has a long history dating back to as early as 3,000 years before Christ.

Linked with this central mystery were countless lesser mysteries. Among these were the doctrines of purgatorial purification after death, salvation by countless sacraments such as priestly absolution, sprinkling with holy water, the offering of round cakes to the queen of heaven as mentioned in the book of Jeremiah. Scripture condemns this false religion repeatedly (Jer. 7: 18; 44: 1719, 25; Ezek. 8: 14). The worship of Baal is related to the worship of Tammuz.

The ancient cult was propagated under the name of the Etruscan Mysteries, and eventually Rome became the headquarters of Babylonianism. The chief priest when established in Rome took the title Pontifex Maximus.

Crowns in the shape of a fish head were worn by the chief priests of the Babylonians cult to honor the fish god. The crowns bore the words "Keeper of the Bridge," symbolic of the "bridge" "between man and Satan." This handle was adopted by the Roman emperors, who used the Latin title "*Pontifex Maximus*," which means "Major Keeper of the Bridge." And the same title was later used by the bishop of Rome. The pope today is often called the "*pontiff*," which comes from "*pontifex*." When the teachers of the Babylonian mystery religions later moved from Pergamum to Rome "they were influential in paganizing Christianity and were the source of many so-called religious rites."

The pope today, who is thus declared to be, not the successor of the fisherman apostle Peter, but the direct successor of the high priest of the Babylonian mysteries, and the servant of the fish god Dagon, for whom he wears, like his idolatrous predecessors, the fisherman's ring.

Babylonian practices and teachings had been so largely absorbed by that which bore the name of the church of Christ, that the truth of the Holy Scriptures on many points had been wholly obscured, while idolatrous practices had been foisted upon the people as Christian sacraments, and heathen philosophies took the place of gospel instruction.

The Lords Response to this Issue

Revelation 18: 18; "for by your sorcery all the nations were deceived." (vs. 8) – Therefore her plagues will come in "<u>one day</u>" – death and morning and famine. And she will be utterly burned with fire, for strong *is* the Lord God who judges her. (vs. 10, 17, 19) – "<u>For in one hour she is made desolate.</u>"

"The Most Terrifying Events Yet To Come"

"The Battle of the Great Day of God Almighty"

"ARMAGEDDON"
"The Final Battle Between Good and Evil"

Revelation 19: 19; "And I saw the beast, the kings of the earth, and their armies, gathered together to make war against Him who sat on the horse and against His army."

Revelation 19: 2021; "Then the beast was captured, and with him the false prophet who worked signs in his presence, by which he deceived those who received the mark of the beast and those who worshiped his image. These two were cast alive into the lake of fire burning with brimstone. And the rest were killed with the sword, which proceeded from the mouth of Him who sat on the horse. And all the birds were filled with their flesh."

The Location of the Campaign of Armageddon

The hill of Megiddo, is located precisely west of the Jordan River in north central Palestine, some ten miles south of Nazareth and fifteen miles inland from the Mediterranean seacoast, this was an extended plain on which many of Israel's battles had been fought. There are other geographical locations involved in this campaign; "the valley of Jehoshaphat," which extends the area east of Jerusalem (Joel 3: 2, 13). "The valley of the passengers," which may be relevant to the valley of Jehoshaphat spoken of in Ezekiel 39: 11. The book of Isaiah declares in chapter 34 and 63, that the Lord is seen coming from Edom or Idumea, south of Jerusalem, when He returns from the judgment. It is mentioned that Jerusalem itself is seen to be the center of conflict (Zech. 12: 211; 14: 2). The campaigns expand from the plains of Esdraelon on the north, down all the way through Jerusalem, then extending out to the valley of Jehoshaphat on the east and to Edom on the south. This area covers the entire land of Palestine, just as Ezekiel said, "the invaders will cover the land" (Ezek. 38: 9, 16). This area also conforms to the extent pictured by John in the book of Revelation 14: 20.

In the Holy Scriptures identifies the book of Revelation as "apocalypse" (or "revelation," chapter 1: 1) and as prophecy (1: 3; 22: 7, 10, 18, 19; you can also see 10: 11; 22: 9).

"Apocalypse" is derived from the Greek noun *apocalypses*, meaning, "revelation, disclosure, unveiling" – that is, the disclosure of unseen heavenly or future realities.

There are features in the scriptures that include visions that dramatize the prophet's admission to God to reverse present injustices.

Apocalyptic literature divided humanity into two immutable camps: (A) the holy minority who await God's deliverance, and (B) their persecutors (unbelievers) destined for wrath and beyond the reach of redemption. It is acknowledged that apocalyptic literature saw the present as so pervaded by corruption that no saving work of

God could possibly be expected before his cataclysmic intervention at the end.

Revelation sees "believers as conquerors," through endurance under suffering and fidelity to the testimony of "Yahshua as our Lord and Savior." Even their persecutors (unbelievers) are called to salvation through repentance and faith.

In this conflict, Yahshua the Lamb has already won the decisive victory through his sacrificial death, but his church continues to be assaulted by Satan, in its death throes, through persecution, false teaching, and the allurement of material affluence and cultural approval.

As revealed in a study throughout Scripture, the events of the end time follow the Rapture of the church and culminate in the second coming of Christ. Immediately after the Rapture of the church, there will be a time period which may be called a period of preparation. In this period there will emerge a ten nation group forming if not already formed a political unit in the Middle East. A world dictator will emerge who will gain control first of three nations and then of all ten nations (cf. Dan. 7: 8, 2425). From this position of political power *he will be able to enter into a covenant* with Israel, bringing the seven year countdown culminating in the Second Coming of Christ Jesus.

The climax will be the second coming of Christ. Revelation 618 deals with the last seven years or, more specifically, the last three and a half years preceding the Second Coming. *The wrath of God will commence with the breaking of the seals.*

Though many have attempted alternate views, probably the best approach is the view that the seven seals are the major events, or time periods, that out of the seventh seal will come a series of events described as seven trumpets, and out of the seventh trumpet will come a series of seven bowls of wrath: devastating judgments on the world just preceding the Second Coming. The effect is a crescendo of judgments coming with increased severity and in increasing tempo as the Second Coming of our Lord and Savior approaches.

The First Seal: World Conquest

The "*World government begins*" at the middle of the seven years. The antichrist comes to power, leading to war.

The Second Seal: War

In the reference to war, it is not necessary to presume that this has in mind a particular war but rather that there are a series of wars in the end time. The pursuit of conquest brings bloodshed.

The Third Seal: Famine

The aftermath of war, which apparently continues to some extent throughout this entire period, brings famine, especially in the areas where war has devastated their crops. A heavenly voice comments on the scales' significance, citing inflated grain prices (8 to 10 times more than normal). Siege and continuous disruption of commercial routes will produce scarcity, driving prices extremely high.

The Fourth Seal: Death

Their authority to kill is limited to a fourth of the entire earth: God's providence restrains both his own wrath and humanity's violence. If the earth's population at the time this occurs is 6 billion, one fourth would mean the loss of life for 1.5 billion of the entire world's population. This would be more than if all of the people in North America, Central America, and South America were all killed within moments. It still will not equal what is described here. The death of a fourth of the entire earth would be a "great tribulation," "such as has not been from the beginning of the world until now." *The "world" is headed for unprecedented trouble*, are you ready? Or should I say are you saved?

The Fifth Seal: Martyrs

The Lamb will restrain his wrath against his witnesses' assailants until the last martyr has been slain. Rev. 20: 4; John saw the souls of those who had been beheaded for the testimony of Yahshua and for the word of God, and those who had not worshiped the beast or its image and had not received its mark on their foreheads or their hands. Speculation has highly risen from society in the United States in relevance to government internment camps that are already built throughout this nation for the purpose of detaining U.S. citizens for whatever reason the government wishes. This time it will not be like it was in World War II, instead of getting out after two and one-half years, the only way out will be through martyrdom, exactly what the word of God says. This is just another sign showing society across the world how close we really are to "the end times."

At least those that were martyred for standing up for Yahshua will have eternal life in the kingdom of heaven. But the ones that rejected Yahshua, and accepted the antichrist and received the mark of the beast, will receive God's wrath for eternity (Rev. 19: 2020: 3, 10).

Revelation 21: 78; the one who conquers will have this heritage, and I will be his God and he will be my son. But as for the cowardly, the faithless, the detestable, as for murderers, the sexually immoral, sorcerers, idolaters, and all liars, their portion will be in the lake that burns with fire and sulfur, which is the second death.

"Those who obey are a royal priesthood for the Lord (Rev. 1: 6; 5: 9, 10) and will reign with Him (Rev. 20: 4, 6)."
The Sixth Seal: Catastrophic Judgment

Revelation 6: 12‑17; I looked, and behold, there was a great earthquake, and the sun became black as sackcloth, the full moon became like blood, and the stars of the sky fell to earth as the fig tree sheds its winter fruit when shaken by a gale. The sky vanished like a scroll that is being rolled up, and every mountain and island was removed from its place. Then the kings of the earth and the great ones and the generals and the rich and the powerful, and everyone, slave and free, hid themselves in the caves and among the rocks of the mountains, calling to the mountains and rocks, "Fall on us and hide us from the face of him who is seated on the throne, and from the wrath of the Lamb, for the *great day of the wrath has come,* and who can stand?"

The luminaries that have marked earth's times since creation (Gen. 1: 14) will be removed. All of this communicates the "truth" that "the end has arrived." Though this scene is not the final judgment as recorded in Revelation 16 under the seventh bowl of wrath, it indicates that the entire last three and a half years up to the second coming of Christ will be a period *of unprecedented trial* and *trouble for the world* as God deals in direct judgment on the world and all of its sin.

"For the church to be forced to endure such a dramatic judgment can hardly be described as a blessed hope."
The question raised at the close of chapter 6, "who can stand?" (Rev. 6: 17) made clear that only those who respond to the grace of God would be able to have a "victorious" climax, only those who are saved conquer and are victorious.

The Seventh Seal: The Sounding of the Trumpets

If you are a child of God, you have been *sealed by the Holy Spirit to be delivered to Christ* when the church goes out of the world before the Great Tribulation Period. This is what is called "the blessed hope" of the church.

The seven trumpets will bring us to the full intensity of the Great Tribulation. The seven seals bring judgments, which are the natural results of the activities of sinful man apart from God. The six seals bring the judgment of nature. The seven trumpets reveal that is directly and supernaturally judging a rebellious race.

Revelation 8: 1: When He had opened the seventh seal; there was silence in heaven about the space of half an hour.
Absolute silence for such a period was ominous and an indication of *"terrifying events*

yet to come." The effect is a grand crescendo, which indicates that each judgment will come with *increased severity* and rapidity in the time just before the Second Coming of Yahshua. As in the case of the first four seals broken, so the first four trumpets form a unit, and one follows the other in somewhat complementary fashion. Visions of woe initiated by the last three trumpets disclose *intensified demonic activity* and global violence as the consummation approaches, at which time; "the kingdom of the world" will have "become the kingdom of our Lord Yahshua (Rev. 11: 15), and every rebel (unbelievers) against his reign will endure eternal condemnation and severe punishment. Therefore *fire from the alter,* from which the saints' prayers rise, will be flung to earth in judgment, indicating that the saints prayers are answered.

The Seven Trumpets of 8: 711:19
Restrained judgments from heaven are sent in response to the saints' prayers.
- Trumpet 1 – Rev. 8: 7; hail, fire, and blood cast on land – one third burned.
- Trumpet 2 – Rev. 8: 89; burning mountain cast into the sea – one third bloodied.
- Trumpet 3 – Rev. 8: 1011; burning stars fall on rivers and springs – one third embittered.
- Trumpet 4 – Rev. 8: 12; sun, moon, and stars – one third darkened.

- Trumpet 5 – Rev. 9: 1-11; (the first woe commences) demons from the Abyss (their king 'Apollyon').
- Trumpet 6 – Rev. 9: 13-21; (the second woe is mentioned) invasion from the east – one third of mankind killed.
- Trumpet 7 – Rev. 11: 15-19; (the third woe is sounded) kingdom of world becomes kingdom of God.

Woe, woe, woe. "The last three trumpets signify escalating judgments on rebellious humanity as the clock ticks the end approaches closer and closer." The increase of demonic activity, plunging rebellious humans into desperation, as the era of God's patient restraint draws to a close. *"Satan can do nothing apart from God's permission."*

Demonic spirits (with Satan as their leader, v.11), released to "torment their own worshipers" (v. 20), who serve their king, the "Destroyer" ('Apollyon'). Satan's demonic hordes "wage war against his own human subjects."

Although those unrepentant unbelievers that rebel against God have been tortured by the very demons they worshiped, the survivors will take no warning from these final trumpet blasts. "The mystery of God will be fulfilled" as mentioned in the scriptures (Rev. 10: 7; cf. 1 Cor. 15: 52; 1 Thess. 4: 16), and *"the last opportunity to repent will be history"* (Rev. 9; 20-21).

Events That Occur at Midnight

Exodus 12: 2930; at *midnight*, (vs. 30) there was not a house where someone was not dead.

Job 34: 16; 34:20; "If you have understanding, hear this; listen to what I say. (Vs. 20) In a moment they die; at *midnight* the people are shaken and pass away, and the mighty are taken away by no human hand.

Judgment on the Nations

Psalm 110: 16; "The Lord says, sit at my right hand, until I make your enemies your footstool." (Vs. 4) The Lord has sworn and will not change his mind. (Vs. 5) he will shatter kings on the day of his wrath. (Vs. 6) He will execute judgment among the nations, filling them with corpses; he will shatter chiefs over the wide earth.

"Many teachers of scripture have mentioned that Psalm 110 would be relevant to the year 2010."

Isaiah 34: 16; "For the Lord is enraged against all the nations, and furious against their entire host; *he has devoted them to destruction, has given them over for slaughter.*"

Isaiah (continued)

(Vs. 3): "Their slain shall be cast out, and the stench of their corpses shall rise; the mountains shall flow with their blood." (Vs. 4) "All their host of heaven shall rot away, and the skies roll up like a scroll." (Vs. 6) "The Lord has a sword; it is sated with blood."

Zechariah 14: 12; *"Their flesh will rot while they are still standing on their feet," "their eyes will rot in their sockets, and their tongues will rot in their mouths."*

Other Occurrences at Midnight

Matthew 25: 1; "But at *midnight* there was a cry, 'Here is the bridegroom! Come out to meet him."
Cross Reference

1 Thessalonians 4: 1518; "For this we declare to "you" by a word from the Lord, that we who are "*alive*," who are left until the coming of the Lord, will not precede those who have fallen asleep." For the Lord himself will descend from heaven with a cry of command, with the voice of an archangel, and with the sound of the trumpet of God. And the dead in Christ will rise first. "Then we who are "*alive*," who are left, will be "*caught up*" together with them in the clouds to *meet the Lord in the air*, and so we will always be with the Lord. Therefore encourage one another with these words.

Mark 13: 35; "Therefore stay awake (on guard) for you do not know when the master of the house

will come, in the evening, or at *midnight*," .....
"Stay on guard or be ready."

Events That Are Predicted In Relevance to the Nations

- The United Nations had organized the first step toward *world government or a One World Order* in 1946. In which CIA agent Ernest Garcia was present at that meeting.
- Israel is formed as a recognized nation in 1948; a historical and biblical event takes place.
- Europe is rebuilt after World War II, setting the stage for its role in the future of the Revived Roman Empire.
- Now comes the rise of Russia as a world military and a strong political world power.
- The world movements such as the Common Market and the "Renown World Bank" set the stage for the grand finally for future (which is now currently under way) lawless political and financial events.
- Red China has become a military power, with unprecedented amount of soldiers.
- The Middle East and the nation of Israel become the focus of worldwide tension (all eyes are on Israel today).
- The Arab oil embargo in 1973 results in world recognition of the power of wealth and energy in the Middle East.

- On October 14, 2009 China and Russia announced $3.5 billion worth of trade agreements and reaffirmed their commitment to a huge *natural gas* deal (wealth and energy control).
- Lack of a powerful political leader prevents the Middle East from organizing as a political power.
- The Rapture of the church removes such a major deterrent to expansion of political and financial power of the Mediterranean world.
- The rise of a new leader in the Middle East who later is identified as the Antichrist who secures power over first three nations and then all ten nations, as he units them into a Mediterranean confederacy.
- This new Mediterranean leader (the antichrist) imposes a peace settlement for seven years on Israel; a peace covenant is currently being negotiated.
- Russian army accompanied by several other nations invades Israel and the invaders are destroyed by judgment from God. (No matter if Israel attacks or does not attack Iran's nuclear facilities, the Gog and Magog war of Ezekiel 38 and 39 "will take place").
- The peace settlement in the Middle East will be broken.
- Just after the Gog and Magog war the Antichrist then becomes the world dictator.

- The world dictator (the antichrist) claims to be God and demands that all worship him or be placed in camps and be killed.
- The world dictator defiles the temple in Jerusalem.
- The commencing of the terrifying judgments of the Great Tribulation described in the seals, trumpets, and bowls of the wrath of God will be poured out on the entire world as written in the book of Revelation.
- Worldwide discontent at the rule of the world dictator resulting from many catastrophes causing rebellion and gathering of the world's armies in the Middle East to fight it out with Armageddon as the center of the conflict, while death continues to spread.
- Second coming of Christ occurs accompanied by the armies from heaven (the saints).
- The armies of the world lead by the antichrist (Satan) attempt to fight the armies from heaven but are totally destroyed by the breath of God.
- Yahshua's millennial reign will now be established, the climaxing judgments on all the unsaved and the final disposition of Gentile political power.
- The blessing of salvation that the saved receive from both Jews and Gentiles when they are placed in the "New Jerusalem" in

the earth where they will spend eternity with Yahshua.

The Fall of Lucifer (Satan, The World Dictator, The Antichrist)

Isaiah 14: 1221; "How you are fallen from heaven, O Lucifer, son of the morning! *How* you are cut down to the ground, you who weakened the nations! For you have said in your heart: I will ascend into heaven, I will exalt my throne above the stars of God; I will also sit on the mount of the congregation on the farthest sides of the north; I will ascend above the heights of the clouds, *"I will be like the Most High."* Yet you shall be brought down to Sheol, to the lowest depths of the Pit. "Those who see you will gaze at you, *and* consider you, *saying*: *Is* this the man who made the earth tremble, who shook kingdoms, who made the world as a wilderness and destroyed its cities, *Who* did not open the house of his prisoners?" All the kings of the nations, all of them, sleep in glory, everyone in his own house; but you are cast out of your grave *like* the garments of those who are slain, thrust through with a sword, who go down to the stones of the pit, like a corpse trodden underfoot.

"You will not be joined with them in burial, because you have destroyed your land and slain your people." The brood of evildoers shall never be named. "Prepare slaughter for his children, because of the iniquity of their fathers."

Fallen from heaven is a figure of speech meaning cast down from an exalted "political position." Yahshua said, "And you, who are exalted to heaven, will be brought down to Hades" (Luke 10: 15), and apparently with the same meaning, "I saw Satan fall like lightning from heaven" (Luke 10: 18). "This is an apt summary of the *failed goal* of the world dictator (Satan, the antichrist) who wanted to grasp universal and eternal domination and fails."

I will be like the Most High is the most outrageous of the arrogant desires of this world dictator (Satan). He wanted to surpass the Most High, a term for the Lord that is often used in connection with the nations of the world (see Ps. 87: 5; 91: 1, 9; 92: 1).

Ezekiel 28: 2; "Because your heart is lifted up, and you say, I *am* a god, I sit in the seat of gods, in the midst of the seas, yet you *are* a *'man'* not a god, though you set in your heart as the heart of a god."

Ezekiel 28: 1415; "You *were* the anointed cherub who covers; I established you; You were on the holy mountain of God; You walked back and forth in the midst of fiery stones. You *were* perfect in your ways from the day you were created, till iniquity was found in you.

Greed and pride lead to materialism, violence, and sinfulness in business and religion.

Isaiah 24: 2122; "It shall come to pass in that day *that* the Lord will punish on high the host of exalted ones, and on the earth the kings of the earth." They will be gathered together, as prisoners are gathered in the pit, and will be shut up in the prison; after many days they will be punished.

Isaiah 29: 57; "Yes, it shall be in an instant, suddenly." You will be punished by the Lord of hosts with thunder and earthquake and great noise, *with* storm and tempest and the flame of devouring fire. Ezekiel 28: 19; " You have become a horror, and *shall be* no more forever."

Was Satan Unleashed In the CIA

John 10: 10; "Satan comes to steal and kill and destroy."

Through *"Project Sunshine"* Satan worked through the government to *"steal our children,"* Satan worked through the government to *"kill our children,"* Satan is working through the "One World Government" to *"destroy all of God's children."*

Revelation 12: 9; "the great *dragon* was thrown down, that ancient serpent, who is called the *devil and Satan*, the deceiver of the world – he was thrown down to earth, and his angels were thrown down with him."

John 12: 31; "Now is the judgment of this world; now the *prince* (ruler, Satan) of this world will be cast out." 16: 810; "And when Yahshua has come, He will convict the world of sin, and of righteousness, and of judgment: of sin because they do not believe in Me."

John 16: 810 (continued)

"Of righteousness, because I go to My Father and you see Me no more; of judgment, because the *prince* (ruler, Satan) of this world is judged."

"*Of judgment:* Satan, the *prince*, the ruler of this world, rules in the hearts of unregenerate people and "blinds their minds" (1Corinthians 2: 68). Satan was judged at the Cross, and the Holy Spirit would convince people of *"the judgment to come." Satan has been judged, so all who side with him will be judged with him.* "There is now no room or 'time' for neutrality, for *he who hesitates has lost.*" "A person is either a *"child"* of God or a *"child"* of Satan."

One point of prophetic revelation that it is essential to clarify in dealing with *Israel* in the tribulation is the identity of the "woman" (Israel) in Rev. 12. The major emphasis in Rev. 11: 19; 20: 15; is the attack of Satan against the people with whom God is dealing with at the time. "This '*attack*' comes in chapter thirteen through the *beasts*, who offers a *false Messiah* and a *false fulfillment of the Abraham covenant.* It comes in chapter seventeen and eighteen through an *apostate religious system*, which *falsely claims to* be the Kingdom of God. It comes in chapter nineteen *"through the alliance of nations"* which is formed against this people and their King, which *the Lord destroys at His coming.* Satan is the prince of the world – its virtual ruler. *"The Revived Roman Empire is the instrument through which he (Satan) acts."*

"This shows us that *Satan is seeking a "governmental authority"* over the woman's (Israel) "remnant" (12: 7), which *authority rightly belongs to Yahshua Himself."*

The thief, that is, a false shepherd, cares only about feeding himself, not building up the flock or caring for others. He *steals* in order to *kill* them, thus *destroying* part of the sheep. But Yahshua has come to benefit the sheep. Yahshua gives *life,* which is not constricted but overflowing. The thief takes *life; "Yahshua gives life to the full."*

"The Journey of Life"

"The journey of *life* started from the origins of heaven and earth, of the human race, including the creation of matter, space, and time, as God being the creator of all things that exist." The awesome beauty and power of God's creation by *His word,* reflects the *"breathtaking beauty"* of what we know *of His appearance* described in the blessed Holy Scriptures of God. And yet *"He opened His arms at the cross to embrace us with His love,"* and offers us to partake of the wonderful *"blessed gift"* of *eternal life* with *"our blessed hope"* Yahshua. There is one word that describes all of this awesome beauty and that word is *"Love"* and He offers it, all of *"His love to you."* Will you take it, and embrace "Him" in return?"

"Only through Faith in "Yahshua" are you saved, and only through Love, you will have Hope, He Love's you."

The research, documents, and interviews were established for the purpose of education and awareness of *"terrifying events yet to come,"* which are relevant to Biblical Eschatology, which is the "capstone of systematic theology." The field of investigation must necessarily embrace both fulfilled and unfulfilled prophecy, the former providing an important guide to the character of prediction embraced in the latter.

January 20th, 2012

Iran Calls for Israel to Be "Punished"
Senior Iranian official Larijani says; *demands* retribution for assassination of nuclear scientist attributed to Israel.
    "This may set the stage for "Gog's war spoken about in Ezekiel 38 and 39 of the Holy Scriptures.

Possible Peace Treaty in the Near Future with Israel and Palestine

"The moment the peace covenant is confirmed the 7yr. tribulation will then commence, but not only that the world dictator known as the antichrist will confirm the peace treaty." – Daniel 9:27.

The Economy

The economy is collapsing 'deliberately' worldwide by the one world order for the purpose of setting the stage for the rise of the antichrist whom will declare that he can save the economy worldwide and then implement the mark of the beast 666. Those that receive this mark will lose their soul to Satan and obtain eternal life in Hell. – Revelation 13: 17.

17

"Deceived," in Jesus name

John 5: 43-44

"I have come in my Father's name, and you do not receive me. If another comes in his own name, you will receive him. How can you believe, when you receive glory from one another and do not seek the "glory" that comes from the "only" God?"

Matthew 1:21

"She will bear a son, and "you shall call his name Yahshua," for he will save his people from their sins."

The Angel messenger could not have given the name Jesus to Mary and Joseph for the simple reason the name, JESUS, did not exist then – no one, not the Romans, nor the Greeks, and most of all not the Jews had ever heard the name Jesus before.

The letter "J" did not exist at the time our Savior was named by the angelic messenger from heaven. In fact this letter "J" , as we are familiar with today, came into being around the 14th to 15th century, a corruption of the Greek, and Roman /

Latin. It was used interchangeably with the letter i and was not considered a consonant until around the 17th century, then coming into its own as a letter and pronounced completely different with a sound of its own. The name of JESUS could not have existed at the time of the Saviors birth, much less at the time of His death.

The name "Jesus" is an English transliteration of the Latin (*Iesus*) which in turn comes from the Greek name Iesous. The name has also been translated into English as "Joshua."
Since most scholars hold that Jesus was an Aramaic – speaking Jew living in Galilee around 30 AD/CE, it is highly improbable that he had a Greek personal name.

The name, the identity, of the God of the Old Testament is presented in the Hebrew writings of the Holy Scriptures by the hand of the scribes of Israel, writing out of the name of the Living Creator over six thousand times (*6,800, the count varies some, depending on who is doing the counting*) They did not change the name, no, but they did something in their own righteousness that ultimately denied that part of their mission to the world, *making the name of God of Israel great in all the world* (Romans 9:17, Ex 9:16). They were to perpetuate the record, which they did, and His Name, which they did not. Instead they covered the Name, they profaned the Name and identity of the greatest force in all creation – instead of glorifying His Name they put up vowel points to indicate the pronunciation of a different word or term, a term that is equivalent to a common term,

"Lord" (Master, or Boss). They did this attempting to avoid saying, or using the sacred Name of the Creator as being too holy to pronounce and to keep from violating the third commandment (Exodus 20:7), at least that is their excuse, and remember I said, in their own righteousness. Our Creator says, *"He will make His name great among nations"* (*Mal 1:11, 14 – John 12:28*). Why? Because Israel would not and did not. It was turned over to the Christians to do it and they did, in the beginning, then as soon as the governing powers of this world adopted Christianity as the state religion that came to an end and like the Jews they found ways to deny His Name by ignoring it. It is a certainty that the "Adversary" (Satan) as the "god of this world" (2Cor 4:4) clouded the minds in this project of covering up and hiding His Holy Name, and the Name by which we must all be saved "Yahshua" (Acts 4:12).

The letters the scribes copied have their counterpart in the English letters, YHWH. They, the Israelite scribes and priest, mistakenly decided not to say, or pronounce it, (The Name) making "The Name of the Mighty God of no use, they profaned the name. It is the Christians that have done the most damage to the Sacred Name, for they have used substitution, they have, in the wisdom of man, helped the Jew to profane (*treat as useless, show contempt, discard – Strong's #2490, to bore, to wound, to dissolve*) the name. The Jews were accused of profaning the Holy Name, yet they did not remove it from their writings (Ezekiel 36:20-23), but the Christians did.

Ezekiel 36:20-23

"But when they came to the nations, wherever they came, *they profaned my holy name*, in that people said of them, "These are the people of the Lord, and yet they had to go out of the land." But I had concern for my holy name, which the house of Israel had profaned among the nations to which they came."

"Therefore say to the house of Israel, Thus says the Lord God: It is not for your sake, O house of Israel, that I am about to act, but for the sake of my holy name, which you have profaned among the nations to which you came. And I will vindicate the holiness of my great name, which has been profaned among the nations, and which you have profaned among them. And the nations will know that I am the Lord, declares the Lord God, when through you I vindicate my holiness before their eyes."

The Bible of the Israelite descendants of the Tribe of Yahudah in the first century AD consisted of 12-20 scrolls of varying lengths. None of these scrolls contained the writings that are now in the Roman Catholic "Greek New Testament."

Marcion a wealthy Greek heretic would combine (most probably) the Gospel of Luke with some of Paul's writings that would eventually become the replacement for Yahshua's Bible. We now have a Canon (a standard) and authority that would eventually replace the authority of Yahshua's Bible for the developing Messianic Community.

After Yahweh makes contact with the natural realm by His messengers, and imparts His message to us, the resultant message is called a "revelation." The accumulation of "revelations" over time becomes the cornerstone of what a community or groups of people come to understand about Yahweh. Such a group of revelations is called the community's "Canon" or "standard." Their "Bible' in turn becomes the authority for their Religious Belief System of the community. Their Religious Belief System now becomes the "Standard" of measurement for all other religious data, information and practice of the community. The Canon becomes the authority to judge and correct all other Canons and all other religious beliefs (regardless of whether it is right or wrong, true or false).

Question: Who determined the Standard?

Unfortunately since the death and resurrection of Yahshua the Roman Catholic Church has for the most part determined the "Standard" of Christianity to be used in evaluating revelation, both past and present. Little consideration is given to Yahshua and His teachings as the true "Standard." Few seem to realize that in reality Yahshua is the "Standard" and His Religious Belief System (his teachings and interpretations) which happen to be that of historical "Israelism" found only in the Tanakh (the Hebrew Scriptures) make for the correct Canon and the true Bible, both yesterday and today!

We can easily see that a new "Standard" becomes a potential source of enormous power for those who control it (as newly organized religions). Priests, preachers, ministers, translators, evangelists, rabbis, etc. have used such "Standards" to control and manipulate people to do their organization's bidding, even if it may not be Yahweh's.

However, it is a false system that now begins to amalgamate both Israelite and non-Israelite into one new religious system. This new religious system well, in the span of three hundred years, becomes a Hellenized (Greek influenced – Roman) Religious Belief System which would begin to serve as the replacement foundation for the Assembly – Ekklesia (called-out-ones of Yahshua). This false counterfeit "Greek influenced" replacement Roman system of Christianity remains in existence today as the Canon (Bible) for most of Modern Christianity.

The Roman Catholic Canon consisted of two major divisions, which contained 75 books instead of the original 38-39 of Yahshua's Bible. Notice very carefully that those who were in charge of creating the Roman Catholic Canon chose to alter the Bible of Yahshua, and add to it, thereby violating Yahweh's law.

They destroyed the primary authority of the Torah by lumping all the books of Yahshua's Bible into one group which was then the title of "Old Testament," thus signifying that Yahweh was giving something "new" to replace the "old." They added nine new books to the books of Yahshua's Bible: Tobit, Judith, I and II Maccabees, The Book of Wisdom, Ecclesiasticus, Baruch, Susanna, and Bel and the Dragon. They created an entirely new division of Canonical books which they called "The Greek New Testament" conveniently replacing the Bible Yahshua used with the Bible that the Popes have approved.

You guessed it, **"a new revelation."** It would be this "new revelation," based upon the old revelation that was to be added to, deleted, changed, and reinterpreted into the replacement Canon of the Roman Catholic Church. This would give them power and authority to replace the religion of Yahshua with the religion of Jeroboam (which Yahweh hates). It is religion of Jeroboam that has come to us today as a mixture of Gentile Paganism and "Israelism."

The new variations in Canons produced very erratic religious practices and inconsistencies. The Roman Catholic leaders felt they had better quickly take action concerning such diversity. They quickly went to work to decide and identify which writings were considered sacred or inspired. This continued in Christianity for over 300 years. Finally, the official Canon of the Roman Catholic Church was agreed upon in 380 CE, over 240 years after Marcion and 350 years after Yahshua.

The last two books to admitted to the Roman Catholic Canon were Hebrews and Revelation. The debate over inclusion of Revelation lasted over 600 years, and continues to a large extent even today! The newly created Roman Catholic Canon provided the authority for the Roman Catholic Church to propagate their anti-Yahshua and anti-Israelite doctrines and dogmas. The power of the Roman government gave the Roman Catholic Church the power to deal with those who opposed them. At last the embarrassment could stop, now there was a single Roman Catholic Canon and it would remain the sole authority for the next 700 years.

Matthew 24:4

"And Yahshua answered and said unto them, Take heed that no man deceive you. For many shall come in my name, saying, I am Christ; and shall deceive many."

He says He will make the Father's Name known to those given to Him (Hebrews 2:12, John 17:25).

Satan used what appeared to be good reasoning and logic, feeding man's wisdom, in order to profane the use, or lack there-of, the Creator's Holy Name. This has been a process that Satan has had in the works from the beginning.

My brothers and sisters there is some serious research suggesting the name "Jesus" is connected to the infamous 666. Try this test, pull the vowels from the name Jesus and you have, Jss, or Iss. Now, pronounce it. Did you know that the number for the Egyptian goddess Isis was 666? This connection can be found under the work of E.W. Bullinger, in his book "Number in Scripture," in the foot note on page 49.

SIX HUNDRED AND SIXTY SIX

Is "the number of a name" (Rev 13:17,18). The gematria of the name of Antichrist is the number 666. But this number has, we believe, a far deeper reference to and connection with the secret mysteries of the ancient religions, which will be again manifested in connection with the last great apostasy.

If six is the number of secular or human perfection, then 66 is a more emphatic expression of the same fact, and 666 is the concentrated expression of it; 666 is therefore the perfection; the culmination of human pride in independence of God and opposition to His Christ.

The number, however, has to be computed (yhfizw (pseephizo), to reckon, to calculate, not merely to count or enumerate). See Revelation 13:18.

666 was the *secret symbol* of the ancient pagan mysteries connected with the worship of

the Devil. It is today the secret connecting link between those ancient mysteries and their modern revival in Spiritualism, Theosophy, etc. The societies for the re-union of Christendom, and the Conferences for the re-union of the Churches, are alike parts of the same great movement, and are all making for and are signs of the coming Apostasy. During this age, "Separation" is God's word for His people, and is the mark of *Christ*; while "union" and "re-union" is the mark of *Antichrist.*

The number 6 was stamped on the old mysteries. The great secret symbol consisted of the three letters SSS, because the letter S in the Greek alphabet was the symbol of the figure 6, a = 1, b = 2, g = 3, d = 4, e = 5, but when it comes to 6, another letter was introduced! Not the next --- the sixth letter (z, zeta) --- but a different letter, a peculiar form of S, called "*stigma*" (V). Now the word stigma (stigma) means a *mark*, but especially a mark by a brand as burnt upon slaves, cattle, or soldiers, by their owners or masters; on devotees who thus branded themselves as belonging to their gods.

This letter is becoming familiar to us now; and it is not pleasant when we see many thus marked (ignorantly, no doubt) with the symbolical "S," "S," especially when it is connected, not with "salvation," but with *judgment,* and is associated with "blood and fire," which in Joel 2;30 31, is given as one of the awful signs "before the great and terrible day of the Lord."

Apostasy is before us. The religion of Christ has, in the past, been *opposed* and *corrupted,* but when it once comes, as it has come in our day, to be *burlesqued,* there is nothing left but judgment. There is nothing more the enemy can do before he proceeds to build up the great apostasy on the ruins of true religion, and thus prepare the way for the coming of the Judge,

It will be seen from this that the number 666 is very far-reaching, and is filled with a meaning deeper, perhaps, than anything we have yet discovered. One thing, however, is certain, and that is, that the triple 6 marks the culmination of man's opposition to God in the person of the coming Antichrist.

Further illustration of the significance of this number is seen in the *fact* that; "The Duration of the Old Assyrian Empire" was 666 years before it was conquered by Babylon. "Jerusalem Was Trodden Down" by the Roman Empire exactly 666 years from the battle of Actium, BC 31, to the Saracen conquest in AD 636,* And according to Daniel 2 and Revelation 13 and 17, Rome is the last of four Gentile world empires and rules to the consummation.

THERE ARE THREE MEN

Which stand out in Scripture as the avowed enemies of God and of His people. Each is branded with this number six that we may not miss their significance:

1. GOLIATH, whose height was 6 cubits, and he had 6 pieces of armor;* his spear's head weighed 600 shekels of iron (1 Sam 17:4-7).
2. NEBUCHADNEZZAR, whose "image" of the prophet Daniel which he sat up, was 60 cubits high and 6 cubits broad (Dan 3:1), and which was worshipped when the music was heard from 6 specified instruments,** and
3. ANTICHRIST, the pope of Rome, the number of whose name, VICARIVS, FILII DEI (Vicar of the Son of God) counts to 666.

*This letter V (called Stigma) is used for the number 6. Why this letter and number should be thus associated we cannot tell, except that both are intimately connected with ancient Egyptian "mysteries." The three letters SSS (in Greek SSS) were the symbols of *Isis,* which is thus connected with 666. Indeed the expression of this number, CxV, consists of the *initial* and *final* letters of the word Xristo V (*Christos*), Christ, viz, X and V, with the symbol of the serpent between them, X—x—V. number04.htm.

"The "Keeper of the Bridge," that is the bridge between man and Satan; and in recognition of this, the priest wore crowns in the form of a head of a fish," (the Catholic Church).

Acts 4:12

"There is "salvation" in no one else, for there is no other name under heaven given among men by which we must be saved."

Jesus comes from the Greek Iesus, a name that dates 1,000 B.C. representing the "Son of Zeus," and the Ur-Babylonian Eagle God.
Diana (Juno, Victoria, Nike, Minerva, Venus, Isis) Zeus (Jupiter), and Iesus (Iesius) = Pagan Trinity. The translations were in Latin and the Iesus, son of Zeus, the Eagle God, became the Catholic "Jesus."
Eagle – God Son's 666 Greek name is "Iesus" (i.e. = son of, and sus = Zeus) "Jesus." This is the 666 *name* to overcome and repent of in Revelation.
According to Masonic books, their Double Headed Eagle God actually represents Satan and Son. "Iesus-Jesus" image (idol) is the Eagle (God), according to a "Bishop/priest over Greek Orthodox (Syrian) Church" off Habbad St., in Old City, Jerusalem.
Keep in mind that the Jesus image (idol) is the "Eagle Son" of "Zeus."

Daniel 11:31

"Forces from him shall appear and profane the temple and fortress, and shall take away the regular burnt offering. And shall set up the abomination that makes desolate."

"Syrian" forces came back to suppress the Jewish religious practices in earnest. "They entered the temple" (possibly called the temple and fortress because it was the religious strength of the people). They stopped the regular burnt offering, and on the fifteenth day of Chislev (December), 167 BC (1 Macc. 1:59), they set up an alter or idol (image) devoted to "Zeus" (*Jupiter*) in the temple (the abomination that makes desolate; cf. Dan. 9:27; 12:11).

"Now do you see how the Catholic Church and Daniel 11:31, have relevance and/or resemble each other, at the End Times." Now tell me, where does the antichrist rise from? Now tell me what idol or image may be "set up for the abomination that makes desolate?"

Revelation 22:18-19

"I warn everyone who hears the words of the prophecy of this book: if anyone adds to them, God will add the plagues described in this book, and if anyone takes away from the words of the book of this prophecy.
God will take away his share in the tree of life and in the holy city, which are described in this book."

Look how many ministers deceive people, by using the name of Jesus for salvation! The work of Satan!

Hosea 4:6

"My people are destroyed for lack of knowledge; because you have rejected knowledge, I reject you from being a priest to me."

Acts 2:21

"It shall come to pass that everyone who calls upon the "<u>name</u>" of the Lord shall be saved."

John 8:32

"You will know the <u>truth</u>, and the <u>truth</u> will set you free."

(This is the Love of Yahweh, and the sacrifice of His son Yahshua, for you). Amen to that.

But you must remember, the facts are already recorded, just open your Bible and you will see the name of Jesus there, and you know who placed that name there (the Catholic Church). The proof is before your eyes. Now repent, and call out on his true name (Yahshua) and you shall be "saved." The choice is yours, at least someone cares (author Marcel L. Garcia Jr.) I pray for your salvation.

2 Peter 1:21

"For no prophecy was ever produced by the will of man, but men spoke from God as they were carried along by the Holy Spirit."

The Holy Scriptures tells us that God inspired man through the Holy Spirit, perfectly and accurately, to write the true words of God almighty, for the church. The church did not "inspire" anything. The holy scriptures were produced by men of God, not by "the church." But they were produced for the church.

The Roman Catholic church has had only one aim from its earliest, pagan and political origins in this life and that is: To destroy the true Christians, and to destroy their Bible. That is why the Catholic church substituted the corrupt Alexandrian perversions of scripture, instead of using the preserved, prophetic and apostolic Words of God as found in Antioch of Syria, where "the disciples were first called Christians" (Acts 11:26). That is why they also added the Alexandrian writings we now call "Apocrypha" to their perverted bible. This is an indication to why they used their Jesuits to infiltrate the Protestant Seminaries, Colleges and Bible Schools. Their Jesuits became the "teachers" and planted seeds of doubt in the Christians' minds. These doubt-ridden Christians then taught at other colleges and schools. All the while they planted that same seed of doubt of God's word in their students, Satan moves on.

The stage was set: Once people no longer believed in God's Preserved Words, they were ripe for destruction.

2 Th. 2:3

"Let no man deceive you by any means, for *that day shall not come,* except there come a falling away first, and that man of sin be revealed, the son of perdition."

Now, 120 years after the switch from God's Holy Word to the devil's lies (the King James abandoned for the Alexandrian texts), while pretending to "improve" our copies of God's words, they really set up the abandonment of God's words. Now almost every Bible in the English-speaking world (and most other languages) is just another re-translation of the Alexandrian *"polluted stream."*
Jeremiah 2:13

"For my people have committed two evils: they have forsaken me, the fountain of living waters, and hewed them out cisterns, broken cisterns that can hold no water."

And that is exactly the point: The bible spewed out by the Catholic church, which now almost all Protestants and other Christians use, ... *"simply doesn't hold water."*

Romans 1:16
"For I am not ashamed of the gospel, for it is the power of God for salvation to everyone who believes, to the Jew first and also to the Greek."

The rapid declension, which is the great mark of these last days, comes from an ignoring of this great principle. God is shut out, and man is exalted. Hence "the gospel of God" is being rapidly and almost universally superseded by the gospel of man, which is the gospel of sanitation, and indeed is now openly called *"Christian Socialism."* But it is a socialism *without Christ.* It does not and cannot end in any real good to man. It begins with man; it's object is to improve the old nature apart from God, and to reform the flesh; and the measure of its success is the measure in which man can become "good without "God."

Man's ways and thoughts are the opposite of God's. God says, *"Seek first."* Man says, "Take care of number one." He is in his own eyes "number one," and his great aim is to be independence of God.

Independence, in God, is His "glory." Independence in man is his sin, and rebellion, and shame.

Now, How Close Are We to the End Times?

Arutz Sheva – 7
www.IsraelNationalNews.com
Shevat 21, 5773, 01/02/13

Exclusive: A seat for the Pope at King David's Tomb

"*Israel seems to have sold Jerusalem to the Vatican*!!!"

An historic agreement has been drafted between Israel and the Vatican. The Israeli authorities have granted the Pope an official seat in the room where the Last Supper is believed to have taken place, on Mount Zion in Jerusalem, and where David and Solomon, Jewish kings of Judea, are considered by some researchers, to also be buried.

The Catholic Church has long wanted control over part of the area on Mt. Zion so as to turn it into an "international religious center" for Catholics. Now, after the Muslim Waqf authority expelled the Christians from the Temple Mount and turned it into a mosque, it's the turn of the Vatican to lay its hands on the Jewish Jerusalem.

The Custody of the Holy Land, the Franciscan order who, with Vatican approval, is in charge of the holy sites, campaigns with the Arabs against Israel.

Should the Vatican gain sovereignty over Mount of Zion, millions of Christian's pilgrims will flock to the site, and this will threaten the Israeli presence in the Old City's Jewish Quarter and Jewish access to the Western Wall.

The Vatican wants the Jews out of the Old City and apparently Israel's government is agreeing with them. Turning the Cenacle into an active church is also a way of desecrating the holiness of the site known as the Tomb of David. The Catholic Church wants Israel relinquishing sovereignty at the Western Wall and the Temple Mount.

Daniel 9:27

"He shall make a strong covenant with many for one week."

The peace treaty starts the tribulation!!! We must move quickly, in bringing others to Yahshua, this is the next headlines. Please look closely to the politicians involved.

The Jewish Press.com
News of the Jews & the world
Published: April 25th, 2013

"Peres and Pope to team up for Peace Process Resurrection"

Agenda includes the "eternal pursuit for peace in the Middle East.

Ansamed *news*
Monday, 17 June 2013

"Pope Francis is good shepherd," Patriarch of Constantinople Orthodox leader in historic visit to Francis' inauguration"
"This pope is a good shepherd of his faithful," the spiritual leader of the Orthodox Church, Bartholomew I, Ecumenical Patriarch of Constantinople, told ANSA.

The first time an Orthodox Pope has done so for almost a thousand years. "The Catholic Church needs a shepherd."
Ansamed *news*
Monday, 17 June 2013

"Pope: Bartholomew I, hope to unite Eastern churches and Rome, Francis can reform Vatican"
Pope Francis believes the reunification of the Orthodox and Rome Churches 1,000 years after the Great Schism of 1054 is possible. Bartholomew I, 73, has been since 1991 the spiritual leader of the Greek Orthodox Church, the first patriarch of Constantinople to be present at the inauguration of a new pontification since 1054.
"Pope Francis and Pope Bartholomew, according to Hurriyet, will meet in Jerusalem on January 4-6, 2014, during the Orthodox Christam, 50 years after the historic meeting between Paul VI and Patriarch Athenagoras."
Bringing the Eastern and Western Churches closer, one of Pope Francis' priorities.
Archbishop Bartholomew I of Constantinople said that he heard Pope Francis indicate that he (Pope Francis) was going to change the shape of the papacy.

What do we know of this Archbishop Bartholomew?

Bartholomew, Archbishop of Constantinople, *New Rome* and Ecumenical

Patriarch is the 270th successor of the 2,000 year-old local Christian Church founded by St. Andrew the Apostle.

He works to advance reconciliation among Catholic, Muslim and Orthodox communities, and is supportive of *peace* building measures to diffuse global conflict in the region.

The Ecumenical Patriarch has the historical and theological responsibility to initiate and coordinate actions among the Churches and numerous archdioceses in the old and "new worlds." He co-sponsored the *Peace* and Tolerance Conferences in Istanbul (1994-2006) bringing together Christians, Muslims and Jews.

The Ecumenical Patriarchate has existed in what was known as Asia Minor, modern-day Turkey, since the fourth century A.D. when Emperor Constantine moved the capital of the *"Roman Empire"* to Constantinople (new Istanbul), a city that he built. Bartholomew has led the world's 300 million Orthodox Christians, *"quietly bringing together major religious leaders"* and intervening in wars and conflicts and the environmental crisis.

Revelation 16:13-14

"And I saw out of the mouth of the dragon and out of the mouth of the beast and out of the mouth of the false prophet, three unclean spirits like frogs. For they were demonic spirits, performing signs, who go abroad to the kings of the whole world, to assemble them for battle on the great day of God the Almighty."

The head of the Orthodox Church worldwide, the Ecumenical Patriarch's full title is Archbishop of Constantinople, *New Rome* and Ecumenical Patriarch. When Constantinople became the seat of the *"Roman Empire," "all the principle teachings of Christianity"* were put down in "seven" ecumenical councils held in or near the city, the principle doctrine being the Nicene Creed set down in 325 A.D.

Ecumenical Patriarch Bartholomew convened "for the first time in history" the Primates of all the *world's* Orthodox Churches with the goal of a Pan-Orthodox Synod and a true expression of "unity," as well as the *"first ever World Clergy-Laity meeting of all Greek Orthodox under his jurisdiction."*

KEEP IN MIND, Daniel 11:32, the abomination that makes desolate, the alter or idol devoted to the *"Greek god known as Zeus."*
Did the Israeli Politicians Really Get Involved?
All information comes from documented reports:

Edgar Bronfman is in a league with Yossi Beilin and Shimon Peres: They all acted as agents for the Vatican while appearing to work for the benefit of the Jews!!!

After 15 whole years of Gaining Jewish confidence, first approaching the subject of land and church properties in Israel! It is noteworthy that the Vatican, despite claiming to NOT interfere with territorial and political issues, in fact CONSTANTLY INTERFERES and intervenes, through intrigue, letters, pressure on political leaders, etc.

In the summer of 1991, even before the labor party was in power, and before the Madrid Conference, the Church already approached Yossi Beilin, via the Meshumad Israeli Fr. David Yaeger, to start negotiations about Jerusalem; according to Yossi Beilin himself, the only thing that really interested the Church was properties, land, things, while Israel wanted recognition – and while the Diaspora Jews wanted freedom from persecution.

Most deceptively, a ILC Conference took place in Baltimore in 1992, in which the head of the Jewish delegation, "happened" to be Edgar Bronfman (CFR member), who simultaneously "happened" to interfere in the Israeli elections, By arranging meetings between Yossi Beilin and Arafat's men, to promise the PLO some sort of a state in "Palestine" in exchange for the Arab vote for the Labor Party in Israel! Bronfman, as agent of the Vatican, and acting as a go-between, actively interfered in the Israeli election process and helped elect Yitshak Rabin and Shimon Peres!
And the whole purpose of this choice was so that the transfer of Jerusalem and other properties to the Church could proceed!

The Vatican interfered with the Israeli elections, and then "used the Diaspora Jews to influence Israel"; also used the concerns of the

Diaspora Jews-anti-Semitism, and the concern of the Israeli Government-recognition of Israel, as bargaining chips "for the land of Israel"!

Right after putting Peres and Beilin in office, the Church got their cooperation to start the "transfer of Church properties to the Vatican." It seems that Rabin just "happened" to be part of the whole deal; an "expandable item," <u>an obstacle</u>, for all practical purposes.

That would certainly explain his murder in 1995, for all of those who "don't believe" the official version of his assassination, and "do believe that Peres was behind it." Peres, in other words, Rome, you decide.

Within one month of the election of Rabin and Peres in June 1992, in July, the Vatican already started "active negotiations about Church properties – illegal, secret and illegitimate, - with Yossi Beilin. Now don't forget that Yossi Beilin was Deputy Foreign Minister, and Shimon Peres was the Foreign Minister, so obviously Peres was in on the deal.

It is important to mention that these talks were "done in secret," and not approved by the Knesset, yet left "footprints" in the form of Documents Drafted, albeit with deception, I would even say under duress, and illegally.

What *"was not supposed to leave"* a footprint were the Parallel Talks of Shimon Peres going on directly with the Pope, about Church properties. Those talks took place at the Vatican between Peres and the Pope, or in form of "Secret" hand-delivered letters written by Peres, or later in 2006, in a letter from Olmert hand-delivered by Peres directly to the Pope.

With absolutely no media coverage in Israel, on December 30th, 1993, an *"historic agreement with the Vatican"* is publicly acknowledged. Called: "The Fundamental Agreement between the Holy See and the State of Israel," it declares:

"Mindful of the singular character and universal significance of the Holy Land. Aware of the unique nature of the relationship between the Catholic Church and the Jewish people, and of the historic process of reconciliation and growth in mutual understanding and friendship between Catholic and Jews";

"Having decided on 29 July 1992 to establish a 'Bilateral Permanent Working Commission,' in order to study and define together issues of common interest, and in view of normalizing their relations."

A letter from Peres to the Pope in September, 1993 in which Peres promised to "Internationalize Jerusalem," granting the UN political control of the Old City of Jerusalem, and the Vatican hegemony of the holy sites within.

Isaiah 28:14-18

Therefore hear the word of the Lord, you scoffers, who rule this people in Jerusalem! Because you have said, "We have made a covenant with death, and with hell we have an agreement, when the overwhelming whip passes through it will not come to us, for we have made lies our refuge, and in falsehood we have taken shelter." Vs14.

"Then your covenant with death will be annulled, and your agreement with hell will not stand; when the overwhelming scourge passes through, you will be beaten down by it." Vs18.

Jerusalem's leaders yielded to expediency for the sake of security. Without directly admitting it, they are taking refuge in deceit and falsehood. The Jerusalem leaders are simply trusting in other god's to save them from the coming scourge; this message of judgment would bring sheer terror.

On the 10th of September, 1993, just three days before the signing of the Oslo Accords Washington, the Italian newspaper *La Stampa* reported that then Foreign Minister Shimon Peres concluded a *secret deal* with the Vatican to hand over sovereignty of Jerusalem's Old City to the Vatican, the agreement and it was included in the *"secret clauses"* of the Declaration of Principles signed on September 13th, 1993 in Washington, DC.

In the same week that Israeli Foreign Minister and chief Oslo architect Shimon Peres signed the Declaration of Principles with Yasser Arafat in Washington, the Israel-Vatican commission held a "special meeting" in Israel. Under the Vatican agreement the Israelis would "give control" of the Old City to the Vatican before the year 2000.

The plan also calls for Jerusalem to become *"the Second Vatican of the World"* with *"all three major religions represented, but under the authority of the Vatican." "Jerusalem will remain the capital of Israel but the Old City will be administered by the Vatican."*

March 1995

A cable from the Israeli Embassy in Rome to The Foreign Ministry was in Jerusalem is leaked to a radio station *Arutz Sheva,* confirming the handover of Jerusalem to the Vatican. Two days later the cable made front page of Haaretz.

A member of Knesset Avraham Shapira announced in the Knesset that he had information that all Vatican property in Jerusalem was to become tax exempt and that large tracts of real estate on Mount Zion were given to the Pope in perpetuity.

On November 10th, 1997, the State of Israel and the Vatican sign the 'Legal Personality Agreement" whereby the State of Israel agrees to "assure full effect law to the legal personality of the Catholic Church itself."

The Church, with its prelates, bishops, cardinals popes, and its *"Canon Law,"* all of a sudden became a big "Devotee of International Law" and "International Agreements."

In addition, the Church, this ever combative and dictatorial political entity, responsible for the killing and murder of countless "millions of Jews, Protestants," and other undesirable persons, suddenly becomes "the voice of love, peace and reason."

January 2001

Israel TV journalists *secretly* filmed under the Shrine of Omar, the 7th century Islamic building which may have been deliberately constructed over the Holy of Holies, the most sacred prayer room of the ancient Jewish Temple. The video revealed a new and massive tunnel aimed directly at the most sacred core of Solomon's and later, Herod's Temples. During the Crusades the early 12th century chivalric order, The Knights Templar, dug under the ruins for nine years and found a network of tunnels where the Jewish priests hid their treasures from the marauding Romans in 70 CE. It was also assumed that the original records of the Jewish Church which prove that the Vatican was not practicing Christianity as its founders had intended, was buried in this spot. A pope with exclusive rights of divine interpretation was not part of G-d's plan. If these scrolls were made public they would jeopardize Rome's legitimacy. Thus it is imperative to The Vatican that the Jews be removed from the Temple Mount so that they don't find these important scrolls. The RA is serving as the Vatican's "building contractors" in this arrangement in the hope that the Vatican will side with the Palestinians in the conflict with Israel.

For centuries the Vatican has been pushing its *"replacement"* doctrine which states that the Catholic has replaced Israel as *"the New Israel."*

The Roman Catholic Church wants Israel to lose sovereign control over the Old City of Jerusalem so that "the promises to the literal descendants of Abraham will be applied to the *New Jerusalem*." If Israel controls Jerusalem it is evidence that Rome's claim are not legitimate and that the literal interpretation of Scriptures is correct. There is no place for the restoration of the nation of Israel in its theology. How can the Vatican claim to be "the New Jerusalem" and "rightful heir to the Kingdom of God" if the Jews control Jerusalem?

How is the Catholic Church going to convince the world that their version of theology is correct?

The Vatican is going to have everyone believe this "mysterious individual who will 'unite the faiths' and appear in Jerusalem which will be under the control of an authority headed by the Vatican.

The ancient dreams of revival of the Holy Roman Empire of Charlemagne with its seat in Jerusalem never died, as a matter of fact, are alive as ever in this pope's mind. *"To Supplant Judaism and Make The Pope The Supreme Religious and Temporal Power of The Renewed Holy Roman Empire Is The Goal."*

The Times of Israel
July 18, 2013

"The European Union's Settlement guidelines"

New directives prohibit Israeli companies located beyond the 1967 lines from receiving prizes, grants, or financing.

Commission Notice:

Section A. General Issues

1. These guidelines set out the conditions under which the Commission will implement key requirements for the award of EU support to Israeli entities or to their activities in the territories occupied by Israel since June 1967. Their aim is to ensure the respect of EU positions and commitments in conformity with *"international law"* on the non-recognition by the EU of Israel's sovereignty over the territories occupied by Israel since June 1967.
2. These guidelines are without prejudice to other requirements established by EU legislation.
3. The territories occupied by Israel since June 1967 comprises the Golan Heights, the Gaza Strip and the West Bank, including East Jerusalem.

4. The EU does "not" recognize Israel's sovereignty over any of the territories referred to in point 2 and *"does not consider them to be part of Israel's territory,"* irrespective of their legal status under domestic Israeli law. The EU has made it clear that it will not recognize any changes to pre-1967 borders, other than those agreed by the parties to the *Middle East Peace Process (MEPP)*. The EU Foreign Affairs Council has underlined the importance of limiting the application of agreements with Israel to the territory of Israel as recognized by the EU.

The Jerusalem Post
August 30, 2013

"US intelligence report holds Assad government responsible for Syria chemical weapons attack"

A Syrian chemical weapons attack killed 1,429 Syrian civilians, including 426 children, an unclassified report by US intelligence agencies concluded on Friday.

BBC News
August 30, 2013

"US plans 'limited act' against Syria over chemical claim"

President Barack Obama has said the US is considering a "limited narrow act" in response to the alleged use of chemical weapons by the Syrian army.

But Russia – a key ally of Syria – has warned that "any unilateral military action bypassing the UN Security Council" would be a "direct violation of international law."

The Jerusalem Post
August 30, 2013

"Tension and skepticism as Obama nears Syria moment"

As US President Obama and Secretary of State Kerry continue to make the case for intervention in Syria, a new Reuters/Ipsos poll suggests that a majority of Americans still oppose any military involvement in the Syrian crisis.

The Jerusalem Post
August 30, 2013

"Iran commander: US strike on Syria will mean the 'imminent destruction' of Israel"

Iran's Revolutionary Guards chief said a US military attack on Syria would lead to the "imminent destruction" of Israel and would prove a "second Vietnam" for America.

The commander of the Iranian al-Quds Brigades, Maj.-Gen. Qassem Suleimani, told a closed meeting Wednesday that the countries of the Levant "will be the graveyards of the Americans," according to Hezbollah's al-Manar website. He also quoted as saying that any US soldier "entering Syria will have to carry his coffin with him."

An Iranian lawmaker, Abdorlreza Azizi, criticized the US, comparing the country's action to the Hitler's moves.

"Like Hitler who started World War II, the US is igniting World War III," he said according to the report.

MISSILE THREAT
Posted on August 26, 2013
The Washington Free Beacon

"China Launches Three ASAT Satellites"

China's military recently launched three small satellites into orbit as part of Beijing's covert anti-satellite warfare program, according to a U.S. official.

The three satellites, launched July 20, 2013, by a Long March-4C launcher, were later detected conducting unusual maneuvers in space indicating "*the Chinese are preparing to conduct space warfare*" against satellites, said the official who is familiar with intelligence reports about the satellites.

One of the satellites was equipped with an extension arm capable of attacking orbiting satellites that currently are vulnerable to both kinetic and electronic disruption.

"This is a real concern for U.S. national defense," the official said. "The three are working in tandem and the one with the arm poses the most concern. This is part of a <u>Chinese 'Star Wars' program</u>."

"There is a Star Wars threat to our satellites," the official said. But the official said "<u>the administration does not want the American people to know about it</u>," because it would require plusing up defense budgets."

"The People's Liberation Army (PLA) is acquiring a range of technologies to improve China's space and counter space capabilities," the report said.

"Battlefield monitor and control, information communications, navigation and position guidance all rely on satellites and other sensors," and Chinese military writings emphasize," <u>destroying, damaging, and interfering with enemy's reconnaissance...and communications satellites</u>."

The military writings suggest that satellites could be part of an initial attack aimed at blinding the enemy. "<u>Destroying or capturing satellites and other sensors...will deprive an opponent of initiative on the battlefield and (make it difficult) for them to bring their precision guided weapons into full play</u>," the PLA report said.

"When China gains superiority in any strategic category it will be even less willing to bargain away capability for the sake of 'stability.'

China will not 'reward' any future U.S. nuclear weapon reductions or restraint in developing space weapons."

The Art of Deception: Pres. Obama & the Oil Wars

"The U.S. Embassy in Iraq is the Largest in the World"

Although Obama preaches against the Iraq Oil War, he is only opposed to the Iraq war in his "posturing" – implementing the "Art of Deception" – an old CFR trick designed to mislead the "common people" in one direction while actually implementing actions in the opposite direction. Obama has been deceptively packaged by his CFR handlers with the support of other military industrial complex lobbying firms and nongovernmental organizations who seek further U.S. military operations, particularly to seize and secure more of the world's oil fields and reserves – not for the people of the United States, but for the CFR member big oil corporations who got us into Iraq in the first place.

The U.S. has already constructed massive permanent military bases in Iraq and Afghanistan to serve as hubs for an invasion into Iran. Obama knows that his planned pullout of Iraq is also posturing, and he knows that he is lying to and deceiving the American people. As President, Obama will lead us into another Oil War with Iran, as directed by his CFR advisors.

Meddling in other countries' foreign affairs has spurred backlash against the U.S. before. This phenomenon is referred to by the C.I.A. as "blowback," or the consequences from provoking unwarranted actions (Unfortunately, the C.I.A. itself is strongly influenced by the Rockefeller interests and has close ties to the CFR).

With Paul Volcker and Zbigniew Brzezinski's lead, all of the key staff positions in Obama's White House will be CFR clones, dedicated to a New World Order, a one-world government, and the diminution of the sovereignty, of the USA into a repressive socialist USSA – The United States of Socialist America! In order for the CFR to expand the U.S. war-making capabilities in the Oil Wars, expect to see a new "crisis" emerge during the new presidency creating a need for a "draft" to expand the ranks of the U.S. military.

If President Barack Obama makes an impassioned mesmerizing TV address urging young Americans to answer their country's call to bear arms, Obama will have the full support of the liberal media, and our children will be brainwashed into fighting and dying in another war that should never have been created. "Change you can believe in?" or more of the same from the CFR controlled New World Order White House? Now you know why Barak Obama is the chosen New World Order Candidate. Only when and if the control of the CFR is fully exposed and eliminated will the voters have a real democratic choice!

"This Sets the Stage for Ezekiel 38:39"
"Prophecy against Gog"

Included in the section dealing with Israel's blessing is the description of the deliverance of Israel from the invaders from the north in Ezekiel 38-39 led by Gog.

The prophecy against Gog is one of the most dramatic predictions of Ezekiel. Many details of the prophecy are not entirely clear, but the main thrust of the prediction is not difficult to understand. The passage predicted an invasion of Israel by a great army that will attack Israel from the north.

This passage is a part of the prediction of the great world conflict which will characterize the years before the Second Coming of the Lord Yahshua. Though Bible expositors have differed as to when this fits into the prophetic picture, it is plausible that preceding this event the predictions of the revived Roman Empire, a ten nation confederacy, will be fulfilled. This will be considered in the prophecies of Daniel 2 and chapter 7, and after the "Peace Treaty" is confirmed.

A political leader will arise who will head up the ten nations and make the Mediterranean Sea a Roman lake as it was in New Testament times. He is referred to in Daniel 9:26 as "the ruler who will come." This ruler will be associated with the people who destroyed the city of Jerusalem in A.D. 70, that is, the "Roman people" and accordingly, he will fulfill the role of a "Roman leader" in the "end times" as heading up this ten-nation confederacy. This ruler will be featured in the first of three "major phases of prophetic fulfillment," climaxing in the second coming of Christ my Lord and Savior. The anti-Christ will rise and the formation of the ten-nation confederacy will set the stage for what will follow.

The second phase of this struggle with a duration of three-and-one-half years was described by Ezekiel in these two chapters, Though variously interpreted, it may be the forerunner and major event that leads to the world government predicted for the last three-and-a-half years leading up to the Second Coming. As the battle described here is a disaster for the invading countries, it may change the political structure to such an extent that it will be possible for the "Roman leader" of the ten nations to become a world dictator.

The third phase of the period leading up to the Second Coming will be this world-empire stage, including all nations of the world (Daniel 7:23; Rev. 13:7-8). The third phase, ending in the Second Coming, will be a time of the Great Tribulation. The Great Tribulation also records another mammoth world war (Dan. 11:40-45; Rev. 16:12-16) which "will occur" just before the Second Coming.

This should be distinguished from the war described in Ezekiel 38-39 which is not a world conflict but a war between a select group of nations attacking Israel.

In the quarter of a century since World War II Russia has risen to be one of the great military powers of the modern world. To a far greater extent than ever before Russia has become a prominent nation, especially in its influence on the Middle East. The "possibility of Russia attacking Israel is a modern concern of the United States and other nations. With both Russia and Red China constituting a major political bloc, the question of a future war between Russia and Israel becomes a "great possibility."

The word "Russia" never occurs in Scripture, but the description of this war connects these two important chapters of Ezekiel with the future outcome of Russia as a world power.

Ezekiel 38-39 reveals a future invasion of the land of Israel by the armies of Russia and five other nations. According to the Holy Scriptures the invaders *"will be totally destroyed by the great hand of God"* which, undoubtedly, will have an effect on the world power struggle in which Russia now is a major factor.

Ezekiel 38:23

"So I will show my greatness and my holiness and make myself known in the eyes of many nations. Then they will know that I am the Lord."

The point of view adopted here places this war in the first half of the last seven years, probably towards its close.

A few have advanced the theory that this war must occur before the Rapture. The situation described here does not come to pass until after the Rapture. The scene is one of peace which has its best explanation with the seven-year covenant enacted by the ruler of the ten-nation confederacy. "This can only occur after the restraint of the presence of the Holy Spirit has been removed at the Rapture (cf. 2 Thes. 2:6-8). Further, it would contradict the doctrine of the imminency of the Rapture.

Daniel's Vision of the Four Beasts

If Daniel 7 had closed with 14, based on other Scripture, one could almost understand a portion of the vision. Like the "image" in chapter 2, the four beasts represented four kingdoms (cf. chart of World Empires in the Bible at Dan. 2).

The first kingdom with characteristics of a lion and an "*eagle*" represented Babylon, where all false religion started. There "*soon*" will be a world war between the forces of the pseudo-Christian West and the radical Islamic nations. Now look around you, how many empires, nations and organizations use the Greek "image" or symbol of Iesus "Son of Zeus," which represents the Ur-Babylonian "*Eagle God*," now tell me, whom do they truly represent (Satan).

The second kingdom represented the Medo-Persian Empire (Iran) which conquered Babylon.

The third kingdom represented Greece, who conquered all of Western Asia were fulfillment of the leopard.

The fourth kingdom was not named but was historically fulfilled by the Roman Empire. The ten horns represented a "future" Roman Empire which will *"reappear in the end times."*

The little horn represented a ruler who would come up last in the fourth kingdom who would be a world conqueror. Just as the image was destroyed in Daniel 2, so the fourth beast was destroyed by fire (7:11). The first three beasts were distinguished from the fourth in that instead of being cut off, they were allowed to continue for a time, that is, each was absorbed in the kingdom that followed in contrast to the fourth kingdom which will be suddenly destroyed (v. 12).

Daniel 7:11

"I looked then because of the sound of the great words that the horn was speaking. And as I looked, 'the beast was killed' and given over to be burned with fire."

Revelation 19:20

"And the beast was captured, and with it the false prophet who in its presence had done the signs by which he deceived those who had

received the mark of the beast and those who worshiped its image. These two were thrown alive into the lake of fire that burns with sulfur."

Closing Statements

Personal pride is serving Satan oh excuse me, the elites of the world, those that demand a "one world order" which consist of the control of the people, and for the people to bow down before them (the mark of the beast and those that worshiped the image). The mark of the beast also goes back to the word of God, when He declared in Leviticus 19:28 "You shall not tattoo yourselves: I am the Lord." This mark identified the people that are followers of Satan. They work hand and hand with one verse of the Bible that says; Satan comes but to still, kill and destroy, human beings, for the purpose of taking them to Hell with him, before they turn their lives to Yahshua for salvation. This administration is opening the gates for a complete annihilation of the United States of America. The gamble is, when and if, will the terrorist and/or the sleepers set their nuclear/plutonium bombs off in America, for the purpose of destroying the U.S. from the inside out? The finale signs or harbingers of Isaiah 9:10 have been completed, and now it is time for God's judgment on our nation, as well as the rest of the world.

"Apostasy is before us." The religion of Christ has, in the past, been *opposed* and *corrupted*, but when it once comes, as it has come in our day, to be *burlesqued*, "there is nothing left but judgment." There is nothing more the enemy can do before he proceeds to build up the "great apostasy" on the ruins of true religion, and thus prepare the way for the "coming of the Judge."

We all condemn Syria for what they did in killing innocent children with their chemicals. But why wasn't America condemned for "Project Sunshine," after all many O.S.S./C.I.A. agents and scientist's just happened to disappear, not to mention the children that were killed by the hundreds if not the thousands, for the sake of science, and how about the other countries that were also involved, "everyone got off scoot free." Now you will understand why I gave this book the title that it has.

"These are the most critical moments in human history"

"I stand strong as a warrior for "Yahshua," my Lord and my Savior," whom do you stand for; the final choice may need to be before a twinkle of an eye."

"No One Has the Right to Change the Name of God, By Using the Word of 'Translation' for Their Own Glory!!! For the Glory Belongs "Only" to Yahshua My Lord and Savior, Thanks Be to God, Amen."

Redeemed

"We (believers) were crucified with Christ (Gal. 2:20). When Yahshua died the law died with Him and so did we. (Col. 2:20) we were buried with Him (Rom.6:4). We were made alive with Him by His resurrection (Eph. 2:5) we were joint heirs with Christ and will be glorified with Him (Rom. 8:17).

Blood purchased us (Rom. 3:25; Eph. 1:7). Bought with His blood (1 Cor. 6:20; 1Pt. 1:18-19; Col. 1:14).

Hebrew 7:27, "Yahshua has become a surety of a better covenant."

Hebrew 9:15, "And for this cause Yahshua is the mediator of the new testament, that by means of death, for the redemption of the transgressions that were under the first testament, they which are called might receive the promise of *"eternal inheritance."* Hebrew 9:16, for where a testament is, there must also of necessity be the death of the testator."

Hebrew 9:12, He entered once for all into the Holy places, not by means of the blood of goats and calves but by means of His own blood, thus *"securing"* an *"eternal redemption."*

Romans 5:9, "Since, therefore, "_We_" have "_Now_" been justified by His blood, much more shall "_We_" be "_Saved_" by Him from the "_Wrath_" of God." Amen.

Yahshua the Christ, proclaimed;

"I am the Way,

The Truth and

The Life."

The End

~ 522 ~

Ernest Garcia

A Secret Hero
Former O.S.S./C.I.A. Covert Actions Operator

Born August 7, 1928

Deceased: September 3, 2008

Ernest Garcia passed away of a heart attack, just twelve days
after his last interview with the author and script-writer, his
cousin; Marcel L. Garcia Jr.

"I thank God for giving Ernest Garcia the strength and
perseverance to petition the American Congress and win the
right to tell his classified story and fulfill his dream.
His dream was to tell you his side of the story."
And as for me, I'm just a messenger, giving the message of
"Hope and Salvation."

"May the grace of God be with you as my love is with you."

Marcel l. Garcia Jr.
Author

~ 523 ~

www.ingramcontent.com/pod-product-compliance
Lightning Source LLC
Chambersburg PA
CBHW060102170426
43198CB00010B/741